Sacred Mandates of Conscience
Interpretations of *The Baptist Faith and Message*

Edited by
Jeff B. Pool

SMYTH & HELWYS
PUBLISHING, INC.
Macon, Georgia

ISBN 1-57312-165-7

Sacred Mandates of Conscience
Interpretations of The Baptist Faith and Message (1963)

Edited by
Jeff B. Pool
©1997
Smyth & Helwys Publishing, Inc.
Peake Road
6316 Peake Road
Macon, Georgia 31210-3960
1-800-747-3016

All right reserved.
Printed in the United States of America.

The paper used in this publication meets the minimum
requirements of American Standard for Information Science–
Permanence of Paper for Printed Library Materials.
ANSI Z39.48-4

Library of Congress Cataloging-in-Publication

Sacred mandates of conscience:
    interpretations of the Baptist faith and message/
    Jeff Pool, editor.
    vi + 186 pp.   6" x 9" (15 x 23 cm.)
    Includes bibliographical references.
    ISBN 1-57312-165-7   (alk. Paper)
    1. Baptist faith and message.
    2. Southern Baptist Convention–Creeds.
    3. Baptists–United States–Creeds.
    4. Southern Baptist Convention–Doctrines–History–20th century.
    5. Baptists–United States–Doctrines–History–20th century.
    I. Pool, Jeff B., 1951-.
BX6462.7.S33   1997
238'.6132–dc21   97-11346
                                                                   CIP

Contents

Acknowledgments	v
Prologue	1
Conscience and Interpreting Baptist Tradition	
Jeff B. Pool	
Chapter 1	37
Chief Article of Faith	
The Preamble of *The Baptist Faith and Message (1963)*	
Jeff B. Pool	
Chapter 2	102
God, the Bible, and Authority in	
The Baptist Faith and Message (1963)	
William L. Hendricks	
Chapter 3	121
God's Way with Wayward Humanity	
Protology, Anthropology, and Hamartiology in	
The Baptist Faith and Message (1963)	
Molly T. Marshall	
Chapter 4	133
"Rooted and Grounded in Jesus Christ"	
Christology and Soteriology in	
The Baptist Faith and Message (1963)	
Warren McWilliams	
Chapter 5	146
Mirror of Doctrine	
Personal Morality and Social Ethics in	
The Baptist Faith and Message (1963	
N. Larry Baker	
Chapter 6	161
In Search of the One, True Church	
Ecclesiology in	
The Baptist Faith and Message (1963)	
Bill J. Leonard	
Chapter 7	173
Principles Implicit in the Concept of Religious Liberty in	
The Baptist Faith and Message (1963)	
William R. Estep	
Contributors	184

Therefore, since we have this ministry, as we received mercy, we do not lose heart, but we have renounced the things hidden because of shame, not walking in craftiness or adulterating the word of God, but by the manifestation of truth commending ourselves to every man's conscience in the sight of God. (2 Cor 4:1-2 NAS)

Acknowledgments

As the editor of this book, I assume responsibility for its final form and content. Still, like all books, but especially a book written by a group of authors, this project eventually became a book due to the efforts of several people. Those people deserve public recognition.

First, and most importantly, I thank the contributors to this small volume of studies. I had no idea that my original invitations to the authors of the articles, which have since become this book's chapters, would ever have led finally to this. I regret any discomfort, inconvenience, or suffering that this project may have caused for any of the authors. I am very happy, however, that we have had the opportunity to participate together in this endeavor, despite all of the obstacles.

Second, I thank the editorial board of *Southwestern Journal of Theology* (*SWJT*) for two decisions: (1) for inviting me to edit an issue of *SWJT* on the *Baptist Faith and Message* and, as a consequence, for authorizing me to invite the authors of this book to write the original articles; and, (2) after suspending the journal's publication, for releasing the authors of this book from their contracts to publish in *SWJT*. I also express appreciation to the members of the editorial board who resisted in various ways the suspension of the journal's publication.

Third, I especially thank William M. Tillman, Jr., managing editor of *SWJT*, for his enthusiasm about the original project for the journal, his generous editorial efforts to polish each author's contribution, especially my own, his courageous stand to prevent the suspension of the journal's publication, and his sincere encouragement to me as I sought to publish these studies elsewhere. I regret any sense of loss that he has experienced due to this turn of events. Nevertheless, perhaps he also will experience at least some satisfaction in the new phoenix that has arisen from the ashes of the previous project.

Fourth, I am grateful to R. Alan Culpepper, former editor of *Perspectives in Religious Studies*, for permission to reprint portions of my recent article: " 'Sacred Mandates of Conscience': A Criteriology of Creedalism for Theological Method among Baptists," *Perspectives in Religious Studies* 23 (Winter 1996). Although that article appeared prior to my chapter in this book, I produced the two studies within a few weeks of one another.

Fifth, I also thank David Dinkins, pastor of Burchill Baptist Church, for his passionate interest in the publication of this book's content. Due to his letter to the editor of the *Baptist Standard*, the larger Baptist world became aware of the curtailment of academic freedom at Southwestern Baptist Theological Seminary.

Sixth, in addition, I express my gratitude to Miriam Harden, who serves as secretary for me and two other professors. She has helped me enormously with correspondence, records, and telephone messages, since the inception of this project with *SWJT*.

Seventh, I must thank several members of my family for supporting me in numerous ways during this project. I thank my brother, David Bryan Pool, and my sister, Karen Dansby, for sharing their strength with me, during the initial turmoil around the studies now contained in this book. I thank my daughter, Kristen Pool, for helping me to think about other important things in life during my work on this book. Due to some of her telephone calls from the University of Chicago, where she is a second-year student in the College, I gratefully shifted to discussing her questions and comments about the ideas of Jean-Jacques Rousseau, Max Weber, Emile Durkheim, and others. As always, I thank my wife, Laurinda Lynne, for the atmosphere of peace, gentleness, and compassion that she carries in her beauty and shares with me. I am also again grateful for my seventeen-year-old son, Jonathan Pool, and his sense of humor during this project. He made a creative suggestion for an epigram to this book: "Dude, tell 'em, I'll go crazy, for real. . . ! For the epigram, however, I chose instead the more appropriate text from the Christian scriptures. Although I think that I made the right decision about the epigram, given this book's origin, Jonathan's suggested possibility may contain an element of truth as well!

Finally, I thank Cecil Staton and David Cassady of Smyth and Helwys Publishing for their interest in this project. Their efforts have enabled the studies in this book to have a public life together, rather than separate lives as articles published in various scholarly journals. Baptists who love their freedom should thank God often for such friends of freedom.

Prologue

Conscience and Interpreting Baptist Tradition

Jeff B. Pool

Introduction

This book interprets several of the most central affirmations in the *Baptist Faith and Message*, the confession of Christian faith adopted by the Southern Baptist Convention in 1963.[1] Because of this book's very specific focus on the SBC's present confession of faith, the authors have addressed this volume of studies to Baptists and Baptist churches, primarily either those still participating in the SBC or those formerly in the SBC, but now with new commitments to other organizations, such as the Cooperative Baptist Fellowship or the Alliance of Baptists. Nonetheless, because the studies of this book interface with the larger history of Baptists, the authors also offer these studies to all persons with interests in Baptist history, doctrine, ethics, and theology.

I. Interpreting a Baptist Confession of Faith

With this book, the authors primarily intend collectively to supply a fresh interpretation of the *Baptist Faith and Message (1963)*, through critical analyses and appraisals, in order to assess that confession's significance for contemporary life, theology, and ethics among Baptists.[2] Second, the authors of this book intend to confirm the traditions of confessionalism among Baptists, while simultaneously issuing another warning against credalism.

Hence, the main title of this book, *Sacred Mandates of Conscience*, originates from the book's purpose. This book borrows its main title from the SBC's first confession of faith, adopted in 1914.[3] Although the SBC specifically addressed its earliest confession to the issue of Christian union, the previous phrase expresses a dual conviction at the root of every Baptist Christian's experience. First, all Christian confessions of faith arise from each person's liberating experience with God through Jesus Christ: articles of faith become written expressions of the convictions of Christian consciences. Second, because such documents arise from each individual's living faith, written confessions of faith never subsume the authority of the Spirit's presence in each believer, the very divine impetus for the written expressions themselves: as a consequence, the community's collective voice, as expressed through confessional documents, can never legitimately dictate terms, doctrines, or policies to the individual's conscience. The phrase, "sacred mandates of conscience," aptly condenses the conviction on the basis of which the SBC originally formulated the *Baptist Faith and*

Message: the competency of every person before God, as realized in the affirmations of God alone as Lord of every human's conscience, the priesthood of every Christian, and the autonomy of every local church. This conviction, in all of its derivative corollaries, supplies the most prominent presupposition for the critical studies in this book. Thus, similarly, this book's interpretations of the *BFM (1963)* also arise from the informed Christian consciences of the authors.

This book's subtitle, *Interpretations of the Baptist Faith and Message*, suggests the genre of this book. First, this book focuses on one object of study, the SBC's current and most comprehensive confession of faith: the *Baptist Faith and Message*. Second, because several authors interpret the various articles of the *BFM (1963)*, the plural noun, "interpretations," more accurately describes the studies in this book. Although these studies reflect a significant and general consistency among themselves, they do not arise from a single ideological, political, or theological perspective, certainly not a perspective required of the authors from any other sources than the object of study itself, on the one hand, and its contemporary context, on the other hand. Third, as a group of interpretations of a historic document, this book qualifies as a commentary on the *BFM (1963)*. As also happens to interpretations of Christian scriptures, this book's interpretations of the *BFM (1963)* will also differ significantly from, hence coming into conflict with, other interpretations of this document, at least interpretations of the *BFM (1963)* by those who presently control the politics and theology of the SBC. For this reason, the interpretations in this book should also be understood as critical. The following chapters do not merely summarize the contents of the *BFM (1963)*. Rather, they engage the confession with an evaluative attitude. Thus, the interpretations in this book also sometimes make proposals for the improvement of the *BFM (1963)* in future revisions. In this sense, these studies do not simply try to understand the document in order to legitimize or to justify the present dominating political and theological ideology of the SBC.

Essentially, this book's chapters contain expositions of several major components and articles of the *BFM (1963)*. These expositions include historical analyses and critical assessments of the *BFM (1963)*, as well as constructive proposals for formulating and interpreting specific Christian doctrines from Baptist perspectives. Hence, as careful expositions of a historic doctrinal confession of the SBC, this book qualifies as *historical* theology. Because the studies in this book interpret the meaning of this historic document in light of and for the sake of contemporary Baptist experience, however, this book also qualifies as *constructive* theology. Furthermore, since the studies of this book also examine the major doctrines of the *BFM (1963)*, following much of the traditional order derived from the logic of the Christian narratives themselves, this book also qualifies as *systematic* theology. In light of the previous hermeneutical approaches to the *BFM (1963)*, the genre of this book ultimately qualifies as *confessional*, but not dogmatic, theology. However significant the SBC's resolutions and pronouncements may be, historically, the SBC has not possessed (at least, perhaps, until recently) the constitutional authority or the ecclesiastical polity to formulate, pronounce, and enforce dogmas. Thus, the studies in this book interpret a confession of Baptist beliefs, not Baptist dogmas.

However properly or improperly the SBC has used the *BFM (1963)*, that revision of the SBC's confessional statement from 1925 has served the SBC for more than thirty years. The SBC's present situation, nonetheless, invites new and even urgent appraisals of this important confessional statement. Although the following interpretations of this document will sometimes identify its weaknesses, these inquiries into the *BFM (1963)* tend to accentuate and to retrieve that document's most significant strengths. The following chapters contain careful expositions of the *BFM (1963)*, expositions of the text in terms of both its historical or contextual sense and its theological significance in contemporary Baptist life. Thus, often the authors will invite Baptists in the SBC to return to some of the powerful emphases in the *BFM (1963)*, even though occasionally suggesting alternatives to some of the document's formulations in light of contemporary concerns. Although every reader may not agree with all conclusions reached in the chapters of this book, the authors of these studies have succeeded in identifying many of the most important questions and issues, both relative to the *BFM (1963)*, specifically, and relative to issues about Baptist confessions of faith, generally.

This book contains only seven expositions of several major segments of the *BFM (1963)*. The *BFM (1963)* itself, the history of its interpretation and usage, and current revisions of it deserve much more critical and comprehensive attention.[4] Although the Sunday School Board of the SBC has recently completed a revised edition of the older interpretation of the *BFM (1963)* by Herschel H. Hobbs, the SBC's current situation begs for contemporary and more thorough interpretations of this confessional statement by the present generation of Baptists. This book of studies represents one collection of efforts directed toward that very end. Nonetheless, while this book attempts to supply readers with a comprehensive interpretation of the *BFM (1963)*, the studies in this volume do not address every doctrinal emphasis or issue found in the *BFM (1963)*. Because the *BFM (1963)* belongs to every Baptist who participates in the SBC, the authors of the following chapters have tried to encourage further expositions of this doctrinal statement by other theologians, ministers, and members of local Baptist churches.

The authors of the chapters in this book accepted assignments for studies of specific portions and doctrinal foci of the *BFM (1963)*. These authors represent the diversity among Baptists in the SBC. All of the scholars have published previous studies about Baptist life, history, or theology; most of them have published quite extensively in one or more of these areas. All of these writers possess at least one graduate degree from one of the SBC's seminaries. All of the writers for this issue have attempted to interpret the *BFM (1963)* in light of both broader Baptist confessional traditions and the SBC's own more specific confessional history.

I contribute the first chapter, an interpretation of the confession's introductory paragraphs, paragraphs collectively and commonly designated as the Preamble of the *BFM (1963)*. William L. Hendricks, Lecturer in Theology and Director of the Baptist Studies Program at Brite Divinity School, wrote an exposition of the doctrines of God, the Christian scriptures, and authority in the *BFM (1963)* as the second chapter. Molly T. Marshall, Professor of Theology, Worship, and Spiritual Formation at Central Baptist Theological Seminary, in a third chapter, carefully examines the doctrines of creation, human life, and sin in this confessional statement. Warren McWilliams, Professor in the Ingram School of Christian Service at Oklahoma Baptist University, contributes the fourth chapter, a study of the christology and soteriology of the *BFM (1963)*. Bill J. Leonard, Dean of Wake Forest University Divinity School, in the fifth chapter, supplies an exposition of the confession's ecclesiology. N. Larry Baker, Pastor of First Baptist Church in Pineville, Louisiana, and at one time Executive Director of the SBC's Christian Life Commission, wrote the sixth chapter, a study of the moral and social visions in the *BFM (1963)*. William R. Estep, Professor Emeritus of Church History at Southwestern Baptist Theological Seminary, in the seventh and final chapter, examines the concept of religious liberty in the *BFM (1963)*, which he places within the context of this concept's larger history among Baptists.

II. Attesting to Dangerous Memories

The studies in this book, while valuable in themselves for their scholarship, have received their real significance largely both from the circumstances of their conceptions and, finally, from their births into publication. While the birth of every infant involves struggle, trauma of transition, and sometimes extreme suffering, midwives for the delivery of the studies in this book even had to fight to prevent the murder of these studies just as their births began. In the following account of the circumstances surrounding the production and publication of this book, I both describe the event of censorship as well as its initial repercussions and reconstruct the seminary's administrative rationalization for its actions. I have reconstructed this story from my own records and notes, newspapers, letters, memos, and conversations. Thus, my attestation also qualifies as an interpretation, as one perspective. Other persons, without a doubt, have experienced these events and will interpret their meanings very differently. I only hope that other interpreters will also take care to document their claims, unlike several of the people who made many of the statements in the course of the events about which I have written.

A. An Event of Academic Censorship

Early in 1996, the editorial board of *Southwestern Journal of Theology* (*SWJT*) officially invited me to edit an issue of that academic journal for the spring of 1997, the thematic focus of which was to be the *Baptist Faith and Message (1963)*.[5] I accepted that invitation. *SWJT's* editorial board intended for that thematic issue to parallel the SBC's doctrinal study for 1997 on the *BFM (1963)*. As the issue-editor, in consultation with William M. Tillman, Jr., the managing editor of *SWJT*, I developed the plan for the journal, secured authors for the articles, and corresponded with them about their contracts or related matters. This project proceeded as planned, with the completed articles in my hands by the end of September 1996. Upon receiving the completed articles from the authors, I also did the preliminary editorial work on their articles.

After I had edited the articles, *SWJT's* copy-editor worked on them. *SWJT's* editorial staff then delivered these articles to the printer. When the managing editor had received page-proofs of the articles from the printer, he sent an outline of the issue (including, of course, the names of the authors) for the spring of 1997 to the editor-in-chief of *SWJT*, also the president of Southwestern Baptist Theological Seminary (SWBTS), Kenneth S. Hemphill.

In mid-November of 1996, I received official notification from the managing editor of *SWJT* that the journal's editorial board had temporarily suspended that particular issue of the journal. Without any explanation for this decision, the letter simply stated that "the articles originally planned" for *SWJT* in the spring of 1997 "are to be rescheduled" and "will be published at a later date than originally intended."[6]

Unofficially, in conversations with members of *SWJT's* editorial board, I learned a little about the reason for the editorial board's decision. In a special meeting of the editorial board, on 8 November 1996, Hemphill had raised concerns about that particular issue of *SWJT*, specifically due to its inclusion of contributions from three authors: Hendricks, Marshall, and

Leonard. According to members of the editorial board, Hemphill did not want to publish that particular issue of the journal in its projected format. Hemphill worried about how readers would or might perceive SWBTS for including articles by these three authors in the seminary's theological journal. Hemphill apparently suggested at least two major alternatives: (1) redesign the format of that particular issue of *SWJT*, by including authors from "the other" perspective (presumably, that meant the perspective held by non- or anti-moderate Baptist theologians), and publish the issue at a later date; or (2) publish the articles separately from one another in several later issues of the journal. Following those discussions, under genuine pressure from Hemphill and his administrative advisers, the editorial board agreed to delay publication of that issue of the journal, while the journal's board considered options for the publication of the articles at a later date or later dates.[7] The editorial board's delay in the publication of those articles, nevertheless, effectively canceled the issue of *SWJT* for the spring of 1997.

To that point, none of SWBTS's administrators had yet communicated with me in any way about this problem. Furthermore, except for the official letter from the managing editor informing me of the action taken by the editorial board of *SWJT*, until 13 December 1996, I received no communications, either verbal or written, from any of the administrators who had pressured the editorial board of *SWJT* to suspend that particular issue of the journal.

B. Initial Repercussions

The editorial board's temporary suspension of *SWJT's* publication had several initial repercussions. First, the authors of the suspended publication began to respond. Larry Baker asked the managing editor, in a letter dated 21 November 1996, to return his manuscript. On 27 November 1996, I also requested the return of my own manuscript from the managing editor of *SWJT*. Since I had received no written explanation from the editorial board for its decision, I responded to that which I had learned from conversations with members of the board. Although other and more substantial reasons existed, my letter gave several technical reasons for my request, two of which held the most importance, but all of which supported the premise that, by its decision, the editorial board had modified my contract to publish in *SWJT*. First, by delaying publication of these articles, the board nullified the original purpose of the articles, which had been to function as parallel resources for the SBC's doctrinal study of the *BFM (1963)* in 1997. Second, by projecting the addition of articles by other and more politically-correct writers to balance the contributions by the three authors in question, the editorial board placed all of the original authors (without their consent) at a scholarly disadvantage, since they had written their articles without reference to any proposed adversarial or polemical context.[8] Shortly thereafter, both William L. Hendricks and William R. Estep sent similar letters to the managing editor of *SWJT*. In the face of this growing negative response to the officially unexplained delay of publication, yet in a gesture of goodwill, the editorial board of *SWJT* voted to return the articles, to release the authors from their contracts, and to allow the authors to retain their honoraria. The editorial board communicated its decision to all of the authors in letters dated 11 December 1996.[9]

Second, as news of the editorial board's action spread, the newspapers received and printed various versions of the event and the seminary's official explanations for it. Also on 11 December 1996, both the *Baptist Standard* and the Associated Baptist Press released stories about this event at SWBTS. These stories had been prompted mainly (although not exclusively) by a letter to the editor from David Dinkins, a recent graduate from SWBTS, the pastor of a Baptist church in Fort Worth, Texas, and a student at Brite Divinity School. On 13 December 1996, I received a letter from Kenneth S. Hemphill, dated 12 December 1996. Although a courteous explanation of his construal of this situation, Hemphill's letter really amounted to little more than a personalized version of the institution's official press releases. Additionally, on 13 December 1996, the *Fort Worth Star-Telegram* published an account of this incident.[10]

Third, these events had a divisive impact on the seminary's faculty. A regularly scheduled faculty meeting for SWBTS's School of Theology, on 12 December 1996, followed the initial publicity in the newspapers about this situation. Although the agenda for the meeting contained several items, the faculty used most of the meeting discussing the school's theological journal. During the meeting, the managing editor of *SWJT* insistently and clearly articulated the reason for the temporary suspension of the journal's publication, as he had learned it during the editorial board's meeting with Hemphill. The problem was the group of writers, not the content of the articles nor the stated concern to redesign the entire journal. With only a few significant exceptions, most comments during the meeting of the faculty reflected concerns either that one issue or several issues of the journal would not be published or that a redesigned theological journal would not continue to be an academic publication, not that the seminary had committed an overt act of academic censorship. Most members of the faculty in attendance remained silent about, either by ignoring (for whatever reasons) or by failing to perceive, the most serious problem. As an illustration of this point, one senior member of the faculty did articulate his agitation about the incident, although he directed his anger at those who had communicated with reporters from the *Baptist Standard*. In a scolding manner, he asserted that those members of SWBTS's faculty had "tattled to Toby Druin" (editor of the *Baptist Standard*), rather than addressing this problem within the privacy of the seminary's confines. Of course, that assertion did not reflect the actual situation, since members of the seminary's faculty communicated to the press only in response to inquiries from reporters, rather than by initiating those contacts. Finally, after declaring that members of the faculty who publicized such problems only hurt the seminary, he concluded with an insult: "We don't need any Benedict Arnolds here at Southwestern!" During that meeting, I remembered one of Pascal's observations about the disciples in the garden with Jesus before his arrest. Pascal's thoughts even now retain genuine relevance for that moment:

> Jesus, totally abandoned, even by the friends he had chosen to watch with him, is vexed when he finds them asleep because of the dangers to which they are exposing not him but themselves, and he warns them for their own safety and their own good, with warm affection in the face of their ingratitude. And warns them: "The spirit is willing but the flesh is weak."
>
> Jesus, finding them asleep again, undeterred by consideration either for him or for themselves, is kind enough not to wake them up and lets them take their rest.[11]

C. Justifying the Unjustifiable
Official Administrative Rationalization
for the Act of Academic Censorship

The public's knowledge of, and initial reactions to, this act of academic censorship at SWBTS appeared to take Hemphill and the subordinate administrators of SWBTS by surprise. In any case, SWBTS's administration certainly demonstrated poor preparation for its own public statements about this incident. The initial public responses by SWBTS's administrators, as a result, tended to obfuscate the actual reasons for the temporary suspension of the journal's publication.

On 11 December 1996, Hemphill stated in the *Baptist Standard* that "the need for 'an improved format and design to enable us to feature our faculty and other authors' was the overriding factor in canceling the spring issue, which was to be published in January."[12] Two days later, however, the *Fort Worth Star-Telegram* published an article on this incident. In that story, SWBTS's administrators did not refer at all to the president's intent to redesign the seminary's theological journal, although Scotty Gray, the seminary's vice-president for academic administration, insisted that "academic freedom was not impinged."[13] An article published on 19 December 1997 in the *Baptist Messenger*, however, repeated comments about the journal's redesign. That story, however, did not describe the "redesign of the journal" as the principal factor behind the suspension of the journal's issue for the spring of 1997. Nonetheless, by its inclusion of the seminary's initial rationalization as the journal's redesign, the *Baptist Messenger's* story still tended to cloak the more important rationalization for the editorial board's decision.[14]

Only subsequent reports in the newspapers began to disclose the real motivation behind the seminary's delay of *SWJT's* publication. According to those news releases, Hemphill identified a very different reason for the suspension of the journal's publication: the question of the "possible perception of unbalanced treatment" of the journal's topic for the spring of 1997, specifically due to the inclusion in that issue of contributions by Hendricks, Marshall, and Leonard.[15] This problem reflected two main concerns: (1) concern regarding possible perceptions about the authors themselves; and (2) concern regarding possible perceptions about the selection of those specific persons as contributors to that issue of the journal.

1. Possible Perceptions about the Authors

Even in the earliest publicity about this incident, Hemphill had commented about his problem with these three authors. In a letter from Hemphill to me as an author of one of the canceled articles, dated 12 December 1996, he corroborated his public comments about those three writers and elaborated on the rationale for his actions. On the basis of both his public comments and his letter to me, the following rationalization emerges. (a) Hendricks, Marshall, and Leonard "were former faculty members at Southern [Baptist Theological] Seminary." (b) They "were highly visible in some controversial issues." (c) They "now teach at 'non-SBC' schools." (d) According to Hemphill in his letter to me, Scotty Gray, Tommy Lea (dean of the seminary's School of Theology), and *SWJT's* editorial board "did not consider it appropriate for Southwestern to be put in an unnecessarily adversarial relation with our sister seminary [Southern Baptist Theological Seminary or SBTS] . . . ." (e) Furthermore, according to the *Fort Worth Star-Telegram*, Hemphill stated that " '[i]t would have been inappropriate for Southwestern to provide these authors with such a platform without opportunity for balanced response.' " (f) Additionally, according to Hemphill's letter, Gray, Lea, and the journal's editorial board "did not consider the writers as a whole to really represent [*sic*] the broad spectrum of either our readership or the convention." The *Baptist Standard* quoted a similar and more ideological comment by Hemphill on this point: "In the perception of the SBC, he said, 'these do not stand for a strongly conservative view of the Baptist Faith and Message Statement.' "[16]

2. Possible Perceptions about Selection of Authors

Hence, on the basis of his previous concern, Hemphill and the journal's editorial board arrived at the following conclusion, on which finally they based their decision to suspend publication of the articles. In his letter to me, Hemphill stated that, after sharing his "observations" with the journal's editorial board, "it was the consensus of the board that the group of writers would not be perceived as a carefully balanced group." In his letter, Hemphill did not clarify exactly what he meant by "a carefully balanced group." In an early statement to the press, however, Scotty Gray had attempted to clarify this ambiguity: " 'The concept of balance deals with the possible perceived lack of balance in the selection of contributors.' " However strange it may appear, Gray supplied the following elaboration, which tended to reconjure clouds of ambiguity: " 'The decision was based on the possibility that those who heard about the journal articles but did not read them would assume they were unbalanced.' " Gray's first comment indicates the administration's concern that some people might perceive the seminary's selection of authors, or the seminary's motives (as represented, of course, by the work of the issue-editor), as favoring moderate rather than fundamentalist Baptist voices. Gray's second and elaborative comment, however, seems to oscillate back to the administrative concern that some people might perceive the content of the articles themselves as unbalanced.[17]

Setting Gray's confusing elaborative comment aside for the moment, the administration's concern about how people would perceive the seminary's selection of moderate Baptist contributors to the journal purportedly reflects a larger goal, according to Hemphill's letter to me: "I have been making every effort to keep Southwestern out of the political controversy and to let us focus on the matter of theological education." The story in the *Baptist Messenger* also identified this pretension to avoid the SBC's political controversy. According to that article, echoing Hemphill's perspective, Tommy Lea "felt the discussion of the editorial board reflected a need to protect the seminary from being cast into a political role." That article quoted Lea as saying, " 'Dr. Hemphill is apolitical when it comes to leading this institution.' "[18] Speaking for the seminary's administrators and the journal's editorial board, in his letter to me, Hemphill supported his purportedly greater goal with the following judgment: "We simply considered that in the highly symbolic time in which we live it would be in the best interest of Southwestern and our convention that we not publish the journal as configured."[19]

III. Opposing the Torture of Testimony

Both the administration's act of academic censorship and the administrative rationalization for it invite more than a journalistic response. The seminary's administration has systematically distorted, on the one side, its explanations of its own motivation as well as its justification for its own actions and, on the other side, the images of the authors as well as their interpretations of the *BFM (1963)*. Such systematic distortions of communication essentially constitute and perpetuate an ideology.[20]

A. Unmasking an Ideology

As a prelude to the interpretations around which this incident has occurred, I offer the following critique of the seminary's administrative rationalization for its act of academic censorship or its ideology. Although I have not addressed every aspect of this ideology, I have tried to expose and answer its major features.

1. On the Purported Intention to Redesign the Journal's Format

Even if one accepts Hemphill's initial explanation for suspension of the journal's publication as the administration's genuine motive for its act of censorship, then a far from adequate administrative management of the journal's operations emerges. I repeat that initial explanation. Hemphill identified the "overriding factor" as "the need for 'an improved format and design to enable us to feature our faculty and other authors.'" Furthermore, according to his letter to me, Hemphill had "for more than a year been discussing with various persons on our staff the need to redesign our approach to the journal."[21]

First, even if Hemphill had considered redesigning the journal's format for more than a year, prudence and diligence would have required the administration to monitor the projected contributions to the journal in consultation, at least, with the journal's managing editor. With such an idea in mind, as the editor-in-chief and a member of the editorial board, Hemphill should have discussed this possibility with the journal's editorial board. The exercise of such supervision would have alerted administrators, as early as 14 February 1996, to the incipient thoughts about the plan for the issue of *SWJT* for spring of 1997. On that date, following conversations about contributors to that issue of the journal between myself and the journal's managing editor, I received a message by telephone from the managing editor, authorizing me to contact the contributors whom he and I had discussed.[22] At that point, I had not yet contacted any of the potential authors about writing articles for the seminary's journal. Incidentally, I did not send official written invitations to the authors until 9 March 1996. Furthermore, after receiving my plan for that issue of *SWJT* (dated, 13 March 1996) as well as copies of the letters that I had mailed to the authors, the managing editor sent a memorandum of appreciation to me for my "conscientious attention to the spring 1997 Southwestern Journal of Theology. . . ," concluding with the following sentence: "You have gone above and beyond on working to assure [*sic*] the spring 1997 Southwestern Journal of Theology is of high quality."[23] In a letter to the editor of the *Baptist Standard*, one person from Fort Worth, Texas, later rightly noted the following about Hemphill's purportedly longstanding interest to redesign the journal's format: "[s]uch a change should have been made prior to the planning of an issue, not after articles had been written."[24]

Second, Hemphill claimed to want " 'an improved format and design *to enable us to feature our faculty and other authors.*' " What other choices did Hemphill envision? Either the contributors to *SWJT* are members of the seminary's faculty or they are non-SWBTS ("other") authors. If one examines the numerous volumes of *SWJT*, one will discover that, in its original format and design, the journal has always featured SWBTS's faculty and "other authors." *SWJT* has always contained contributions by the seminary's faculty. As a matter of fact, two contributors to the disputed issue presently teach at SWBTS (Pool, for four and one-half years; and Estep, for more than forty years), while two of the authors formerly taught at SWBTS (N. Larry Baker, for over three years; and Hendricks, for twenty years). Also, five of the seven authors hold at least one graduate degree from SWBTS: Estep, the Th.D.; Hendricks, the M.Div. and Th.D.; Baker, the B.D., Th.M., and Th.D.; Leonard, the M.Div.; and Pool, the M.Div. Of the authors chosen to contribute to the disputed issue of the journal, several had previously published articles in *SWJT*, while both Estep and Hendricks had previously served as editor of *SWJT*.[25] Not that long ago, the journal's editorial board had even published a thematic issue of *SWJT* as a *Festschrift* for Estep.[26] Additionally, not only has the journal included contributions by Baptists from other institutions of the SBC, but it has included contributions by Baptists in the SBC labeled as "moderates," and even articles by non-Baptists.[27]

Third, although the editorial board had invited me to edit the now controversial (though nonexistent) issue of *SWJT*, and even though I had developed that issue, none of the administrators ever mentioned any of their problems with this issue of the journal to me. If Hemphill had communicated to me his problems with the selection of contributors early enough, together we could have developed another mutually-acceptable format or he could have chosen another editor for the issue. As it stands, to date I have received only one communication from the seminary's administration: Hemphill's letter of explanation for the editorial board's decision.

2. On Contributors as Former Members of SBTS's Faculty

As one of the criteria that Hemphill and SWBTS's other administrators used to justify their act of censorship, they noted that Hendricks, Marshall, and Leonard had formerly taught at SBTS. All three persons, however, had distinguished themselves during their years of service at SBTS. One would think that including contributions by these three authors would endear SWBTS to SBTS, rather than possibly engendering an adversarial relationship between the two seminaries. Most importantly for Hemphill, however, these three teachers left SBTS due to conflicts with the school's leadership over SBTS's "new direction." More accurately, however, Leonard, Marshall, and Hendricks left at different times, but largely as a result of pressures, threats, or affronts from the school's fundamentalist leadership.[28] Rather than an "adversarial" relationship with a "sister seminary," the administration of SWBTS appears to be more afraid of angering or insulting SBTS's president, R. Albert Mohler, Jr.: Mohler has exhibited his domineering style and behavior on more than one occasion. If Hemphill's purported intention to avoid an adversarial relationship with SBTS does not disclose his fear of Mohler's political power in the SBC, perhaps it does suggest Mohler's quiet yet explicit influence on Hemphill and, thus, Mohler's interference in SWBTS's supposedly independent operations.

3. On Visibility of Contributors in Controversial Issues

According to Hemphill, as another criterion with which to justify SWBTS's act of censorship, Hendricks, Leonard, and Marshall "were highly visible in some controversial issues."[29] From Hemphill's perspective, such decisions exhibit only administrative or organizational (neither academic nor political) concerns, principally to avoid controversy or agitation in or around the institution. Certainly, these three authors were involved in controversies, specifically controversies at SBTS. Nevertheless, even though SBTS succeeded in ridding itself of these three teachers, that school's successful expulsion of these people did not automatically or necessarily prove its leadership to be either right in its actions or truthful in its claims—unless, of course, "might makes right"! Furthermore, if Hemphill chooses to employ high-visibility-in-controversy as a criterion by which to eliminate persons from participation in the academic life of SWBTS, then several of the speakers whom the administration had scheduled to speak in SWBTS's chapel during the spring semester of 1997 would not qualify for the seminary's campus either: W. A. Criswell, O. S. Hawkins, Carl F. H. Henry,

Chuck Kelly, R. Albert Mohler, Jr., especially Paige Patterson, Morris Chapman, Richard Land, and now even Hemphill himself.[30] If the gospel of God in Jesus of Nazareth ever becomes genuinely controversial (a stumbling block or scandal—σκαϖνδαλον) again in the SBC or even at SWBTS, the seminary's leadership may need to consider an administrative decision to ban the gospel from the campus as well.[31]

4. On Current Service of Contributors in "Non-SBC" Schools

Hemphill supplied an additional criterion to justify SWBTS's act of censorship: Hendricks, Leonard, and Marshall "now teach at 'non-SBC' schools." Exactly what did Hemphill mean by "non-SBC" schools? In the previous statement, Hemphill most probably referred to independent universities or seminaries, institutions neither owned by the SBC nor managed by trustees appointed through the SBC. Technically, of course, Hemphill is correct—if his statement held that meaning. Although Hemphill made an accurate statement, it obscures several important factors about these individuals.

Leonard left SBTS after a lengthy tenure there but took a position at Samford University as chairperson of the Department of Religion and Philosophy. Samford University, although not owned and operated by the SBC, is a Baptist school and relates indirectly to Baptists in the SBC through the state convention in Alabama. Presently, Leonard serves as dean of Wake Forest University's Divinity School, another similar Baptist school. Hemphill received his own undergraduate degree from Wake Forest University. On the surface, Hemphill also spoke correctly about Hendricks. As the director of Baptist Studies at Brite Divinity School, Hendricks does not teach in one of the SBC's seminaries. Nonetheless, Hendricks has taught more than thirty-five years in three of the SBC's seminaries: twenty years at SWBTS, six years at Golden Gate Baptist Theological Seminary (GGBTS), and ten years at SBTS from which he retired. Such a distinguished career more than supplies Hendricks with the qualifications to meet Hemphill's criterion.

Incidentally, immediately following the initial publicity about this event of academic censorship, during the faculty meeting of SWBTS's School of Theology (12 December 1996), one of Hemphill's adjutants made a revealing comment. This administrator gave two examples of contributors whose contributions would have balanced the disputed issue of the journal: Timothy George and David Dockery. Of course, however, neither George nor Dockery serve schools either owned or controlled by the SBC, at least not in the sense noted previously. As a matter of fact, George currently serves as dean of Beeson Divinity School, Samford University, while Dockery presently serves as president of Union University. Both of these persons also formerly taught at SBTS. SWBTS's administrators themselves apparently consider this criterion (no one from a "non-SBC" school) applicable only when it does not affect their own political and theological allies.

5. On the Possibility of Adversarial Relationship between SWBTS and SBTS

Hemphill and his administration, for some reason, decided that scholarly studies of the SBC's confession of faith by Hendricks, Marshall, and Leonard would place SWBTS in an "unnecessarily adversarial" relationship with SBTS. Again, one should understand this statement as a reference to SBTS's president, Mohler. Still, how would scholarly studies of the *BFM (1963)* make Mohler the adversary of SWBTS (or, rather, Hemphill)?

A comment by Hemphill in one of his press releases contains a clue, however. Since Hendricks, Leonard, and Marshall formerly taught at SBTS, according to Hemphill, " '[i]t would have been inappropriate for Southwestern to provide these authors with such a platform without opportunity for balanced response.' "[32] Although no further elaboration accompanies this comment, the statement implies at least one major assumption: that these authors would develop their interpretations of the *BFM (1963)*, in order to attack the present fundamentalist leadership of SBTS, specifically, Mohler. Hemphill, or his adjutants at least, could have easily verified the falsity of that assumption, simply by reading the articles in question. Apparently, they had no real interest in the truth or falsity of the assumption. Those who formulated this specious claim with its obvious yet unstated assumption, like many other leaders of the SBC since 1979, designed the claim for its rhetorical effect, not for its truth or accuracy. SWBTS's administration designed that statement only to cast the shadow of suspicion over the articles, thus justifying the delay or cancellation of their publication in the journal.

Since the writings in question do not contain anything like the specters suggested by SWBTS's administration, what did Hemphill mean by "balanced response" to those articles? Clues for an answer to this question, of course, occur in other statements made by SWBTS's administration, statements to which my following observations refer.

6. On Contributors Not Representing SWJT's Readership or the SBC

According to Hemphill's letter to me, SWBTS's vice-president for academic administration, the seminary's dean for the School of Theology, and the journal's editorial board "did not consider the writers as a whole to really represent [*sic*] the broad spectrum of either our readership or the convention." In his initial comments to the *Baptist Standard*, Hemphill made this evaluation more specific: "In the perception of the SBC, he said, 'these do not stand for a strongly conservative view of the Baptist Faith and Message Statement.' "[33] Again, these comments reflect at least two major problems.

First, how can SWBTS's administration plausibly claim that the writers as a whole do not represent either the journal's readership or the SBC? Several thousand graduates from SWBTS have taken courses with Hendricks, Baker, Estep, and Pool. Several thousand more graduates from SBTS and MWBTS took courses from Leonard, Marshall, and Baker; and at least several hundred more graduates from GGBTS took courses from Hendricks. Certainly, those graduates, even if half of them reflect perspectives similar to their teachers, comprise a significant portion of the broad spectrum of both the journal's readership and the SBC itself. Furthermore, even though these authors may not agree with the fundamentalist leaders who dominate the SBC and its institutions, this divergence in perspective does not automatically mean that the authors in question do not represent a large proportion of Baptists in the SBC or even of *SWJT's* readership.

Second, even if Hemphill were correct in his claim about the SBC's perception of either the authors in question or their writings, perception is not necessarily reality. A seminary's educational task is not to protect itself from antagonism based on either accurate perceptions or misperceptions of its efforts to fulfill its commission. Baptists have produced seminaries to educate men and women for ministry. The educational process involves dispelling false perceptions, not reinforcing misperceptions and prejudices. In order to teach those who need education, every educational institution will challenge unfounded assumptions and bias. Nothing an institution can do will prevent those who do not read, or those who fear education, from arriving at false conclusions. When an educational institution refuses to allow the expression of alternative perspectives (whether in its publications or in its classrooms), in order to avoid antagonistic responses through open declarations of uninformed biases by nonreaders or those against education, then that school also reinforces both the very prejudices and mean-spirited behavior that inhibit the institution's educational process.

Third, again, even if Hemphill were correct in his claim about the SBC's perception, and even if the SBC's perception about the authors in question were correct, should Baptists in the SBC not know, and would they not benefit from learning, both that legitimate or historically supportable alternative interpretations of the *BFM (1963)* do exist and that Baptists in the SBC actually do interpret the SBC's confession of faith in these ways? The issue here does not concern whether or not the SBC and these authors affirm the same confessional document, but whether or not either SWBTS or the SBC itself will allow every Baptist both to understand the *BFM (1963)* according to the dictates of her or his own conscience and to express freely that interpretation (whether in writing or speaking) as a Baptist in the

SBC. The seminary's censorship of the journal undermines this foundational Baptist principle.[34]

Fourth, following from the previous problem, how can Hemphill or his administrative adjutants presume to speak for the SBC or all Baptists in the SBC? The SBC has not authorized Hemphill or his adjutants to speak for all Baptists in the SBC. More importantly, not every Baptist in the SBC has authorized, as his or her official voice, the administrators of SWBTS with that privilege. In Baptist ecclesial polity, no one speaks for all Baptists. Genuine Baptists accept no official magisterium, or teaching office, as the final or authoritative source for every question about either faith or practice. Genuine Baptists, after careful study, decide for themselves. If Hemphill and his administration genuinely trusted and expressed the SBC's historic perspectives, they would allow Baptists to read, to discuss, to argue, if need be to complain, and finally to decide for themselves, how they will evaluate interpretations of the *BFM (1963)*. Instead, the administrators of SWBTS have decided not to allow Baptists in the SBC to exercise their prerogatives as participants in a common priesthood. Neither such a repressive posture nor such manipulative behavior represents the broader and most authentic heritage and piety of Baptists in the SBC.

7. On Possible Perceptions about the Selection of Authors

As I mentioned previously, SWBTS's vice-president for academic administration had attempted to explain the administration's decision to suspend the journal's publication. According to Scotty Gray, the administration's concern revolved around " 'the *possible perceived* lack of balance in the selection of contributors.' "[35] Perhaps the administrators were genuinely concerned about "possible" *perceptions* of imbalance in the selection of authors. If so, then my previous comments about education and perceptions apply to this statement as well. More than likely, however, the *actual selection* of contributors really troubled the administrators. If so, then the administrative mention of "the possible perceived lack of balance in the selection of contributors" contains the reference to possible perceptions largely as a mask to disguise the administrative posture of the seminary, such as, the administration's own evaluation of the selections as unbalanced, its own distaste for the selections made by the issue editor, and its own desire to remedy the situation. Some of the administrative language, at least, appears to imply that message. That implicit message, whether intentional or not, requires a response.

After I had accepted the editorial board's invitation to edit *SWJT* for the spring of 1997, the journal's managing editor and I discussed possible authors for that issue of the journal. I did not contact any of the authors until the managing editor had approved my recommendations and had authorized me to make the initial contacts.

I used a variety of criteria for my selection of possible contributors for the journal. First, I looked for highly competent scholars of Baptist history, theology, and ethics. All of the possible contributors fit this category, with four theologians, two historians, and one ethicist.

Second, I searched for scholars with substantial connections to, interests in, or relationships with SWBTS. Each of the authors finally invited to contribute, except for one person, either had taken at least one graduate degree from SWBTS, or had previously contributed an article to *SWJT*, or had taught at SWBTS, or presently teaches at SWBTS. Some of the authors fit into more than one of those categories.

Third, I tried to find scholars who reflected the diversity of Baptist experience and history. The group of scholars finally chosen filled that requirement.

Fourth, I avoided choosing writers from only one or two Baptist schools or institutions, looking for authors who represented a wider institutional spectrum: thus, Baker, pastor of a Baptist church in Louisiana; Estep, professor of church history at SWBTS; myself, assistant professor of systematic theology at SWBTS; Marshall, professor of theology and spirituality at Central Baptist Theological Seminary; Leonard, dean of Wake Forest University's Divinity School and formerly chairperson of Samford University's Department of Religion and Philosophy; Hendricks, director of Baptist studies and lecturer in theology at Texas Christian University's Brite Divinity School; and McWilliams, professor of theology at Oklahoma Baptist University.

Fifth, I wanted this slate of authors to contain female as well as male perspectives. Fortunately, Molly Marshall accepted my invitation to write for the journal. Although I also asked one other female Baptist theologian, she declined the invitation to contribute to *SWJT*.

Sixth, I aimed to enlist both senior and junior scholars. Estep, Hendricks, and Baker represent the senior end of this spectrum, while Leonard and McWilliams represent the middle range, with Marshall and myself barely representing the lower end of this spectrum.

Seventh, I sought to avoid any person committed to the theological ideology of conquest and domination so characteristic of the SBC's leadership since 1979. None of the authors selected came from that category.

My use of the several previous criteria indicates at least three things. First, I considered the sensitive nature of both the SBC and the journal itself. Second, with these selections, I made a genuine effort to enhance the academic reputation of SWBTS. Third, as the previous criteria demonstrate, I endeavored to select a balanced group of contributors. When it comes to genuine scholarship and the academic process, however, "the concept of balance" involves far more than whether or not one agrees with or submits to those who dominate the SBC.

8. On the Alleged Best Interest of SWBTS and the SBC

About the benevolent intentions behind the seminary's act of academic censorship, Hemphill made similar claims in various press releases: "that he thought he was 'doing what is right for Southwestern Baptist Theological Seminary and the Southern Baptist Convention' "; and that the editorial board had canceled the articles " 'in the best interests of Southwestern and the Southern Baptist Convention.' " Similarly, in his letter to me, he claimed that he, the vice-president for academic administration, the dean for the School of Theology, and the journal's editorial board thought that "it would be in the *best interest* of Southwestern and our convention that we not publish the journal as configured."[36]

No one would dispute the claim that an institution's administrative leadership exists to promote the "best interests of" or to do "what is right for" that institution. Two questions arise, however, about Hemphill's claims. (1) Did Hemphill rightly perceive that which is right or proper for SWBTS? (2) Do Baptists in the SBC need or want an institutional leader to decide for them that which is right or in their best interests to read?

In answer to the first query, I offer another question: Is academic censorship ever right or in the best interests of an educational institution, especially when those who contribute to the academic enterprise, either by publications or by teaching, do so responsibly? As a response to the second question, comments from a letter to the *Baptist Standard* answer most forcefully. "As a graduate of Southwestern, I find it amusing to learn that Hemphill is able to discern what is in my best interests. I also found it humorous to read that he and William Tolar both excuse censorship on the basis of needing 'a new format and design.' "[37] Genuine Baptists neither appreciate nor desire leaders who attempt to usurp the prerogatives of each individual's conscience. Not only does such arrogant behavior strike at the heart of religious freedom, but in an academic context such actions actually distort and erode academic freedom.

9. On the Purported Nonimpingement of Academic Freedom

Since one of the seminary's accrediting agencies has recently released SWBTS from probation (which the agency had imposed, after the seminary's trustees had terminated Russell Dilday's employment as president, partially due to concerns about academic freedom at the seminary), the seminary's administrators desperately tried to avoid any appearance of academic censorship. For instance, in his letter to me, Hemphill comments as follows: "I have not read the articles and have not discussed the content with those who have." Furthermore, according to the *Fort Worth Star-Telegram*, Scotty Gray claimed that ". . . the *content* of the articles was not the basis of the decision." Also in that story, Gray claimed that "academic freedom was not impinged."[38]

Had the seminary's administrators, other members of the faculty, or even all members of the editorial board read the articles and found them to be deficient in research or reasoning, then to delay or even permanently to cancel their publication would have genuinely protected or even enhanced the seminary's academic standards. Oddly, however, the seminary's administration claimed that the content of the articles did not influence the decision to suspend the journal's publication. The administrators seemed to think that, with such an explanation, they had avoided any threats to or violations of academic freedom. Thus, they could avoid any investigations by the seminary's accrediting agencies.

Academic freedom in an educational institution, however, does not apply only to the content communicated in publications or classrooms. Academic freedom also belongs to the voices or persons that communicate that content. An institution also violates academic freedom when it refuses to permit certain qualified people to speak within its context, but will allow other people to speak within its context who contradict or attack those whose voices the institution has silenced or eliminated.[39] Such preferential treatment of some Baptists, and the correlative marginalization of other Baptists who represent alternative perspectives, has glaringly characterized the SBC for almost two decades. Although such abuses of academic freedom have occurred at SWBTS previously, never have they occurred so blatantly nor in such a wholesale way.[40]

10. On Hemphill's Purported Avoidance of the SBC's Political Controversy

According to Hemphill's letter to me, he had "been making every effort to keep Southwestern *out of the political controversy*" and to allow the seminary to "focus on the matter of theological education." The dean of SWBTS's School of Theology, Tommy Lea, reflected Hemphill's perspective in a comment to a reporter: " 'Dr. Hemphill is *apolitical* when it comes to leading this institution.' "[41] With those comments, of course, the seminary's administration implied at least two major conclusions: (1) if the journal were published as configured, the list of authors alone would politicize the seminary in the SBC; and (2) avoidance of the seminary's politicization, therefore, motivated the seminary's administrative decision to suspend the journal's publication. These claims, however, raise several significant problems.

First, by eliminating the content of the articles (or theological and historical evidence) as the basis for its decision, in order to avoid charges of academic censorship, the seminary's administration left only one other real option as a motive for its suspension of the journal's publication: political expediency. Strangely, although Hemphill claimed that he has made "every effort to keep Southwestern out of the political controversy," he admitted that the departures from SBTS by Leonard, Marshall, and Hendricks at least influenced his decision. Those three teachers, however, departed because they differed with the fundamentalist leadership about the direction of that school. Clearly, according to his letter to me, the denominational-political orientation of at least these three authors motivated Hemphill and the other administrators.[42]

Second, the SBC has already politicized SWBTS. Fundamentalists have dominated the seminary's board of trustees for some time, the very board of trustees that fired Dilday and hired Hemphill. The seminary's trustees and administration have openly aligned SWBTS with the fundamentalist agenda and credenda of the present SBC. Hemphill worked to keep SWBTS "out of the political controversy," but only by moving SWBTS more fully into line with the SBC's prevailing fundamentalist regime. The actual result of publishing the journal as configured would have been to re-open the seminary also to moderate political perspectives, thus balancing its own approach to theological education. The seminary's administration and some of its trustees publicly and theoretically tout fair treatment of all perspectives in the institution, but they privately and practically do not permit it.

Third, the seminary's administration did not aim to avoid the seminary's politicization. Rather, Hemphill and his adjutants sought to avoid any appearance of defecting from the seminary's political allegiance to the fundamentalist-dominated SBC. Consequently, avoiding any opportunity at SWBTS for nonfundamentalist, Baptist, denominational political perspectives motivated suspension of the journal's publication. The purportedly "apolitical" posture of the seminary or its president is only apolitical in the refusal of support for anyone with a moderate Baptist perspective. The seminary's administration only concerns itself with any possible politicization of the seminary when that politicization does not favor the SBC's prevailing, fundamentalist status quo.

Fourth, if authors from the SBC's current fundamentalist leadership had written the same articles with the same content, would the seminary's administration have questioned the publication of those articles? Implicitly, the seminary's official press releases seem to suggest a negative answer to that question. To the contrary, however, certain Baptists did not earn the political label, "moderates," as a result of their political methods. Rather, the name, "moderates," arose as a tag for Baptists with nonfundamentalistic theological perspectives. The content of the articles, whoever the authors might have been, also would ultimately have raised theological questions for a seminary's administration with commitments to the SBC's fundamentalist credenda. The seminary's administration openly commits itself, without any public critical perspective, to the political organization of the SBC's fundamentalist oligarchy. No one commits oneself politically to that political regime, however, without a corresponding commitment to the fundamentalist theological credenda or articles of faith. The fundamentalist theology legitimates the fundamentalist political domination of the SBC; the fundamentalist political machine enforces the theology of its own legitimation on Baptists in the SBC. Thus, in the administrative suspension of *SWJT's* publication, due to contributions in it by moderate Baptist scholars, political expediency and academic censorship have coincided.

Fifth, in his letter to me, Hemphill also wrote a related statement: "We simply considered that *in the highly symbolic time in which we live* it would be in the best interest of Southwestern and our convention that we not publish the journal as configured."[43] No further elaboration accompanied this comment. Several times, however, I have conversed with persons at SWBTS who used similar language. Hemphill's comment seems to imply something resembling the following argument. Certain actions, behavior, language, style, attitudes, policies, and even personalities represent far more than something in themselves. Sometimes these things signify something larger or more significant than themselves, even though they also participate in those larger realities they signify.[44] Furthermore, Hemphill then seems implicitly to ascribe this quality to the present time or period of either the SBC's life or the world's existence. In addition, Hemphill also appears to imply a dual conclusion: (1) that this present time is or may be, in some sense, more symbolic than other times; and (2) that such intensified eras of the SBC's history demand or may require, by the SBC's unstated moral standards, both occasional self-contradictory behavior from individuals and even inconsistent administration of institutions. Thus, since Baptists of the SBC presently dwell in a "highly symbolic time," the seminary's administration can justify its efforts to suspend publication of the journal.

Certainly, this present time in the SBC's existence is symbolic, perhaps even more symbolic than other times in the denomination's history. Such a claim, however accurate it may be, can never genuinely justify personal actions or institutional operations that themselves signal either the abandonment of Christian honesty in the behavior of Baptists or the compromise of academic integrity in the operation of the denomination's seminaries. If

Hemphill is correct about "the highly symbolic time in which we live," then he and his adjutants should realize the symbolic density of their own comportment and actions in the suspension of *SWJT's* publication. During this "highly symbolic time," through such administrative decisions and reasons, is it (has it ever been or will it ever be) truly in the best interests of either the SBC or SWBTS to make the seminary a symbol of academic censorship, of enforced fundamentalist ideology, of fear, of persistent retribution toward so-called "moderate" Baptists, of unconditional commitment to the SBC's fundamentalist oligarchy, and finally of compromised Christian piety? Again, Pascal supplies a terse reminder: "It is no doubt an evil to be full of faults, but it is a still greater evil to be full of them and unwilling to recognize them, since this entails the further evil of deliberate self-delusion."[45]

B. The Gray Martyrdom

The studies in this book do not supply a single, official, and definitive or formulaic interpretation of the *BFM (1963)*. The authors of the following chapters have engaged their topics with all of their scholarly abilities, integrity, knowledge, and experience. These authors offer modest, balanced, and sensitive appraisals of their assigned topics. They have not endeavored to destabilize Baptist appreciation for the *BFM (1963)* with ideological attacks on that document or the history of its usage. Yet, the authors of these studies have not hesitated to expose flaws and weaknesses either in the *BFM (1963)* itself or in the employment of that document by Baptist Christians, Baptist churches, institutions of the SBC, or even the SBC itself.

In addition, the authors have written these studies from their perspectives as Christians, specifically, from their perspectives as genuine *Baptist* Christians. These authors have not written about the SBC or its confessional heritage as "outsiders" or external observers. Rather, the authors of the following studies have written as Christians who have invested their lives in the SBC and its institutions, as people whose own personal stories participate in the larger account about the *BFM (1963)*, its history, and its theological meaning. Thus, each author's interpretation of the *BFM (1963)* qualifies also as testimony to her or his own spiritual experience as a Baptist in the SBC. In his own studies of the phenomenon of "testimony," Paul Ricoeur helpfully observes that "a witness may so implicate himself in his testimony that it becomes the best proof of his conviction." Ricoeur expresses this similarly elsewhere: "we especially come to call testimony an action, a work, the movement of a life insofar as these things constitute by themselves the mark and the living proof of a man's conviction and devotion to a cause."[46] The seminary's administrative construal of at least some of the testimonies in this book certainly validates Ricoeur's claims. The administrators who both desired and pressured a decision to suspend the publication of these studies had not even read the texts themselves. Yet, the names of the writers alone so identified those authors with certain perspectives, however wrongly the seminary's administration misrepresented those perspectives, that the institution's leadership believed that it could convince Baptists in the SBC that the journal's editorial board had censored the work of those authors for legitimate or justifiable reasons.[47]

Johann Baptist Metz describes the church as "the public witness and bearer of the tradition of a dangerous memory of freedom in the 'systems' of our emancipative society." In its attestation to this "dangerous memory of freedom," the Christian community attests to the "*memoria passionis, mortis et resurrectionis Jesu Christi.*" This dangerous memory has a double dynamic. Positively, memory of the Christ's freedom appears as "liberating force" for those who suffer oppression and bondage. Negatively, this dangerous memory interrogates and subverts the structures or programs of oppression themselves: "It gives rise again and again to the suspicion that the plausible structures of a society may be relationships aimed to delude." Thus, in the various forms of its testimony to this dangerous memory, the Christian community also participates in the dual movement of that liberation disclosed in and given by the Christ.[48] According to the Gospel of Luke, Jesus identified his own life as the fulfillment of precisely that task, when he read from the scriptures in the synagogue at Nazareth. " 'The Spirit of the Lord is upon me, because he has anointed me to bring good news to the poor. He has sent me to proclaim release to the captives and recovery of sight to the blind, to let the oppressed go free, to proclaim the year of the Lord's favor.' "[49] As Metz also notes, "the Church's teachings and confessions of faith should be understood as formulae in which this challenging memory is publicly spelt out."[50]

The authors of these studies find their own liberty inscribed in Christ's freedom. The studies in this book have originated precisely from each author's experience of Christ's liberating freedom. Hence, in various ways, every chapter of this book attests to that dangerous memory of Christ's freedom—as present in the lives of the authors, as declared in the *BFM (1963)*, and as remembered through each author's interpretation of that confessional document. These authors attest to that which they have heard, seen, handled—or experienced for themselves—the most basic qualities of a witness.[51] As a result, this book's testimonies to that liberating yet subversive memory also contradict every person or institution that oppresses, enslaves, distorts, deceives, malforms, manipulates, or coerces authentic human life. Yet, the leadership of SWBTS decided to initiate the suppression of these testimonies, by softening or eliminating their presence in its own theological journal, even by insinuating problems with the authors and their works. The authors of this book's chapters, once again, know quite well the meaning of Nietzsche's penetrating insight: "One is punished most for one's virtues."[52]

As every writer knows, the task of writing always entails labor, struggle, and suffering. To write about one's faith and its place within a specific tradition, one also often struggles and suffers even more. To write about the faith of one's tradition in the face of opposition and persecution, however, brings suffering to the work of writing in a far more radical sense. The authors of the chapters in this book have suffered in each of the three previous ways, but most deeply in the third way. Those who remain responsible for suspending, and ultimately for canceling, the publication of the articles, by that very administrative action and its rationalization, have cast shadows of suspicion on the interpretations of the *BFM (1963)* contained in this book. In this way, the seminary's leadership, whether fully aware of it or not, has distorted and twisted these interpretations of Baptist faith, by the implications and innuendoes suggested in the administrative language used to discredit some of these authors, specifically Hendricks, Marshall, and Leonard—yet the remaining authors as well through, at least, a sort of guilt by association! If not distortion or perversion or twisting of the interpretations themselves, the seminary's action and self-justification for it at least have distorted, twisted, and perverted "possible perceptions" of those articles, thus bringing pain even to the authors themselves. However indirect such infliction of pain may be, the authors have certainly been the ultimate targets of that distortion. John Proctor, a character in Arthur Miller's play *The Crucible*, asks questions of an inquisitor who searches for witches, questions pertinent to this situation. "Is the accuser always holy now? Were they born this morning as clean as God's fingers?"[53]

From the Latin word "*torquere*," which means "to twist," the English language derives its own word, "torture." Referring to the witness of Jesus before Pilate and the consequences of that meeting, Julia Kristeva insightfully claims that "[t]he avowal of faith is thus from the very start tied to persecution and suffering." As she perceives, "[t]his pain, moreover, has wholly permeated the word 'martyr,' giving it its basic, ordinary meaning, that of torture rather than testimony." As Ricoeur observes, "[w]hen the test of conviction becomes the price of life, the witness changes his name; he is called martyr."[54] Such fortitude certainly begins to demarcate between the true and the false witness. Augustine of Hippo supplied one other important criterion: "*Itaque martyres non facit poena, sed causa*"; "it is not the punishment (or suffering) that makes martyrs, but the cause (for which they are punished)."[55] Those who suffer the penalty for their attestations to a *just cause*, those witnesses qualify as martyrs, since they suffer unjustly.

Most assuredly, I exaggerate if I construe the maltreatment of this book's authors as martyrdom or the most extreme form of persecution. These authors have not paid for their convictions with the termination of their very lives. In another sense, however, they have paid a penalty for their convictions with their lives. An Irish Christian typology of martyrdom from the fifth and sixth centuries helps to clarify the truth in my exaggeration. While "Red Martyrdom" held the traditional meaning of martyrdom by blood or death, "Green Martyrdom" referred to the Christian's voluntary abandonment of ordinary or material comforts, by retreating to remote locations, such as forests, mountains, or islands, in order to "study the scriptures and commune with God." Irish Christians also identified a third type, "White Martyrdom": the permanent exile, a "voyage of no return," of a Christian from her or his homeland in Ireland, either inflicted by the church as punishment for a crime or self-inflicted as a missionary vocation.[56] Perhaps, within the dysfunctional context of the SBC and its institutions, a fourth type of martyrdom emerges: a Baptist community's or institution's intentional marginalization of those Baptists who refuse to ignore the ideologization of the Christian gospel, the silencing of dissenting voices within the community, the exclusion of such Baptists from any and all forms of effective participation in a community's or an institution's operations or programs or development. Such treatment of participants in a community pushes them to the periphery, still within the community, yet in the region of least participation or belonging, as close to the edge of alienation and non-identity as possible. The designation, "gray martyrdom," fittingly describes a Baptist Christian's experience of such attack on life, of exile to a region of such indefiniteness and ambiguity. The seminary's administration has inflicted precisely such punishment, a gray martyrdom, on the authors of the chapters in this book.

Most certainly, the offenses against these authors, even their writings themselves, amount to very small matters in the larger processes of life and the divine Spirit's activity in the creation. Nonetheless, the chapters of this book and the events from which they originated remain unique and valuable, however seemingly insignificant or minor. For that reason, I have written this account, lest the writings be lost, the events be minimized or forgotten, and the disparagement of the authors remain unanswered. Jorges Luis Borges noted the great value in even the most mundane of memories.

> In time there was a day that extinguished the last eyes to see Christ; the battle of Junín and the love of Helen died with the death of a man. What will die with me when I die, what pathetic or fragile form will the world lose? The voice of Macedonio Fernández, the image of a red horse in the vacant lot at Serrano and Charcas, a bar of sulphur in the drawer of a mahogany desk?[57]

Without these unique witnesses, Baptists as well as all Christians lose valuable and dangerous, however minor, memories—dangerous because these memories expose similar forms of oppression and victimization, yet valuable because such memories empower others with the hope for liberation.

Conclusion

Why do the authors of the following chapters continue to write, to teach, to study, and to speak? Why do they publish these small studies of the *BFM (1963)*? The celebrated comment by Karl Marx, his eleventh thesis on Feuerbach, helps to answer the previous questions: "The philosophers have only *interpreted* the world in various ways; the point, however, is to *change* it." The authors of this book continue their work because they hope to end the cycle of dysfunction among Baptists. They hope to change the world. They do not seek merely to understand the world, in order to maintain and to justify the prevailing structures of domination. Thus, these authors know that the actual publication of these articles, the fact of their public inscription, is perhaps more important than the actual content of the chapters themselves. As Bill Leonard remarked in his letter to Hemphill about this situation, "[h]istory often judges us by what we did in the small moments when courage was possible but ignored."[58] The authors of this book have chosen not to ignore the moment when those with power tested the convictions expressed through the following interpretations of the *BFM (1963)*.

Each author has endeavored to stimulate further conversation among Baptists about the doctrinal perspectives inscribed within the *BFM (1963)*. As the editor of this book, I hope that these studies will supply ministers and teachers with another helpful resource for teaching Baptist doctrinal perspectives, both to the many other Christians in the thousands of local Baptist churches and to the many students in Baptist colleges, universities, and seminaries. I also hope that this book's content and the fact of its existence will inspire other Baptists to resist every effort to tear them from their home in Christ's liberty. Most importantly, I hope, along with the other authors, both that this book fulfills scripture's reminder to all Christians and will serve to inspire other Baptist Christians to testify similarly.

> Now who will harm you if you are eager to do what is good? But even if you do suffer for doing what is right, you are blessed. Do not fear what they fear, and do not be intimidated, but in your hearts sanctify Christ as Lord. Always be ready to make your defense to anyone who demands from you an accounting for the hope that is in you; yet do it with gentleness and reverence. Keep your conscience clear, so that, when you are maligned, those who abuse you for your good conduct in Christ may be put to shame.[59]

Notes

[1] See "Committee on Baptist Faith and Message," in *Annual of the Southern Baptist Convention: One Hundred Sixth Session in Kansas City, Missouri, 7-10 May 1963*, ed. Executive Committee, Southern Baptist Convention (Nashville: Southern Baptist Convention, 1963) 63, 269-81 ("Proceedings," Thursday Morning, May 9, Items 112-124) (hereafter, cited as *BFM [1963]*).

[2] Herschel H. Hobbs wrote the standard interpretation of the *BFM (1963)* (Herschel H. Hobbs, *The Baptist Faith and Message* [Nashville: Convention Press, 1971]). Even though the SBC has recently released a revision of this book, it remains essentially unchanged (Herschel H. Hobbs, *The Baptist Faith and Message* [Nashville: Convention Press, 1996]).

[3] "We are also in hearty accord with every movement and cause in which Christians of every name may take part without doing violence to the *sacred mandates of conscience* and without impairing their sense of loyalty to Christ" ("Pronouncement on Christian Union and Denominational Efficiency," from "Report of Commission on Efficiency to the Southern Baptist Convention," in *Annual of the Southern Baptist Convention: Fifty-Ninth Session in Nashville, Tennessee, 13-18 May 1914*, ed. Secretaries, Southern Baptist Convention [Nashville: Marshall and Bruce, 1914] 73 ["Proceedings," Fourth Day, Morning Session, May 16, Item 97] [emphasis mine]). For a brief study of this document, see James E. Carter, "Southern Baptists' First Confession of Faith," *Baptist History and Heritage* 5 (January 1970): 24-28, 38.

[4] Despite a denial of this claim by the document itself, see the following, camouflaged, and perhaps preliminary, revision of the *BFM (1963)*: "The Report of the Presidential Theological Study Committee," in *Annual of the Southern Baptist Convention: One Hundred Thirty-Seventh Session in Orlando, Florida, 14-16 June 1994*, ed. Executive Committee, Southern Baptist Convention (Nashville: Southern Baptist Convention, 1994) 112-18. Also see my rhetorical-theological analysis and ideology-critique of that credal revision of the *BFM (1963)*: Jeff B. Pool, *Against Returning to Egypt: Exposing and Resisting Credalism in the Southern Baptist Convention* (forthcoming, Macon GA: Mercer University Press, 1997).

[5] Bill Tillman, Fort Worth, to Jeff Pool, Fort Worth, 1 February 1996, Transcript in the hand of Jeff B. Pool, Archives, Roberts Library, Southwestern Baptist Theological Seminary, Fort Worth, Texas. The faculty of Southwestern Baptist Theological Seminary's School of Theology established *SWJT* in 1917 and continued its publication until 1924. Thirty-four years later, with permission from the president of Southwestern Baptist Theological Seminary, J. Howard Williams, the faculty of the School of Theology re-established and again began to publish *SWJT* in 1958. Since then, until November of 1996, SWBTS had published *SWJT* continuously (see James Leo Garrett, "Editorial Introduction," *Southwestern Journal of Theology* 1 [October 1958]: 4-7).

[6] William M. Tillman, Jr., Fort Worth, to Jeff B. Pool, Fort Worth, 18 November 1996, Transcript in the hand of Jeff B. Pool, Archives, Roberts Library, Southwestern Baptist Theological Seminary, Fort Worth, Texas.

⁷*WJT's* editorial board during this incident included the following persons: Kenneth S. Hemphill, editor-in-chief; William M. Tillman, Jr., managing editor; Al Fasol, book review editor; Justice C. Anderson; H. Alan Brehm; Karen Bullock; Bob W. Brackney; and William W. Colson. Later, according to the *Baptist Standard*, William B. Tolar, consultant to the president of SWBTS, noted a lack of unanimity in the editorial board's agreement with Hemphill: "One or two on the editorial board of the journal had strong feelings about leaving its content alone, he said, but 'those of us who looked at it with a larger view felt it did not represent a good cross-section and for the sake of the seminary' should be suspended" (Toby Druin, "Southwestern Journal Pulled 'In Best Interests,'" *Baptist Standard* 108 [11 December 1996]: 3). At least one member of the editorial board perceived Tolar's statement as condescending: because members of the editorial board disagreed with the administration's perspective, Tolar's comment implies that those board members did not look at, or were not capable of looking at, this issue "with a larger view." Tolar, however, did not even meet with the editorial board on 8 November 1996.

⁸Jeff B. Pool, Fort Worth, to William M. Tillman, Jr., Fort Worth, 27 November 1996, Transcript in the hand of Jeff B. Pool, Archives, Roberts Library, Southwestern Baptist Theological Seminary, Fort Worth, Texas; N. Larry Baker, Pineville, Louisiana, to William M. Tillman, Jr., Fort Worth, 21 November 1996, Transcript in the hand of Jeff B. Pool, Archives, Roberts Library, Southwestern Baptist Theological Seminary, Fort Worth, Texas.

⁹William M. Tillman, Jr., Fort Worth, to Jeff B. Pool, Fort Worth, 11 December 1996, Transcript in the hand of Jeff B. Pool, Archives, Roberts Library, Southwestern Baptist Theological Seminary, Fort Worth, Texas.

¹⁰Druin, "Southwestern Journal Pulled 'In Best Interests,'" 3; Toby Druin and Greg Warner, "Southwestern Cancels Journal with Controversial Authors," Associated Baptist Press, 11 December 1996; Kenneth S. Hemphill, Fort Worth, to Jeff B. Pool, Fort Worth, 12 December 1996, Transcript in the hand of Jeff B. Pool, Archives, Roberts Library, Southwestern Baptist Theological Seminary, Fort Worth, Texas; Jim Jones, "Seminary President Cancels Journal Issue," *Fort Worth Star-Telegram*, 13 December 1996, 1, 4 (B). Other articles on this event followed this initial publicity. As examples, see the following publications: "Hemphill Cancels Southwestern Journal; Authors Cited," *Western Recorder* 170 (17 December 1996): 2; Craig Bird, "Hemphill Suspends Southwestern Theology Journal," *Baptist Messenger* 85 (19 December 1996): 10; "Journal Blocked; Protests Arise," *Daily Oklahoman*, 21 December 1996, 16.

¹¹Blaise Pascal, "The Mystery of Jesus," in *Pensées*, trans. A. J. Krailsheimer (Middlesex, England: Penguin Books Ltd., 1966) 313 (4.B.919). A few days after this meeting of the faculty of SWBTS's School of Theology, Bill J. Leonard communicated his own questions about the faculty's response in a letter to Hemphill. "My sadness is directed less toward you—you were elected to respond in this way to such issues—than with your faculty. Their silence and acquiescence in this matter is a repudiation of collegiality toward co-laborers, friends, and former students. It is also a distressful model for your current generation of students. What will your students think about the courage and academic integrity of the faculty?

Was there even one righteous person on the faculty who raised the issue of fairness, openness, freedom, or simply good old-fashioned Baptist dissent? I hope such a voice was raised. I am saddened that most of your faculty seems to have missed the point and the moment" (Bill J. Leonard, Winston-Salem, North Carolina, to Dr. Kenneth Hemphill, Fort Worth, 17 December 1996, Copy of Transcript in the hand of Jeff B. Pool, Archives, Roberts Library, Southwestern Baptist Theological Seminary, Fort Worth, Texas).

[12]Druin, "Southwestern Journal Pulled 'In Best Interests,'" 3. Other papers later carried this same story: e.g., "Hemphill Cancels Southwestern Journal; Authors Cited," *Western Recorder* 170 (17 December 1996): 2.

[13]Jones, "Seminary President Cancels Journal Issue," 1, 4 (B).

[14]Craig Bird, "Hemphill Suspends Southwestern Theology Journal," *Baptist Messenger* 85 (19 December 1996): 10.

[15]Jones, "Seminary President Cancels Journal Issue," 1 (B); Bird, "Hemphill Suspends Southwestern Theology Journal," 10.

[16]Kenneth S. Hemphill, Fort Worth, to Dr. Jeff Pool, Fort Worth, 12 December 1996, Transcript in the hand of Jeff B. Pool, Archives, Roberts Library, Southwestern Baptist Theological Seminary, Fort Worth, Texas; Jones, "Seminary President Cancels Journal Issue," 4 (B); Druin, "Southwestern Journal Pulled 'In Best Interests,'" 3; Bird, "Hemphill Suspends Southwestern Theology Journal," 10; "Hemphill Cancels Southwestern Journal; Authors Cited," *Western Recorder* 170 (17 December 1996): 2.

[17]Kenneth S. Hemphill, Fort Worth, to Dr. Jeff Pool, Fort Worth, 12 December 1996, Transcript in the hand of Jeff B. Pool, Archives, Roberts Library, Southwestern Baptist Theological Seminary, Fort Worth, Texas; Jones, "Seminary President Cancels Journal Issue," 4 (B).

[18]Kenneth S. Hemphill, Fort Worth, to Dr. Jeff Pool, Fort Worth, 12 December 1996, Transcript in the hand of Jeff B. Pool, Archives, Roberts Library, Southwestern Baptist Theological Seminary, Fort Worth, Texas; Bird, "Hemphill Suspends Southwestern Theology Journal," 10.

[19]Kenneth S. Hemphill, Fort Worth, to Dr. Jeff Pool, Fort Worth, 12 December 1996, Transcript in the hand of Jeff B. Pool, Archives, Roberts Library, Southwestern Baptist Theological Seminary, Fort Worth, Texas. Hemphill also officially released similar comments to reporters (Druin, "Southwestern Journal Pulled 'In Best Interests,'" 3; Druin and Warner, "Southwestern Cancels Journal with Controversial Authors," Associated Baptist Press, 11 December 1996; Bird, "Hemphill Suspends Southwestern Theology Journal," 10; "Hemphill Cancels Southwestern Journal; Authors Cited," *Western Recorder* 170 [17 December 1996]: 2).

[20]The work of Jürgen Habermas on critical theory significantly informs my ideology-critique of the official accounts and assessments of this situation: see Jürgen Habermas, *Legitimation Crisis*, trans. Thomas McCarthy (Boston: Beacon Press, 1975); idem, *Knowledge and Human Interests*, trans. Jeremy J. Shapiro (Boston: Beacon Press, 1971); idem, *The Theory of Communicative Action*, vol. 1, *Reason and the Rationalization of Society*, trans. Thomas McCarthy (Boston:

Beacon Press, 1984); and idem, "Consciousness-Raising or Redemptive Criticism," *New German Critique* 17 (1979): 30-59. Also see the following studies of Habermas' work: Stephen K. White, *The Recent Work of Jürgen Habermas: Reason, Justice, and Modernity* (Cambridge: Cambridge University Press, 1988); Paul Lakeland, *Theology and Critical Theory: The Discourse of the Church* (Nashville: Abingdon Press, 1990). Also see Paul Ricoeur, "Hermeneutics and the Critique of Ideology," in *Hermeneutics and the Human Sciences: Essays on Language, Action, and Interpretation* by Paul Ricoeur, ed. and trans. John B. Thompson (Cambridge: Cambridge University Press; Paris, Editions de la Maison des Sciences de l'Homme, 1981) 63-100; idem, *Lectures on Ideology and Utopia*, ed. George H. Taylor (New York: Columbia University Press, 1986); and Rebecca S. Chopp, *The Power to Speak: Feminism, Language, God* (New York: Crossroad, 1989) 59-70.

[21]Druin, "Southwestern Journal Pulled 'In Best Interests,' " 3; Kenneth S. Hemphill, Fort Worth, to Dr. Jeff Pool, Fort Worth, 12 December 1996, Transcript in the hand of Jeff B. Pool, Archives, Roberts Library, Southwestern Baptist Theological Seminary, Fort Worth, Texas.

[22]Tillman, Fort Worth, to Pool, Fort Worth, 14 February 1996 (9:20 A.M.), Transcript of Telephone Message, taken by faculty secretary, Miriam Harden, in the hand of Jeff B. Pool, Archives, Roberts Library, Southwestern Baptist Theological Seminary, Fort Worth, Texas.

[23]Jeff B. Pool, Fort Worth, to Dr. Larry Baker, Pineville, Louisiana, 9 March 1996, Copy of Transcript in the hand of Jeff B. Pool, Archives, Roberts Library, Southwestern Baptist Theological Seminary, Fort Worth, Texas; idem, Fort Worth, to Dr. William R. Estep, Fort Worth, 9 March 1996, Copy of Transcript in the hand of Jeff B. Pool, Archives, Roberts Library, Southwestern Baptist Theological Seminary, Fort Worth, Texas; idem, Fort Worth, to Dr. William L. Hendricks, Mill Valley, California, 9 March 1996, Copy of Transcript in the hand of Jeff B. Pool, Archives, Roberts Library, Southwestern Baptist Theological Seminary, Fort Worth, Texas; idem, Fort Worth, to Professor Bill Leonard, Birmingham, Alabama, 9 March 1996, Copy of Transcript in the hand of Jeff B. Pool, Archives, Roberts Library, Southwestern Baptist Theological Seminary, Fort Worth, Texas; idem, Fort Worth, to Professor Molly Marshall, Kansas City, Kansas, 9 March 1996, Copy of Transcript in the hand of Jeff B. Pool, Archives, Roberts Library, Southwestern Baptist Theological Seminary, Fort Worth, Texas; idem, Fort Worth, to Professor Warren McWilliams, Shawnee, Oklahoma, 9 March 1996, Copy of Transcript in the hand of Jeff B. Pool, Archives, Roberts Library, Southwestern Baptist Theological Seminary, Fort Worth, Texas; idem, Fort Worth, to Bill Tillman, Fort Worth, 13 March 1996, Copy of Transcript in the hand of Jeff B. Pool, Archives, Roberts Library, Southwestern Baptist Theological Seminary, Fort Worth, Texas; and Bill Tillman, Fort Worth, to Jeff Pool, Fort Worth, 18 March 1996, Transcript in the hand of Jeff B. Pool, Archives, Roberts Library, Southwestern Baptist Theological Seminary, Fort Worth, Texas.

[24]Beth Shaddai, "Journal Decision Disturbing, Embarrassing," *Baptist Standard* 109 (8 January 1997): 4. As an aside, thanks to a comment by a friend, I

became curious about the identity of this letter's author. Since the Fort Worth telephone directory lists no "Shaddai," either Beth Shaddai has an unlisted telephone number (or no telephone), or this name functions as a pseudonym for someone who thinks she or he cannot write under her or his own name due to threat of reprisal. If the name "Beth Shaddai" does function as a pseudonym, this tactic indicates an oppressive situation from and to which this person writes. The author of this letter has transliterated Hebrew words into English to produce this name. The name can mean "house" ("Beth") of "the Almighty" ("Shaddai"). Genuine voices of Baptist dissent will continue to speak, even when oppressive situations force dissenters to protect themselves with camouflage. In this case, however, the cloak communicates a powerful message as well!

[25]See the following examples: Molly Truman Marshall, "The Doctrine of Salvation: Biblical-Theological Dimensions," *Southwestern Journal of Theology* 35 (Spring 1993): 12-17; N. Larry Baker, "Living the Dream: Ethics in Ephesians," *Southwestern Journal of Theology* 22 (Spring 1979): 39-55; idem, review of *It's Tough Growing Up*, by C. W. Brister, in *Southwestern Journal of Theology* 14 (Fall 1971): 87-88; idem, review of *Pastoral Care in the Church*, by C. W. Brister, in *Southwestern Journal of Theology* 35 (Fall 1992): 45; William R. Estep, "Church and Culture in Latin America," *Southwestern Journal of Theology* 4 (April 1962): 27-47; idem, "The Anabaptist View of Salvation," *Southwestern Journal of Theology* 20 (Spring 1978): 32-49; idem, "A. H. Newman and Southwestern's First Faculty," *Southwestern Journal of Theology* 21 (Fall 1978): 83-98; idem, "The Baptist Struggle for Freedom in the Historical Context," *Southwestern Journal of Theology* 31 (Spring 1989): 42-48; William L. Hendricks, "Stewardship in the New Testament," *Southwestern Journal of Theology* 13 (Spring 1971): 25-33; idem, "All in All: Theological Themes in Colossians," *Southwestern Journal of Theology* 16 (Fall 1973): 23-35; idem, "Theology and Children: Remarks on Relationships between Christian Theology and Childhood Developmental Psychology," *Southwestern Journal of Theology* 20 (Spring 1978): 60-72; idem, "The Nature of Grace: A Baptist Perspective," *Southwestern Journal of Theology* 28 (Spring 1986): 15-17; idem, "Learning from Beauty," *Southwestern Journal of Theology* 29 (Summer 1987): 19-27; idem, "Baptism: A Baptist Perspective," *Southwestern Journal of Theology* 31 (Spring 1989): 22-33.

[26]*Southwestern Journal of Theology, Festschrift for William R. Estep, Jr.: A Statement for Religious Liberty* 36 (Summer 1994).

[27]See the following representative examples: Dale Moody, "The Theology of the Johannine Letters," *Southwestern Journal of Theology* 13 (Fall 1970): 7-22; Charles R. Wade, "Good, But Broken," *Southwestern Journal of Theology* 32 (Spring 1990): 6-9; Joseph Sittler, "Ecological Commitment as Theological Responsibility," *Southwestern Journal of Theology* 13 (Spring 1971): 35-45; Jaroslav Pelikan, "Creation and Causality in the History of Christian Thought," *Southwestern Journal of Theology* 32 (Spring 1990): 10-16; Mark I. Wallace, "Performative Truth and the Witness of the Spirit," *Southwestern Journal of Theology* 35 (Summer 1993): 29-36.

[28]See the following stories: "Baptist News in Brief: Bill Leonard," *Baptist Standard* 103 (9 October 1991): 5; "Dockery Hired, Profs Warned," *Baptist Standard* 104 (12 February 1992): 5; "Virginians Ask Prof's Dismissal," *Baptist Standard* 104 (19 February 1992): 4; "Southern Profs Denied Chairs; 3 Trustees Quit," *Baptist Standard* 105 (28 April 1993): 11; "Embattled Molly Marshall Forced to Resign at Southern," *Baptist Standard* 106 (31 August 1994): 11; Michael Duduit, "Southern Faculty Seek Changes, Affirm Deposed Professor," *Baptist Standard* 106 (7 September 1994): 11.

[29]The SBC employed this criterion long before the fundamentalists conquered and began to dominate the SBC. Langdon Gilkey recalled attending a meeting at Vanderbilt University, in which Herschel H. Hobbs defended the trustees of Midwestern Baptist Theological Seminary for firing Ralph H. Elliott due to the controversy generated by his commentary on Genesis (see Ralph H. Elliott, *The Message of Genesis* [Nashville: Broadman Press, 1961]). "Admitting freely that many other Baptist professors held the views expressed in the book, that they were in fact fairly conservative views, and that the book dealt with materials regularly taught in other Southern Baptist seminaries, Hobbs nevertheless insisted that the expulsion, 'a purely administrative matter,' was justified because of the controversy the book had caused among Baptists, and because Elliott (to his credit, one must think) had refused voluntarily to withdraw the book from further publication because of the controversy" (Langdon Gilkey, *How the Church Can Minister to the World Without Losing Itself* [New York: Harper & Row, 1964] 42 n. 13).

[30]See "Chapel Schedule: Spring 1997," Southwestern Baptist Theological Seminary, Fort Worth, Texas; and Byran McAnally, "Spring Chapel Slate Features Noted Pastors, Southern Baptist Leaders," *The Scroll*, Southwestern Baptist Theological Seminary (27 January 1997) 2.

[31]See 1 Cor 1:18-25.

[32]Jones, "Seminary President Cancels Journal Issue," 4 (B).

[33]Kenneth S. Hemphill, Fort Worth, to Dr. Jeff Pool, Fort Worth, 12 December 1996, Transcript in the hand of Jeff B. Pool, Archives, Roberts Library, Southwestern Baptist Theological Seminary, Fort Worth, Texas; Druin, "Southwestern Journal Pulled 'In Best Interests,'" 3.

[34]Cf. Marv Knox, "Baptist Integrity Rests on Freedom of the Press," in *Defining Baptist Convictions: Guidelines for the Twenty-First Century*, ed. Charles W. Deweese (Franklin TN: Providence House, 1996) 206-13.

[35]Bird, "Hemphill Suspends Southwestern Theology Journal," 10 (emphasis mine).

[36]Jones, "Seminary President Cancels Journal Issue," 1, 4 (B); Bird, "Hemphill Suspends Southwestern Theology Journal," 10; Druin, "Southwestern Journal Pulled 'In Best Interests,'" 3; Kenneth S. Hemphill, Fort Worth, to Dr. Jeff Pool, Fort Worth, 12 December 1996, Transcript in the hand of Jeff B. Pool, Archives, Roberts Library, Southwestern Baptist Theological Seminary, Fort Worth TX (emphasis mine).

[37]Mark L. Beal, "Dislikes 'Journal' Decision," *Baptist Standard* 109 (15 January 1997): 4.

[38]Kenneth S. Hemphill, Fort Worth, to Dr. Jeff Pool, Fort Worth, 12 December 1996, Transcript in the hand of Jeff B. Pool, Archives, Roberts Library, Southwestern Baptist Theological Seminary, Fort Worth, Texas; Jones, "Seminary President Cancels Journal Issue," 4 (B) (emphasis mine).

[39]I made similar comments in a story by the *Fort Worth Star-Telegram* (Jones, "Seminary President Cancels Journal Issue," 4 [B]).

[40]See, as a prominent example, the case of Henry Smith. After Smith published in *SWJT* a provocative article on contemporary challenges to traditional Christian soteriologies, the seminary's administrators construed Smith's article, not as outside the parameters of the *BFM (1963)* (affirmed and signed by every person elected to the faculty of SWBTS), but as not consistent with the seminary's "ethos," whatever that meant. The seminary's administration asked Smith either to write another article in which he would essentially recant or to take his impending sabbatic-leave as his severance-package from SWBTS. Courageously, he took the latter alternative (see Henry N. Smith, "Salvation in the Face of Many Faiths: Toward a Hermeneutic of Optimism," *Southwestern Journal of Theology* 35 [Spring 1993]: 26-31). Also, see my brief account of this incident: George H. Shriver and Bill J. Leonard, eds. *Encyclopedia of Religious Controversies in the United States* (Forthcoming, Westport CT: Greenwood, 1997) s.v. "Southwestern Baptist Theological Seminary," by Jeff B. Pool.

[41]Kenneth S. Hemphill, Fort Worth, to Dr. Jeff Pool, Fort Worth, 12 December 1996, Transcript in the hand of Jeff B. Pool, Archives, Roberts Library, Southwestern Baptist Theological Seminary, Fort Worth, Texas; Bird, "Hemphill Suspends Southwestern Theology Journal," 10 (emphasis mine).

[42]Again, see Kenneth S. Hemphill, Fort Worth, to Dr. Jeff Pool, Fort Worth, 12 December 1996, Transcript in the hand of Jeff B. Pool, Archives, Roberts Library, Southwestern Baptist Theological Seminary, Fort Worth, Texas; Jones, "Seminary President Cancels Journal Issue," 4 (B); Bird, "Hemphill Suspends Southwestern Theology Journal," 10.

[43]Kenneth S. Hemphill, Fort Worth, to Dr. Jeff Pool, Fort Worth, 12 December 1996, Transcript in the hand of Jeff B. Pool, Archives, Roberts Library, Southwestern Baptist Theological Seminary, Fort Worth, Texas (emphasis mine).

[44]According to Tillich, a religious symbol "participates in the reality of that for which it stands" or "participates in the reality which is symbolized" (Paul Tillich, *Systematic Theology* [Chicago: University of Chicago Press, 1951] 1:239; idem, *Systematic Theology* [Chicago: University of Chicago Press, 1957] 2:9).

[45]Pascal, *Pensées*, 348 (4.C.978).

[46]Paul Ricoeur, "Hermeneutic of the Idea of Revelation," *Protocol of the Colloquy of the Center for Hermeneutical Studies in Hellenistic and Modern Culture* 27 (13 February 1977): 12; also as idem, "Toward a Hermeneutic of the Idea of Revelation," in *Essays on Biblical Interpretation* by Paul Ricoeur, ed. Lewis S. Mudge (Philadelphia: Fortress Press, 1980) 113; idem, "Herméneutique

de l'idée de Révélation," in *La Révélation* by Paul Ricoeur, Edgar Haulotte, Etienne Cornélis, and Claude Geffré (Bruxelles: Facultés Universitaires Saint-Louis, 1977) 50; idem, "The Hermeneutics of Testimony," *Anglican Theological Review* 61 (1979): 444; also in *Essays on Biblical Interpretation*, 130; idem, "L'Herméneutique du Témoignage," *Archivio di Filosofia (La Testimonianza)* (1972): 43; cf. idem, "Le sujet convoqué: A l'école des récits de vocation prophétique," *Revue de l'Institut Catholique de Paris* 28 (October-December 1988): 90-99; also cf. Jean Nabert, *Le Désir de Dieu*, Philosophie de L'Esprit Series (Paris: Aubier-Montaigne, 1966) especially 263-311.

[47]In the situation of this book's authors, however, an odd reversal occurs. Rather than a text alerting readers to the character of a life implicated in the testimony of the text, for some of this book's authors, their lives or names alerted potential readers to the character of texts implicated by the movement of the authors's lives.

[48]Johann Baptist Metz, *Faith in History and Society: Toward a Practical Fundamental Theology*, trans. David Smith (New York: Seabury Press, 1980) 89-90.

[49]Luke 4:18-19, 20-21 (NRSV).

[50]Metz, *Faith in History and Society*, 90. The SBC's meeting in 1963, during which the SBC adopted a revision of its previous confession of faith, represents an excellent example of this inscription of the dangerous memory of Christ's freedom in confessions of faith. For that year, the Convention adopted the phrase, "To Make Men Free," as its general theme. Perhaps as a symbol of the focal point for the SBC's concern that year, the Convention opened its meeting with the reading of Jude 1-21, a text traditionally understood as a biblical mandate for writing and adopting articles of faith. For the morning on which the SBC discussed and adopted the *BFM (1963)*, the Convention used the phrase, "Freedom Through Soul Liberty," as its theme. Again, perhaps as a symbol of the source for the freedom to which that theme attested, J. Lloyd Moon read Romans 5:1-10 (*Annual SBC [1963]*, 47-50, 62 ["Proceedings," Tuesday Night, May 7, Items 6, 12; Thursday Morning, May 9, Item 102]).

[51]For example, see 1 John 1:1-4, especially the verbs "ακηκοαμεν" ("we have heard"), "εωραϖκαμεν" ("we have seen"), "εφθεασαϖμεθα" ("we gazed upon"), and "εφψηλαϖφησαν" ("we handled"), which thoroughly elaborate the meaning of the verb, "marturou'men," "we testify." The English word, "martyr," originates from this Greek verb (see Gerhard Kittel, ed. *Theological Dictionary of the New Testament*, vol. 4, *L–N*, trans. and ed. Geoffrey W. Bromiley [Grand Rapids: Eerdmans, 1967] s.v. "μαρτυ♣, μαρτυρεϖω, μαρτυριϖα, μαρτυ–ϖριον" by H. Strathmann).

[52]Friedrich Nietzsche, *Beyond Good and Evil: Prelude to a Philosophy of the Future*, trans. R. J. Hollingdale, rev. ed. (New York: Penguin Books, 1973; 1990) 100 (maxim 132). Consequently, danger also accompanies testimonies to this messianic freedom for another reason. Those who identify with the structures and programs of oppression, those who maintain "the plausible structures of society" through their aims to delude, will also endeavor to prevent the subversion of their dominating activity and tools. Thus, those who would attest to the source of

such subversion become the targets of suppression, repression, or even oppression themselves. The publication of both the censored articles and an account about the event of their censorship permanently inscribes the memory of a controversial situation that the leadership of SWBTS would prefer both to eradicate and to forget. No one who maintains that memory endears herself or himself to those with such preferences.

[53]Arthur Miller, *The Crucible*, Penguin Plays (New York: Penguin Books, 1976) 77 (Act 2).

[54]Julia Kristeva, *Powers of Horror: An Essay on Abjection*, trans. Leon S. Roudiez, European Perspectives Series (New York: Columbia University Press, 1982), 129; Ricoeur, "Hermeneutics of Testimony," 443. Paul Ricoeur, however, does not collapse so quickly the distinction between a witness and a martyr: "the disciple is martyr because he is a witness, not the inverse" (Ricoeur, "Hermeneutics of Testimony," 445).

[55]Augustine *Enarrationes in Psalmos* 34.2.13 (line 12).

[56]See Thomas Cahill, *How the Irish Saved Civilisation: The Untold Story of Ireland's Heroic Role from the Fall of Rome to the Rise of Medieval Europe* (New York: Doubleday, Anchor Books, 1995) 151, 170-71, 183-84.

[57]Jorge Luis Borges, "The Witness," in *Labyrinths: Selected Stories and Other Writings*, ed. Donald A. Yates and James E. Irby (New York: New Directions, 1964) 243.

[58]Karl Marx, "Theses on Feuerbach," in *The Karl Marx Library*, vol. 5, *On Religion*, ed. and trans. Saul K. Padover (New York: McGraw-Hill, 1974) 65 (emphasis mine); Bill J. Leonard, Winston-Salem, North Carolina, to Dr. Kenneth Hemphill, Fort Worth, 17 December 1996, Copy of Transcript in the hand of Jeff B. Pool, Archives, Roberts Library, Southwestern Baptist Theological Seminary, Fort Worth TX.

[59]1 Pet 3:13-16 (NRSV).

Chapter 1

Chief Article of Faith
The Preamble of *The Baptist Faith and Message (1963)**

Jeff B. Pool

Introduction

Baptists in the Southern Baptist Convention (SBC) commonly refer to the introductory paragraphs of the *Baptist Faith and Message (1963)* (*BFM [1963]*) as the Preamble, even though that document does not refer to those paragraphs with that term.[1] The Preamble of the *BFM (1963)* explicitly elaborates principles that distinguish many Baptists from several other Christian communities. Most Baptist confessional documents prior to the *Baptist Faith and Message (1925)* (*BFM [1925]*), however, often permitted these distinctive principles to remain implicit presuppositions or understated doctrinal commitments.[2] The previous claim expresses the broad contours of a central presupposition to the hypothesis of this study. To elaborate, the opening paragraphs of both the *BFM (1925)* and the *BFM (1963)*, or the preambles of these documents, qualify these confessions as unique in the history of Baptist doctrinal statements.[3] With this study, I have focused on the unique character of the Preamble.

This study proceeds on the basis of a threefold hypothesis. Three interrelated claims, the latter two of which function as subsets or elaborations of the first claim, move from the more general to the most specific dimensions of this hypothesis. First, as the initial, general, and guiding claim of this study, then, the Preamble of the *BFM (1963)* constitutes the chief article among the doctrinal articles of this confessional statement, though not explicitly identified as such in either the *BFM (1925)* or the *BFM (1963)*, despite the genuine importance of the later doctrinal formulations themselves.[4]

The second component of this threefold hypothesis supplies the basic rationale for this study's guiding claim. The Preamble occupies such an essential position because, with the content of this introductory statement, the SBC has explicitly elaborated the fundamental and legitimate conditions of possibility for confessional or doctrinal statements among Baptists in the SBC, conditions mostly implicit in previous Baptist confessional documents. The realities to which Baptists faithfully attest with doctrinal articles or statements, as well as those confessional documents themselves, hold within themselves the very conditions of possibility for Baptist confessionalism as roughly characterized by both the *BFM (1925)* and its heir, the *BFM (1963)*. In its positive function, the Preamble explicitly describes the essential characteristics of genuine confessional statements for Baptists in the SBC. As a negative function, then, these introductory comments implicitly supply a criteriology of credalism, or criteria with which to distinguish confessions of faith from creeds.[5]

Finally, as the third component of this study's hypothesis, one basic conviction engenders the conditions of possibility for Baptist confessions of faith as characterized in the Preamble, a principle often formulated by Baptists as "the soul's competency in religion under God." E. Y. Mullins, whom the SBC appointed in 1924 as chairperson of the Committee on Baptist Faith and Message, may have most clearly expressed this claim.[6] According to Mullins, this principle assumes both that God has created humans in God's image, giving to humans a "capacity for God," and that God as a person "can communicate" with or is "able to reveal" God's self to humans.[7] Through its application both explicitly and implicitly, this principle both theoretically and practically supplies the thematic unity for the entire Preamble.

The Preamble itself contains six major interrelated components. The first component contextualizes the *BFM (1963)*, by identifying the origin of both the Committee on Baptist Faith and Message and its commission to produce a confession of faith. With the Preamble's second component, the committee briefly expressed its fidelity to the SBC's doctrinal traditions, specifically as represented in the *BFM (1925)*. The third component characterizes confessional statements among Baptists in the SBC, thus implying a criteriology of credalism within that characterization. The Preamble's fourth component specifies operational guidelines for the committee's use of the *BFM (1925)* in the fulfillment of the committee's commission. The fifth component briefly characterizes the Baptist vision, most specifically the web of authority among Baptists, that this revision of the *BFM (1925)* presupposes. The Preamble's sixth component concisely states the purpose of the report. These six components supply the structure for this chapter. Through the following exposition of the Preamble's six major components, consequently, I will demonstrate the previous threefold hypothesis. For the most part and generally, I will follow the order in which these components appear in the Preamble, rather than forcing the Preamble to conform to an external and alien rationale. In this way, I aim to illuminate, as well as to avoid distortion of, the Preamble's own logic.

I. Context of Commission

In its first major component, the Preamble places the entire confessional document within the context through which the SBC had authorized the production of another confessional statement. By recalling the origins of its task, the committee acknowledged its own role as both representative and servant of the Convention that had invited it to serve and had commissioned it for this task. The committee included, as the first component of its report, the whole text of the SBC's previous recommendation to appoint a committee to produce another statement of Baptist faith and message. J. Ralph Grant had presented this recommendation from the SBC's Executive Committee to the SBC, and the SBC had adopted it during the Convention's annual meeting in 1962.[8] This recommendation contains several significant elements.

First, the recommendation arose in the midst of a controversy in the SBC. Ralph H. Elliott, then a professor of Old Testament at Midwestern Baptist Theological Seminary, had written a commentary on the book of Genesis that Broadman Press had published.[9] Several leaders in the SBC incited a severe reaction among Baptists against both Elliott's use of critical methods to study scripture and some of his exegetical conclusions.[10] Incidentally, during the SBC's annual meeting in 1962, and following the SBC's adoption of the Executive Committee's recommendation, messengers submitted several motions expressing both explicit and implicit negative responses to Elliott and his book.[11] Consequently, the controversy about Elliott's book supplied the immediate background for the Preamble to the *BFM (1963)*. More than any other factors, this controversy precipitated the call in 1962 for a reinterpretation or revision of the *BFM (1925)*.[12] Nonetheless, although hints appear, the Executive Committee's original recommendation itself does not *explicitly* refer to this controversy over biblical interpretation and theological education. For example, while the recommendation suggests the need for either an "overall statement" of faith that "might be helpful *at this time*" or "some similar statement . . . which may serve as *guidelines* to the *various agencies of the Southern Baptist Convention*," the text does not refer to the precipitating occasion of this recommendation.[13] Hence, that recommendation aimed to chart the possibility of a positive and constructive rather than a negative and reactionary course for the Convention.

Second, the recommendation reflected concern for faithfulness to the SBC's historic doctrinal traditions. In the text of that recommendation, the SBC's Executive Committee identified the need for a contemporary review and revision of the Convention's previous confessional statement, the *BFM (1925)*. The recommendation both suggested the need for either an "overall statement" or an "introductory statement which might be used as an interpretation of the 1925 statement" and recommended that a committee "present" to the SBC's annual meeting in 1963 "some similar statement."[14] The recommendation acknowledged the SBC's occasional adoption of "various [confessional] statements" since 1925, but did not refer specifically to any of them.[15] The Executive Committee focused on the *BFM (1925)* as its primary point of reference, both because that document represented the most comprehensive of the SBC's recent confessional statements and because the SBC had fashioned the *BFM (1925)* from the previously popular *NHC (1833)*. Without a doubt, in the adoption of this recommendation, the SBC intended for the Committee on Baptist Faith and Message in 1962 to exercise the SBC's fidelity to its own doctrinal traditions by interpreting and revising the *BFM (1925)*.

Third, the Executive Committee recommended the appointment of a large committee, one intended to reflect the actual diversity in the SBC. Admittedly, this recommendation proposed a committee with a very executive or pastoral composition, with the suggestion for the SBC to request its own president, then Herschel H. Hobbs, to convene a meeting of the current presidents in the various state conventions for this task. Nonetheless, the Executive Committee endeavored to temper the rather episcopal disposition of its proposed committee with the explicit addition of a congregational assumption: "It is understood *that any group or individuals may approach this committee to be of service*."[16] In principle at least, the articulation of that assumption both supplied every Baptist in the SBC with access to the proposed committee and prevented the proposed committee from operating completely behind closed doors or without listening to the constituencies that would commission it.[17] Incidentally, when Hobbs reported to the SBC about the committee's work in March of 1963, prior to the Convention's meeting in May, he informed the SBC that not only had the committee solicited aid and suggestions from seminaries, theological professors, pastors, and state secretaries, but the committee had also gratefully received and prayerfully considered suggestions from a variety of individuals and groups as well.[18]

Fourth, the Executive Committee aimed for the future report from its proposed committee to function descriptively not prescriptively toward the churches in the SBC. The recommendation asked for its proposed committee to "present" a doctrinal statement (resembling the *BFM [1925]*) during the SBC's next meeting "which *shall serve as information* to the churches, and which *may serve as guidelines* to the various agencies of the Southern Baptist Convention."[19] The recommendation distinguished between "information" and "guidelines," intending for the doctrinal statement only to function informatively or descriptively rather than prescriptively in relation to the churches in the SBC.

Fifth, nonetheless, in the recommendation's additional distinction between churches in the SBC and the SBC's "various agencies," the Executive Committee both suggested that the SBC possessed a more authoritative relationship with agencies or institutions of the SBC and implied the possibility that the revised doctrinal statement *might* function prescriptively for the SBC's agencies or institutions. This distinction allowed the possibility for agencies of the SBC to alter the function of the revised doctrinal statement, from regarding its contents as mere "information" to employing its contents as "guidelines." Nonetheless, that possible alteration did not represent a harsh prescriptive comportment in the Executive Committee's recommendation, insofar as the term "guidelines" suggested less rigidity than a term such as "parameters," for example. In this way, when adopted by the SBC, the recommendation avoided a governing posture toward the churches, yet assured the churches of the Convention's desire to satisfy Baptist concerns about the doctrinal commitments of those employed by the SBC's agencies, without explicitly requiring creeds for the SBC's entities.

By incorporating this recommendation into the Preamble of the *BFM (1963)*, the Committee on Baptist Faith and Message demonstrated its fidelity to its original commission from the SBC, thus underscoring the congregational character of its service. In addition, by including this recommendation in the Preamble, the committee indirectly affirmed both every human's competency before God and every Christian's priesthood in the Christian community. Consequently, inclusion of this recommendation as the first structural component of the *BFM (1963)* both begins to inform, even if indirectly and suggestively, Baptists in the SBC about the unique character of the *BFM (1963)* in the history of Baptist confessional documents and begins to suggest the foundational role of this Preamble for the *BFM (1963)*. In very important ways, the remainder of the Preamble merely makes explicit and then expands several aspects of this first major component.

II. Fidelity to Baptist Heritage

With the Preamble's second component, the committee briefly expressed, in an introductory fashion, its own fidelity to the SBC's doctrinal traditions, specifically as represented in the *BFM (1925)*. More specifically still, in this short paragraph, the committee quoted two sentences from the third paragraph of the introductory statements to the *BFM (1925)*. "Christianity is supernatural in its origin and history. We repudiate every theory of religion which denies the supernatural elements in our faith."[20] For the *BFM (1925)*, those two sentences expressed the SBC's response to the then "present occasion for a reaffirmation of Christian fundamentals," an occasion described as "the prevalence of naturalism in the modern teaching and preaching of religion."[21]

Thus, the committee that produced the *BFM (1963)* implicitly and virtually equated the confessional situation in the 1960s with the SBC's stated occasion for the adoption of the *BFM (1925)*. Although the cultural situations differed dramatically from one another, the Preamble of the *BFM (1963)* itself does not address those differences. In his report on the committee's work in the March meeting prior to the Convention's meeting in May of 1963, nonetheless, Hobbs acknowledged that the differences between the theological climate in 1925 and that in 1963 necessitated more work on the article about the doctrine of God.[22] He did not discuss those differences, however. Although the Committee on Baptist Faith and Message did not completely ignore those differences in its revision of the *BFM (1925)*, the committee did not explicitly identify those differences or the issues that necessitated another confession of faith.

Nonetheless, the committee demonstrated its commitment to the SBC's historic doctrinal foundations with this initial use of the *BFM (1925)*. Furthermore, by employing those two sentences, the committee in 1963 also implicitly addressed some of the major issues that had emerged in relation to Elliott's commentary on the book of Genesis, such as the alleged historical and naturalistic reductionism in Elliott's hermeneutical methods.

Certainly, this particular way of affirming fidelity to the SBC's historic doctrinal perspectives modified those traditions. Such modification, however, did not misrepresent or misconstrue those historic perspectives. The SBC's historic perspectives included a commitment to the revision of doctrinal statements as required by the appearance of new situations and issues. In this instance, then, the committee in 1963 used these comments from the *BFM (1925)* to introduce both its own use and its own revision of that statement.

At this point, the *BFM (1963)* exhibits a weakness, especially as demonstrated programatically by the Preamble's acknowledged dependence on the *BFM (1925)*. This document does not explicitly appeal to the SBC's larger and richer history of confessional statements. Rather, the Preamble seems to assume that the *BFM (1925)* already and adequately had summarized or had restated those earlier confessional traditions. If so, however, why did the *BFM (1925)* require revision anyway?

In any case, the Preamble employs those statements from the *BFM (1925)* to contextualize its own further use of that confession's concept of doctrinal statements. Thus, by using the theory of confessionalism contained in the *BFM (1925)*, the Preamble to the *BFM (1963)* continues to deepen its faithfulness to that previous confession of faith. This specific theory of confessionalism constitutes the Preamble's third major component.

III. Characterization of Baptist Confessionalism
(Criteriology of Credalism)

In its third major component, the Preamble characterizes confessions of faith or doctrinal statements, as the SBC has understood such documents historically. For this portion of the Preamble, the committee borrowed completely from the *BFM (1925)*.[23] Although the Preamble subsequently repeats elements from this third major component, this description of confessionalism yields fourteen characteristics, to each of which corresponds an implicit criterion with which to identify a characteristic of creeds. In other words, this characterization of confessionalism implies a criteriology of credalism. These criteria enable Baptists to detect the presence or approach of credalism among themselves and in the SBC itself.[24]

Both this characterization of confessionalism and its implicit criteriology of credalism comprise the heart of the Preamble to the *BFM (1963)*. Without this central component, both the *BFM (1963)* would qualify as a creed, and the *BFM (1925)* would never have permitted revision of itself in any way. This component in both confessions of faith establishes the legitimate conditions of possibility among Baptists in the SBC for articles of faith themselves. Furthermore, when Baptists fail or refuse to interpret and to employ the articles of faith through this component, then they have misconstrued, misused, and distorted the very articles of faith that they supposedly affirm.[25] Thus, the following characteristics of confessional documents and their implicit criteria of creeds remain essential for the most adequate understanding of doctrinal articles among Baptists in the SBC.[26] Although both the *BFM (1925)* and the *BFM (1963)* explicitly identify and enumerate five major characteristics, I have exercised the same freedom operative in the *BFM (1963)* in its revision of the *BFM (1925)*. Building "upon the structure" of those two confessional statements, substituting "words for clarity," adding "sentences for emphasis," "combining" and distinguishing points "with minor changes in wording," I have more systematically described these characteristics and criteria.[27]

A. Emerge from Living Christian Faith

The *BFM (1963)* identifies a first characteristic in confessions of faith: a "*living faith,*" or faithfulness toward the living God, through the resurrected Jesus Christ, by empowerment from the indwelling Holy Spirit, elicits confessions of faith. Confessions of faith result or emerge from, and do not produce, the human experience of salvation through and life in Christ. With confessions of faith, Baptists do not intend "to add anything to the simple conditions of salvation" as disclosed by God: specifically, "repentance towards God and faith in Jesus Christ as Saviour and Lord." The SBC has most often defined faith in terms of a personal relationship between humans and God through Jesus Christ, as trust and trustworthiness, rather than as the cognitive acceptance of theological propositions.[28]

Hence, this initial characteristic of confessionalism suggests a first criterion of credalism. At the very least, credalism equates the faith which is believed (*"fides quae creduntur"*) with the faith by which it is believed (*"fides qua creduntur"*), if it, more seriously still, does not elevate the former above the latter.[29] In such a reversal, principally if not only assent to the cognitive content, as formulated in the creed itself, produces or guarantees the appearance of faith in the second sense: faith as trust in the living God. Although the cognitive content remains soteriologically important, for Baptists, mere mental assent to the particularity of that content produces no soteriological effect in itself: advocacy of such a perspective would express a form of gnostic works-righteousness, that is, one must learn and accept key cognitive elements before God will save that person. Often, to the contrary, very little cognitive understanding accompanies a person's initial salvific experiences. Adequate and significant comprehension of the cognitive content very often only follows the experience of salvation, and then only occurs gradually. Again, faith (in the sense of fidelity or faithfulness) seeks understanding (in the sense of gaining practical wisdom, not amassing information in some cognitive sense alone). When a creed becomes the object of faith, it has ceased to represent trust in and trustworthiness toward the genuine object of faith, the living God. More dangerously, placing faith in such an object, a creaturely object at that, tends to extinguish genuine trust in God alone.

B. Interpret Living Christian Faith

Second, with confessions of faith, Baptist Christians interpret their living faith, their experience with God, other humans, and the remainder of creation. Through written discourse, Christian confessional statements express Christian *understanding* of Christian experience in the form of carefully crafted and organized thoughts, *"concerning those articles of the Christian faith which are most surely held"* by the Baptists who produce and affirm the confessional statements. According to the *BFM (1963)*, "a living faith must experience a *growing understanding* of truth and must be continually interpreted and related to the needs of each new generation."[30] By emphasizing this characteristic of confessional statements, Baptists acknowledge with the broader Christian tradition the impulse of all believers more fully to comprehend life in relation to God through Jesus of Nazareth: life as *fides quaerens intellectum*, faith seeking understanding in every sense, whether cognitively, practically, or aesthetically.

Correspondingly, a second criterion of credalism emerges from this characteristic of confessional statements. The endeavor to make Christian experience conform to precise doctrinal formulations, rather than the effort to express an understanding of that experience through careful linguistic usage, heralds the approach of credalism. The drive toward such uniformity tends either to trim away or to add to life itself, in order to realize Christian experience's perfect fit within the linguistic or conceptual doctrinal container.

C. Represent Christian Beliefs Incompletely

A third characteristic follows from the previous discussion, according to the Preamble of the *BFM (1963)*: Baptists in the SBC "*do not regard*" confessions of faith "*as complete statements*" of their faith. Confessional statements do not possess "any quality of finality." On the one hand, confessional statements can only supply short, summative, and informative, not exhaustive, linguistic formulations about Christian faith. If such documents adequately or sufficiently represented Christian life through and in Christ, both the Holy Spirit and the Christian scriptures themselves would become irrelevant and unnecessary. Obviously, short summaries of Christian doctrine cannot adequately represent either the fullness of Christian experience or the whole wealth of the Christian scriptures. On the other hand, humans in their finitude, even as faithful Christians led by the Holy Spirit, have limitations of knowledge, understanding, ability, and so forth, limitations that can affect and often have affected both the form and content of their confessional statements. As an interpretation of Christian experience with God through Christ, a confession of faith always represents Christian truth as mediated through specific Christians and, therefore, expresses only partial perspectives on that living truth.

This characteristic of confessionalism suggests a third criterion of credalism. Credalism becomes operative when doctrinal statements themselves pretend to be complete or perfect representations of Christian beliefs, when those who produce such statements pretend to have avoided the limitations of finitude in their doctrinal formulations, or when Christians employ doctrinal statements under such illusions. Such illusions blind individuals and communities to the need for a growth in understanding of Christian faith. Furthermore, such illusions often originate in a fundamental refusal to acknowledge the characteristics of creatureliness itself, that is, from the human desire and effort to be "like God."

D. Do Not Infallibly Interpret Christian Faith

According to the Preamble, confessions of faith also exhibit a fourth characteristic. They *never* possess *"any quality . . . of infallibility."* Not only can confessions of faith err as a consequence of finitude's limitations, as the previous characteristic indicates, but human sin itself can also contribute to distortions of the form and content of confessional statements. Christians can represent and often have represented their own biases, prejudices, and selfish intentions as the truth of Christian faith, as pure Christian doctrine. Hence, not only can confessional statements contain theological mistakes or misinformation, but they can contain sinful distortions of doctrine as well.

Thus, a fourth indicator or criterion of credalism emerges. When confessional statements pretend to originate from a complete purity of intention or to exhibit impeccable interpretations of either the scriptures or Christian experience, then credalism stalks the Christian community in the form of idolatry. Such pretensions inhibit, if they do not entirely prevent, revisions in doctrinal statements necessitated by genuine repentance alone.

E. Demonstrate Common Christian Privilege

The Preamble affirms a fifth characteristic of confessionalism. All Christians share the privilege or right to produce and publish confessions of faith. Any group of Baptists or any individual Baptist, in any period of history, whatever the racial, sexual, social, religious, economic, or political status of that Baptist individual or group, has *"the inherent right"* to formulate and to publish confessions of faith for itself, herself, or himself. This characteristic of confessionalism arises from the SBC's consistent commitment to three essential dimensions of religious liberty. (1) The SBC has consistently founded this claim on a historic commitment to the basic human freedom of religious commitment and expression, as a capacity given by God to every human. (2) When affirming every Baptist's inherent right to publish a confession of faith, the SBC has also consistently based its claim on a deep commitment to an understanding of freedom in Christ, in terms of the priesthood of all Christians, or to "the sacred mandates of conscience." (3) The third dimension of religious liberty follows from the two previous dimensions: the theonomous autonomy or self-governance of every local church, from which follows the local church's freedom to associate and to cooperate (or not) with other local churches or organizations.[31] Again, individual Christian freedom to confess one's faith establishes the condition for any group's or individual's right publicly to confess its, her, or his faith in any form.

Thus, the Preamble implies a fifth criterion of credalism. When the group begins to devalue the convictions of the individual Christian conscience over against communal interests, concerns, decisions, and doctrinal formulations, and to subordinate the individual Christian's priesthood to the community itself, whether cognitively or practically or aesthetically, credalism has appeared again. If the voice of the community, the first-person plural pronoun or the "we," absorbs or silences the voice of the individual Christian, the first-person singular pronoun or the "I," then an essential part of credalism's machinery has begun to operate. This principle applies as well to the relationship between the larger community, as represented by the SBC, and the individual local Baptist church. In this light, a question once asked by John Leland deserves both boldly to be posed and conscientiously to be answered again today by Baptists in the SBC. Since Jesus himself did not leave a confession of faith or "a system of religion" for his followers, "why should a man be called a heretick [sic] because he cannot believe what he cannot believe, though he believes the Bible with all his heart?"[32]

F. Register Only Christian Opinions

Sixth, a Baptist group's confessional statement registers that particular group's "consensus of *opinion*" concerning "those articles of the Christian faith" believed by the group. Confessions of faith, according to the Preamble of the *BFM (1963)*, do not contain absolute knowledge either in form or content. From the SBC's historic perspective, pretensions to absolute certainty with regard to doctrinal formulations never produce or accompany confessional statements. Because confessional statements represent *interpretations* of Christian experience in light of *interpretations* of scripture, and vice versa, such documents always remain within the category of opinions about the various doctrines considered—however *informed* such opinions might be. However more probable may be the accuracy and sufficiency of certain interpretations than others as formulated within confessional documents, such statements remain subject to the logic of probability and, hence, open to doubt and further inquiry. Confessions of faith record only the opinions of a group or an individual about various Christian doctrines, not unalloyed truth itself. Only God can possess and express such absolute certainty about the knowledge of anything.

Consequently, this characteristic of confessional documents implies another rather obvious criterion of credalism, one following from several of the previous criteria as well. Credalism encroaches upon the Baptist community when doctrinal statements in any way claim for themselves to come directly from God or when humans make such claims for those statements. When a doctrinal statement expresses absolute claims about itself in whole or in part, such a document discloses this characteristic of credalism. When credal statements contain claims, attitudes, or pretensions to unqualified or absolute certainty about the formulations that comprise those statements, the formulators of such documents have virtually endowed those credal statements with a divine status, in a spectrum of possibilities ranging from divinely-inspired to God's own voice. This characteristic claims for credal statements more certainty than that expressed in scientific reports. Such pretensions signal the presence of credalism.

G. Express Christian Consensus

Seventh, a confession of faith expresses the *"consensus"* of a group of Baptists or a Baptist organization, however large or small, about specific Christian doctrines. The word "consensus" literally means "to feel with or together." In this sense, consensus originates in personal experience and convictions, personal convictions subsequently understood to be shared with other persons. For Baptists, however, such consensus always follows and arises from the individual Christian's experience, not the reverse. The SBC has consistently articulated the conviction that even the character and polity of Baptist Christian communities originate from their roots in the individual human's relationship with God, a relationship understood as equality with one another in "direct access to God."[33] Nonetheless, finally, either one person writes a confessional statement, while a committee changes and approves it for recommendation to the entire community, or various individuals write specific portions of the confession and the whole document proceeds through the same or similar processes. In this way, the group produces a confessional statement, but only the individuals consenting together authorize it as the group's confession of faith. No elite hierarchy produces doctrinal statements to which all the participants in the community *must* adhere.

As a seventh criterion, then, credalism erupts when an elitist individual or a group of elitist individuals relegates to itself the privilege and authority to articulate the doctrinal commitments for an entire community of Baptist Christians. In this respect, credalism depends on a highly efficient and extremely hierarchical social system or community, an organization in which one person makes, or several people make, decisions for the entire community—autocratic, oligarchic, or aristocratic systems of polity in practice, even when denied in principle. In effect, such posturing virtually defines the community as the leadership itself. Such an ecclesiology represents the application to Baptist communities of the famous view held by Ignatius of Antioch: "Wherever the bishop shall appear, there let the people be; even as wherever Jesus Christ may be, there is the catholic church."[34]

H. Employ Christian Scriptures as Primary Resources

Eighth, also characteristic of confessional statements, Baptist Christians employ the Christian scriptures as the primary resources to aid in the interpretation of life in Christ. Because the Christian scriptures constitute the primary and written attestations to and interpretations of God's involvement with creation and humanity, statements "*drawn from*" the Christian scriptures function as the foundational resources for the interpretation of Christian experience or life through and in Christ, or as the primary attestations or witnesses to the history of God's ancient interaction with creation, humanity, and Israel: "the sole authority for faith and practice among Baptists is the Scriptures of the Old and New Testaments." Confessions always remain subordinate in value to the Christian scriptures themselves, never taking the place of scripture. As authoritative, however, even the scriptures remain subordinate to the very person of God as disclosed through Jesus Christ and presently active through God's Holy Spirit.[35] This suggests, at best, that confessions of faith employ biblical language and concepts that represent the broadest or most comprehensive models among the biblical traditions—those that most adequately and sufficiently represent the patterns of biblical faith.

Thus, an eighth implicit criterion of credalism accompanies this characteristic of confessionalism. When doctrinal statements misuse or fail to employ biblical resources, and when such documents usurp either theoretically or practically the place of the Christian scriptures themselves, then credalism operates. When doctrinal formulations misconstrue and misrepresent biblical language or concepts, when such statements only cloak alien concepts with biblical language, as well as when Baptists disallow questions about more adequate or sufficient biblical language, further evidence of credalism's operation has appeared. Most dangerously, credalism also emerges when Christians, either theoretically or practically, place a confessional statement or a group of confessional statements on either an equal level with or a superior level to the Christian scriptures. This characteristic appears when interpretations of Christian faith in a confessional statement supersede in importance biblical attestations themselves. As John Leland commented about all forms of confessionalism, "after all, if a confession of faith, upon the whole, may be advantageous, the greatest care should be taken not to *sacradize*, or make a petty Bible of it."[36]

J. Guide Interpretation of Christian Scriptures

Ninth, confessions of faith characteristically function "*only as guides in interpretation*" of the Christian scriptures. Confessions supply broad, yet concise and dense, renderings of Christian doctrines and practices, in order to aid the interpreter of biblical texts to discover therein attestations to the essential elements that describe the shared Christian experience. Historically, for the SBC, confessional statements have never disallowed the discovery of more or less than that described or claimed by confessions themselves. In other words, Baptists in the SBC do not require either the Christian scriptures or interpretations of biblical texts to conform to the interpretations contained within confessions of faith. Rather, the SBC has consistently claimed that all confessional statements must either conform to the testimony of the Christian scriptures or receive revision in light of those scriptures, in the event that confessional statements fail to conform. Nevertheless, confessional statements can and do function as guides into the vast, diverse, and beautiful terrain of the Christian scriptures.

Thus, this characteristic implies a ninth criterion with which to identify the presence or approach of credalism. Both the restriction of the riches in the Christian scriptures to the boundaries of a confessional document (that is, to specific and presupposed interpretations of the scriptures themselves), by either that document or its use, and the canonization or prohibition of certain methods for the study of the scriptures announce the advent of credalism. Credalism operates when doctrinal statements restrain, inhibit, or prohibit either certain methods for the study of the Christian scriptures or certain interpretations of the Christian scriptures. If a participant in the community obeys the credal rule, then the participant cannot, and must not, find in the scriptures anything that differs from or contradicts the creed itself. The Christian must read the scriptures through the lens of the official creed. Furthermore, the participant in the community must not use methods or approaches that would or might make such discrepancies possible. Thus, when doctrinal statements inhibit or prohibit genuine exploration of the scriptures by Christians, when credal formulations stifle or restrain Christian reflection on and thought about those ancient testimonies of faith, then credalism has appeared.

K. Serve as Educational Instruments

Tenth, with a confession of faith, Baptist Christians in any particular group characteristically teach the broad contours of the cognitive content, *"those articles of the Christian faith,"* shared or held by participants in the community or group. Confessional statements function to educate bi-directionally: first, to and among the members of the group themselves; and, second, "to the world" or to those outside the community, to those who do not yet or who never will participate in the community. In terms of the first direction, a confession of faith functions as a tool with which and as a medium through which the members of the community can articulate to one another various aspects of their Christian experience, thus educating one another about various aspects of their shared life in Christ. In this respect, a confessional statement supplies a common linguistic framework with a vast and broad range of possible combinations for dialogical interaction regarding Christian experience. Furthermore, no single member of the community may legitimately monopolize or control the linguistic medium; among members of the group, mutuality guides the educational dynamic. In the case of the second direction, a confessional statement serves to inform everyone outside the group about the community's cognitive, axiological, and practical commitments. In this second respect, confessions of faith function apologetically, dialogically, hence evangelistically, and even ecumenically.

To this characteristic of confessionalism, corresponds a tenth credal indicator. When doctrinal statements serve as immutable standards for indoctrination, credalism has appeared. Several other characteristics of credalism generate the possibility of this characteristic, especially a credal document's nonrevisability or infallibility. Even though the word "indoctrinate" means only "to teach," specifically referring to various ideas or beliefs, and while not inherently negative, this word has a long history of negative usage. The word "indoctrinate" has often referred to the use of various processes or methods for imbuing allegedly right, proper, or acceptable knowledge or convictions in learners, with the goal of preventing or eliminating all other possibilities from their considerations or thoughts. Hence, I distinguish indoctrination from genuine education. Rather than encouraging learners to think carefully and analytically, as in genuine education, those who use confessional statements to indoctrinate tend to discourage any thinking that might lead to genuine questions about the form or content of Christian doctrinal statements themselves. Such a process tends to protect doctrinal formulas from critical thought, as if such statements had originated from God's own self. In this sense, indoctrination represents the principal aim of credalism.

L. Possess Religious Not Scientific Status

As an eleventh characteristic of confessional statements, because such documents address the content of Christian faith, as *"statements of religious convictions,"* confessions of faith possess *religious not scientific status*. A confessional statement makes claims about God and God's relation to all of reality, claims not necessarily verifiable or demonstrable by empirical, scientific, or logical methods, whether those are the methods of the physical, biological, and social sciences or even the methods of the philosophical disciplines. For this reason, Baptist Christians should not use confessions of faith "to hamper freedom of thought or investigation in other realms of life."[37] Confessions of faith do not demonstrate the validity of their own claims. Rather, they affirm and declare, but do not prove, various aspects of the truth in which Christians participate.

Correlatively, this implies an eleventh indicator or criterion of credalism. Credalism operates when doctrinal statements ignore their own religious status (or when Baptists employ them without regard for this limit) and attack the scientific methods of inquiry or the established results of their applications in other areas of human experience and research. When doctrinal statements contain polemics against various scientific methods or theories, when confessions of faith contain claims intentionally designed to contradict results established through other forms of investigation, then such documents have transgressed their basic limits as confessions of faith, according to the Preamble of the *BFM (1963)*. This does not mean that Baptists refuse to challenge unproved theories. Rather, if Baptists make such challenges, they must prove such theories to be invalid. Such efforts, however, do not occupy doctrinal statements as the SBC has understood the function of such documents.

M. Reflect Historical Conditioning

As a twelfth characteristic, because a human or a particular group of humans, or *"some Baptist body, large or small,"* formulates and publishes a confession of faith, obviously such documents *always reflect historical conditioning*. A confessional statement always contains contemporary formulations or reinterpretations of ancient Christian doctrines and practices, in which those who have written the document have addressed problems, issues, crises, dilemmas, or concerns for a specific group of Christians within its own unique or peculiar historical circumstances. Confessional documents always reflect such particularity linguistically, conceptually, practically, axiologically, epistemologically, and ontologically.

As a twelfth correlative criterion, then, credalism arises also when doctrinal statements deny, minimize, or even fail to acknowledge their own historical conditioning. Various tendencies or claims, either explicit or implicit, disclose this dehistoricizing posture in a doctrinal statement—claims to completeness or finality in expression of credal statements; or claims, whether subtle or blatant, to infallibility in the communication of either the form or content of Christian truth. Of course, the pretension to formulations of culturally unbiased truth also accompanies the pretension to absolute certainty described previously.

N. Remain Open to Revision

Consequently, as a thirteenth characteristic, confessional statements *remain open to revision*. The SBC has considered it a moral imperative for Baptists to maintain a critical posture toward confessional statements or diligently to scrutinize such documents: "as in the past so in the future, Baptists *should hold themselves free to revise* their statements of faith as may seem to them wise and expedient at any time." A bipolar attitude constitutes this critical posture. The first attitude of this critical posture requires Baptists to remain *hermeneutically suspicious* of confessional statements in two respects: (1) by examining such documents carefully for evidence of serious errors in or omissions from formulations of essential dimensions of Christian life with God; and (2) by searching for any evidence or presence of sinful distortions in such doctrinal summaries. This critical posture's second attitude also requires Baptists to analyze their confessions of faith carefully (with both wisdom and expedience), in order to revise them *when historical circumstances change*, to meet the needs of new generations of Baptist Christians. In this respect, a questioning and self-examining faith always operates as the Christian community's self-criticism in light of divine illumination. For example, the apostle Paul alerted the Thessalonian Christians to this principle. "Do not quench the Spirit. Do not despise the words of prophets, but test everything; hold fast to what is good; abstain from every form of evil."[38] Throughout their varied history, most Baptists have consistently acknowledged and exercised this dimension of their faithfulness to God. Although various commitments to the operation of this prophetic principle have consistently appeared in the SBC's confessional documents, the SBC has articulated this prophetic principle no more explicitly and completely than in the confessional statement that it produced in connection with its preparation for and observance of the Third Baptist Jubilee in 1964.[39] According to that document, *Baptist Ideals* (*BI [1963]*), the healthiness and fruitfulness of both local churches and the SBC itself depend upon acceptance by those entities of "the responsibility of constructive self-criticism." Furthermore, only damage to churches and to the SBC will result both from denials of "the right to differ" and pretensions to the finality or perfection of "methods and policies." After affirming the need for "frequent reevaluation" of "methods" as well as of "historic principles and practices as they relate to contemporary life," the *BI (1963)* defends the appropriateness of this principle's operation: "for one to criticize does not necessarily mean that he is disloyal; his criticism may stem from a deep commitment to the welfare of the denomination."[40] Hence, when Baptists revise their confessions of faith, they remain "in historic succession of intent and purpose," as they endeavor to state for their "time and theological climate those articles of the Christian faith" that they "most surely" hold among themselves: "A living faith must experience a growing understanding of truth and must be continually interpreted and related to the needs of each new generation."

A thirteenth criterion with which to identify credalism, then, corresponds to the previous characteristic of confessionalism. Credalism operates when doctrinal statements (or those who affirm them) inhibit, if they do not eliminate altogether, any possibilities for genuine and critical revision, either corrective or elaborative, of those formulations. Given the previous characteristics, the tradition's or the creed's conservators, or the successors of the creed's writer or writers, acknowledge no external perspective from which to examine such authoritative credal statements. Unless the creed contains its own self-critical principle or characteristics, such as the doctrinal statement's admission of its own fallibility or incompleteness, then the creed remains the rule for all evaluation of doctrine and no criterion external to itself, with the exception of God's own Self, exists with which to evaluate the document itself.

O. Exercise No Inherent, Ultimate, Mandatory, or Prescriptive Authority

The previous characteristics of confessional statements imply a fourteenth and fundamental characteristic. Confessions of faith neither possess nor exercise any inherent, ultimate, mandatory, or prescriptive authority over either the individual Christian's conscience or Christian communities. As a key to the interpretation of scripture, a confession of faith offers guidance to Christians and Christian communities into the meaning of biblical texts and Christian experience, but cannot legitimately function to prescribe, command, coerce, or discipline either the Christian's conscience or the Christian community as a whole for refusal or modification of such guidance. "Confessions are only guides in interpretation, *having no authority over the conscience*." Finally, only either the individual

Christian's conscience and attestation or the local Christian community's actions and pronouncements can confer any functional authority to confessions of faith. The ultimate authority or supreme norm, *norma suprema* or *norma non normata*, for Christians and their communities is none other than the God disclosed in Jesus of Nazareth and attested presently by the Holy Spirit. As stated in the Preamble of the *BFM (1963)*, "*the sole authority for faith and practice among Baptists is Jesus Christ* whose will is revealed in the Holy Scriptures." Second to God alone, according to the Preamble of the *BFM (1963)*, the scriptures even remain above confessions of faith. Confessions of faith can only point to or guide into the testimony of the Christian scriptures and to God indirectly through the scriptures. Consequently, confessions of faith *cannot legitimately function* either as "parameters for cooperation" or as tools for ecclesiastical, much less denominational, discipline.[41]

To the previous characteristic of confessionalism, then, corresponds a fourteenth criterion of credalism. When confessional documents prescribe for participants in a given group the contents of their belief or practice, as exhibited by the formulations contained within those documents, or claim that Baptist Christians must affirm those particular formulations to remain in the community, and when Baptists employ various forms of power in order to enforce adherence to such statements, credalism looms most threateningly. Such documents transgress the descriptive limit of doctrinal statements among Baptists in the SBC. By endowing doctrinal or moral statements with this prescriptive character, credalists aim to guarantee every individual's conformity to the group's official definition of its identity, by leaving no doubt about the community's expectations for every individual. The faith as *fides quae*, the cognitive content, becomes the law to obey with one's will and mind. Christian faith then becomes obedience or duty to an inanimate written rule, rather than trust and trustworthiness toward the living Spirit of God. Credalism cannot sustain its previous characteristics, unless, behind the doctrinal formulations, various kinds of real power exist with which to enforce the document's purportedly absolute, immutable, legal, and divine claims on participants in the community. In many cases, creeds invoke anathemas or curses upon those who have understandings that differ from the prescribed doctrines themselves. When political, social, economic, or cultural mechanisms exist through which to coerce participants in the community to conform to the creed publicly, then credalism operates most openly and efficiently. Hence, the community practically makes those anathemas real, in varying degrees and with various methods, in the lives of those in the community who might dissent or have dissented from the creed. The community corrects deviation from the creed with coercion.[42] In Christian history, communities have coerced dissenters with torture, excommunication, and even execution. More recently, Baptist communities have coerced conformity to doctrinal formulations with various threats to the livelihood of dissenting participants.

In this final characteristic, credalism realizes the most negative sense of the original meaning of the word "religion," the sense that pervades the previous characteristics of credalism as well. From the Latin word "*religare*," the English word "religion" originates. The word "*religare*" means "to tie or fasten behind" or "to bind back."[43] Thus, this characteristic of credalism emphasizes the real, raw power to bind, to restrict, or to restrain individuals, the power to make individuals conform to the dictates of a community—perhaps, figuratively, to tie the hands of their freedom in Christ behind their backs.

IV. Hermeneutic of Baptist Heritage

Operating on the basis of the previous convictions, the Committee on Baptist Faith and Message also incorporated a fourth component into the Preamble. With this fourth component, the committee applied the previous theory of Baptist confessional statements and doctrinal articles to the *BFM (1925)* itself. In other words, this component succinctly describes the committee's hermeneutical approach to, or interpretive comportment toward, the Baptist heritage transmitted as the *BFM (1925)*.

This hermeneutic of Baptist heritage again demonstrates the committee's fidelity to the Baptist heritage as represented in the *BFM (1925)*. As the Preamble to the *BFM (1963)* notes, in 1925 the Committee on Baptist Faith and Message, in order to fulfill its own task, employed and recommended for the SBC's approval the *NHC (1833)*, "revised at certain points, and with some additional articles growing out of present needs. . . ." The Committee on Baptist Faith and Message in 1963, as the Preamble to the *BFM (1963)* attests, adopted "the same pattern."[44] This configuration of hermeneutical practices exhibits six general features.

First, according to the Preamble, the committee in 1963 "*sought to build upon the structure of the 1925 Statement*, keeping in mind the 'certain needs' of our generation." The committee exercised a faithful freedom in its use of the *BFM (1925)* as the basis for a restatement of the SBC's interpretations of Christian doctrine. With confidence in the reliability of the heritage transmitted by the *BFM (1925)*, the committee built upon the structure of the *BFM (1925)*, sometimes the larger structure of the document as reflected in the configuration of or the relationship among the articles and sometimes the smaller structures as reflected in the specific formulations of the various articles themselves, without captivity to mere repetition of either the larger or smaller structures. Thus, with the freedom of the universal Christian priesthood, while the committee employed the *BFM (1925)* as the structural foundation for its own confessional study in 1963, the committee modified elements of the *BFM (1925)*, where contemporary circumstances required such modifications. Although the *BFM (1963)* does not explicitly identify the circumstances for its own production, the committee clearly perceived new issues that required such a doctrinal statement. In the confession's larger structure, for example, the committee reduced the twenty-five articles of the *BFM (1925)* to seventeen articles in the *BFM (1963)*.

Second, the committee sometimes "*reproduced sections of that Statement* without change." In numerous places, the committee retained both the content and the form of articles from the *BFM (1925)*. Although the *BFM (1963)* does not express the various rationales for those retentions, such reproduction of the previous confession presumably occurred because the committee perceived no contemporary issues threatening to undermine or to confuse previous affirmations. For example, the committee reproduced the eighth article, "The Lord's Day," almost exactly as it appeared in the *BFM (1925)*.[45]

Third, in some cases, the committee "*substituted words for clarity or added sentences* for emphasis." Again, claiming to avoid modifications of the confession's content, the committee made various changes in the form of numerous articles. Contemporary linguistic, rhetorical, and hermeneutical studies indicate a more intimate relationship between form and content, however, than that suggested by the naïve the committee that produced the *BFM (1963)*. One cannot modify the form of discourse without genuinely, even if minutely, affecting its content or meaning. More importantly, however, did the committee successfully modify the linguistic form of the various articles in the *BFM (1925)* without modifying the meaning of those articles? Only careful linguistic and theological comparisons of each article in the two confessional documents can supply an answer to the previous question.[46]

Fourth, in places, the committee "*combined articles*, with minor changes in wording, to endeavor to relate certain doctrines to each other."[47] With such rearrangements in the *BFM (1963)*, the committee generally clarified the interrelatedness of various Christian doctrines, relationships often obscured by the more atomistic groupings of both the *BFM (1925)* and its precursor, the *NHC (1833)*.

Fifth, in other places, the committee "*sought to bring together certain truths* contained throughout the 1925 Statement in order to relate them more clearly and concisely." One question emerges, however. Did the committee's reduction of those truths to more concise statements actually clarify those truths? Such condensations can produce broader, rather than more specific, statements that invite an even richer variety of interpretations.[48]

Sixth, nonetheless, the committee *never "sought to delete from or to add to the basic contents of the 1925 Statement."* With this principle, the committee attempted to retain the basic meanings of the articles in the *BFM (1925)*. A naivé, however, accompanies this principle. Several changes in wording obviously affected the meaning of several articles.[49] In spite of this naive pretense, such deletions or additions to the meaning of any particular article did not contradict the committee's overall approach to the *BFM (1925)*. The committee's first hermeneutical principle authorized such reconstruals of content, insofar as those modifications indicated the committee's attention to contemporary issues and needs of Baptists in the SBC.

Thus, the Preamble's fourth component, based on the committee's practices, specifies operational guidelines, or principles in a broad hermeneutical framework, for the committee's use of the *BFM (1925)* with which to fulfill the committee's commission. With its outline of these principles, the committee attempted to assuage any fears among Baptists in the SBC that the committee might be trying to alter the historic commitments of the SBC. The committee tried to show that it would faithfully interpret the Baptist heritage of the *BFM (1925)*. To some extent, this effort appeared to mitigate the radical implications of the previous theory of confessionalism at the heart of the Preamble itself. According to that theory, not only may Baptists revise the form but they may also revise the content of their doctrinal statements if they so desire. With its hermeneutic of Baptist heritage, however, the committee actually cloaked some of its own revisions, however minor or slight, of the doctrinal content or meaning of the *BFM (1925)*. At the same time, nevertheless, the committee remained faithful to the Baptist heritage of the *BFM (1925)* in the most radical sense, insofar as the committee refused to eliminate the conditions of possibility for such revisions of the SBC's confessional traditions.

V. Web of Authority in the Baptist Vision

Both the previous hermeneutical approach to the *BFM (1925)* and the previous theory of confessionalism originate from and depend upon the Preamble's fifth component. This fifth component constitutes the web of authority among Baptists in the SBC, as the presupposition of both the Preamble and this confessional document as a whole. Various appearances of the *BFM's* concept of authority in the Preamble invite hermeneutical explorations into other areas of this confessional statement. Therefore, I have reconstructed this component from a variety of elements embedded in both the Preamble and several of the *BFM's* articles themselves.

A. Clarifications: From the *BFM (1925)* to the *BFM (1963)*

Religious authority in the Baptist vision occurs as a web of dynamic interactions between the living God as disclosed in Jesus of Nazareth and attested by the Holy Spirit, the individual human's conscience and conduct, the canon of Christian scriptures, and the Christian community as the body of Christ. I examine this web of authority in the Baptist vision through a study of its appearances in the *BFM (1963)*, in light of comparisons especially, but not exclusively, with its precursor, the *BFM (1925)*.[50] I begin by identifying creative dissonance in the concept of authority contained in the *BFM (1963)*. This dissonance, of course, invites comparisons with the concept of authority in that document's precursor, the *BFM (1925)*. I focus these inquiries, however, through analyses of both the preambles or introductory paragraphs and the articles on the scriptures in those two documents.

1. Concepts of Authority in the Preambles

The conjunction between two affirmations or claims in the Preamble of the BFM (1963) generates the first traces of dissonance within that document's description of the Baptist concept of authority. The dissonance between these two statements, however, produces neither an inconsistent concept of authority nor one disintegrated by sheer internal contradictions. Rather, the dissonance promises a richer and more subtle understanding of authority than suggested by a formal competition between two very different statements.

(a) *Bible as Sole Authority for Faith and Practice.* Initially, the concept of authority in the *BFM (1963)* appears in the fourth of the five major introductory comments retained from the *BFM (1925)*, when the latter document claims "[t]hat the *sole authority for faith and practice among Baptists is the Scriptures of the Old and New Testaments*." In their elaborations of this claim, both versions of the *BFM* remove confessional documents from every necessarily regulative mediating role between the individual human conscience and the Christian scriptures themselves. "Confessions are only guides in interpretation, having *no authority over the conscience*."[51] Accordingly, because God has endowed every human with some capacity to interact directly with God's self ("the soul's competency before God," realized in the Christian as "the priesthood of the believer"), at least in principle, nothing requires humans to approach the Christian scriptures through the interpretive grid of any confessional statement. In their identical articles on religious liberty, both versions of the *BFM* reinforce this claim: "*God alone is Lord of the conscience*, and He has left it free from the doctrines and commandments of men which are contrary to His Word or not contained in it."[52] All Christians may approach the scriptures directly, without an outline of predetermined findings, because the Holy Spirit indwells all Christians and illumines the scriptures for them. The *BFM (1963)*, at least the third section of the article on the doctrine of God, explicitly declares this point. In the *BFM (1925)*, however, the article on sanctification only implies the connection between the Christian's interpretation of scripture and the Holy Spirit's illumination of the Christian's understanding.[53]

(b) *Jesus Christ as Sole Authority for Faith and Practice.* With a second appearance, the *BFM's* concept of authority significantly qualifies the first claim. The authors of the *BFM (1963)* added this qualification to the introductory statement of the *BFM (1925)*. Because Baptists "profess a living faith," one "rooted and grounded in Jesus Christ," "*the sole authority for faith and practice among Baptists is Jesus Christ* whose will is revealed in the Holy Scriptures."[54] This modification, when isolated from its context and placed alongside the first affirmation of the Christian scripture as the sole authority for faith and practice, certainly generates some dissonance, despite the effort in the modification itself to link Christ's authority to the Christian scriptures. Both Christ and the Christian scriptures cannot occupy the position of *sole* authority. The obvious difference between the two concepts of authority resides in one claim: for the second statement, authority for faith and practice originates from the resurrected and living Christ, who remains divine as well as human; for the first statement, authority arises from a book that remains, even though inspired by God and written by humans, nonetheless, neither God nor a living creature of any kind. In spite of this glaring difference, the modification does not necessarily contradict the concept of authority from the *BFM (1925)*. Rather, the statement added in the *BFM (1963)* makes explicit that which the statement from the *BFM (1925)* implied with its emphasis on the freedom of the individual Christian's conscience from the authority of confessional statements. The modification in the *BFM's* Preamble makes the *genuine source* visible in the concept of authority: *a vital relationship with a living person, the God disclosed through and in the resurrected Jesus of Nazareth, the Christ*. With this qualification, the committee in 1963 primarily identified Baptist faith as trust in the living triune God, rather than as loyalty to or knowledge of a book or document.

The Christian scriptures, whatever intrinsic or objective authority they possess as the primary attestations to the history of God's self-disclosure in and to the creation, derive their subjective trustworthiness and authority for the Christian from the human's experience of divine love through Christ. In 1920, the SBC also emphasized this origin in its first fully elaborated summary of doctrinal articles: "Through the Holy Spirit God makes Himself known within the hearts of men, and sanctifies them through the truth as it is revealed in Jesus Christ."[55]

(c) *Concepts of Authority and Ordering the Articles of Faith.* In the Preamble of the *BFM (1925)*, however, its explicit and less adequate concept of authority tended to support the order of the articles of faith in the *NHC (1833)*, an order the authors of the *BFM (1925)* followed when they also included those articles of faith in the SBC's confessional statement. The *NHC (1833)* begins with an article on the authority of the Christian scriptures, then follows it with an article on the doctrine of God. In this pattern, the *NHC (1833)* imitated a Calvinistic pattern that had originated with the *Westminster Confession* in 1646. From that influential Reformed doctrinal statement, the Calvinistic Baptist authors of the *Second London Confession* borrowed that pattern in 1677. In 1742, Calvinistic Baptists of North America also borrowed this pattern when, with minor additions, they adopted the *Second London Confession* as their own *Philadelphia Confession*.[56] Regardless of this pattern's repetition in the Baptist confessional statements cited previously, neither the earliest and non-Calvinistic Baptist confessions of faith nor even the Calvinistic first *London Confession* of 1644 followed that pattern. Rather, those confessions present articles on the doctrine of God prior to articles on the authority of the Christian scriptures. Furthermore, even the SBC's *Fraternal Address of Southern Baptists* from 1920 repeats the earlier pattern, with its article on the doctrine of God appearing prior to its article on the nature of the Christian scriptures.[57]

2. Concepts of Authority in the Articles on the Scriptures

Despite their modification of the concept of authority in the Preamble of the *BFM (1963)*, the authors of that document retained from the *BFM (1925)* the order of its articles on the nature of the Christian scriptures and the doctrine of God. The retention of this arrangement, of course, intensified the dissonance within the web of authority, as presupposed by the Committee on Baptist Faith and Message in 1963. Again, however, the committee attempted to reduce this dissonance with two additions to the article on the nature of the Christian scriptures.

(a) *Scripture as the Record of God's Self-Revelation to Humanity.* In the first addition, the committee restated a concept of the Christian scriptures that the SBC had affirmed in several of its previous pronouncements. While continuing to affirm that "[t]he Holy Bible was written by men divinely inspired. . . ," the committee added a description of the Christian scriptures as *"the record of God's revelation of Himself to man."*[58] As a result, the committee effectively returned to the older Baptist ordering of the relationship between God and the scriptures. This modification, then, implicitly construes the entire creation, including human history, as the context and medium of God's self-disclosure. Hence, God's interactions with all creatures and with humans in their history become the events of God's self-revelation. As the "record" of God's self-revelation, the Christian scriptures attest to those events or narrate the story of those events. This perspective avoids identifying the Christian Bible as the primary event of God's self-disclosure. Yet, with this formulation, the committee retained a concept of this inspired record as the primary written testimony to that history and, therefore, as derivative revelation.[59]

(b) *Christ as Criterion for Interpretation of Scripture.* With its second addition to the article on the Christian scriptures, the committee in 1963 genuinely reinforced the previous addition: *"The criterion by which the Bible is to be interpreted is Jesus Christ."*[60] Although the *BFM (1963)* does not elaborate on this claim, Herschel Hobbs subsequently explained its addition to the first article as a response to Ralph Elliott's interpretation of Melchizedek, in the book of Genesis, as a priest of Baal. According to Hobbs, "[t]hose objecting to this saw it as a reflection upon/against the priesthood of Jesus Christ."[61] In light of that explanation, one might interpret this christological criterion as a purely textual criterion, insofar as this posits the New Testament's attestation, to Jesus as an everlasting "high priest according to the order of Melchizedek," as the measure for accurate interpretations of the Old Testament.[62] Given the validity of such an interpretation of the *BFM's* hermeneutical criterion, then, this criteriological addition to the article on the scriptures identifies a canon within the canon of the Christian scriptures. Such an interpretation of the christological criterion would position some of the scriptures above others, a conclusion certainly not drawn by the *BFM (1963)*. Thus, even Hobbs concluded that "the purpose of this 'criterion' extends far beyond the above instance." Accordingly, "He [Christ] is the full and final revelation of God to man."[63] With the previous concluding comments in his interpretation of the criteriological addition, Hobbs seems to construe the criterion in terms of its actual language in the *BFM (1963)*, not so much as a written, textual, or documentary criterion (that communicated about Jesus as the Christ), but as a living, personal, and dynamic criterion (the very Christ, the resurrected Jesus of Nazareth) to whom the Holy Spirit, who indwells every Christian, attests. In this latter sense, then, the criterion for the interpretation of scripture harmonizes with the Preamble's explicit positioning of its attestation to the triune God's authority, as focused in the living Christ, above scripture's authority—this, of course, in spite of the committee's retention of the article on the scriptures in position prior to the article on God.

B. Redescription
Junctures in the Web of Authority
in the *BFM (1963)*

From the previous analysis, the web of authority in the *BFM (1963)* emerges as a much more vital concept than initially apparent. With the following model, I will briefly redescribe the web of authority as presupposed in the Preamble of the *BFM (1963)*.[64]

The Preamble of the *BFM (1963)* emphatically announces that Baptists "profess *a living faith*," a faith "*rooted* and *grounded* in Jesus Christ who is 'the same yesterday, and today, and for ever [*sic*].'" "Operating on the basis of this conviction, the *BFM (1963)* presupposes authority as a vital and nurturing reality: the living God, the divine reality disclosed most fully through the Christ, Jesus of Nazareth. Because this faith or trust grows from and responds to its source in the living God, the *BFM (1963)* identifies Jesus Christ as the "sole authority for faith and practice among Baptists."[65] The organic metaphors ("living," "rooted," "grounded"), therefore, signal a concept of authority that differs significantly from an understanding of authority as domination or power over others.

The concept of authority in the Preamble of the *BFM (1963)*, as a result, much more adequately reflects the most basic etymological valence or strength of the English term, "authority." The terms "authority" and "author" originate from the same Indo-European root word, *aug*, which means "increase." This root word evolved into the Greek terms, "au[xhsi", which means "growth" or "increase," and its verbal source, "aujxavnw," which means "grow, cause to grow, increase."[66] With the following model, I will briefly redescribe the organic and nurturing concept of authority in the Baptist vision as a web of authority. Insofar as a web exists as tensile relationships between various junctures, seven principal junctures occur in this web of authority.

1. Formative Authority

For the *BFM (1963)*, then, the term "authority" refers to the divine reality that authorizes faithful Baptist Christian experience or Baptist Christian "faith and practice." The book of Hebrews reminds Christians to fix their attention on "Jesus, the author (ajrchgo;n) and perfecter (teleiwth;n) of faith."[67] In this sense, the living God, as disclosed in Jesus Christ, and active in the Holy Spirit, comprises the formative authority, since, from God, originate the possibilities, actual appearances, nurture, and renewal of life. The first Johannine epistle strikingly describes the fecund and nurturing formative authority of the triune God as love: oJ qeo;" ajgavph ejstivn.[68] Without the other junctures in the web of authority, however, the human's affirmation of God as formative authority would not occur. This affirmation becomes possible only because God has initiated a dialogical and interactive relationship with the creation, an overture to which the creation responds in one way or another. Regardless of any so-called "objective" reality that belongs to God as formative authority, the divine reality only actualizes authority as fecundity and nurture of creation (rather than as coercion or domination) in conjunction with the additional junctures in the web of authority.

2. Transformative Authority

Furthermore, according to the Preamble, as persons respond positively in their encounters with the living Christ, God causes legitimate Baptist Christian experience to grow, as well as increases such faith and practice. In this sense, the Preamble portrays the ground or origin of Baptist Christian experience, Jesus Christ, as the *transformative authority*.[69]

On the one side, God lovingly seeks the estranged human, offering reconciliation and renewal of life. In the meeting between the loving God and the unfaithful human, this creative and nurturing power (formative authority) moves across (*trans*) the gulf of estrangement, offering new life to the alienated human (*form*), thus promising change in the character and condition of disordered and distorted human life: "[r]egeneration or the new birth, is a work of God's grace whereby believers become new creatures in Christ Jesus."[70] The first Johannine epistle states this forcefully:

> By this the love of God was manifested in us, that God has sent His only begotten Son into the world so that we might live through Him. In this is love, not that we loved God, but that He loved us and sent His Son to be the propitiation for our sins.[71]

On the other side, only the human acceptance or reception of this healing divine love actualizes the possibility, which the divine formative authority offers—a new relationship of mutual fidelity between humans and God, as transformative authority. Again, according to Johannine theology, "[w]e love, because He first loved us."[72]

The soteriology of the *BFM (1963)* unequivocally affirms these two dynamics of transformative authority: "*Salvation* involves the redemption of the whole man, and is *offered freely to all who accept Jesus Christ* as Lord and Saviour, who by His own blood obtained eternal redemption for the believer"; the Holy Spirit "convicts of sin, of righteousness and judgment," as well as "calls men to the Saviour, and effects regeneration"; regeneration "is a change of heart wrought by the Holy Spirit through conviction of sin, to which the sinner responds in repentance toward God and faith in the Lord Jesus Christ"; "*[f]aith is the acceptance of Jesus Christ* and commitment of the entire personality to Him as Lord and Saviour."[73] On this soteriological basis, the Preamble of the *BFM (1963)* protects the integrity of the Christian's conscience from, thus affirming the inviolability of the priesthood of every Christian, any human doctrinal document or confession of faith: " 'Confessions are only guides in interpretation, having no authority over the conscience' "; "Baptists emphasize the soul's competency before God, freedom in religion, and the priesthood of the believer."[74]

3. Conformative Authority

According to the *BFM (1963)*, the Holy Spirit indwells every human who has accepted the offer of God's forgiving love, each one who has willingly received this healing from God, every disciple of Jesus, the Christ. In every Christian, the Holy Spirit attests to Jesus as the Christ and to the truth disclosed in and through Jesus of Nazareth: the Holy Spirit "exalts Christ." The first Johannine epistle clearly declares this: "And it is the Spirit who bears witness, because the Spirit is the truth."[75]

In the previous sense, the Holy Spirit brings to memory the image of the historical Christ, Jesus of Nazareth. According to the *BFM (1963)*, "Jesus perfectly revealed and did the will of God, taking upon Himself the demands and necessities of human nature," completely identifying with humanity "yet without sin," and honoring "the divine law by His personal obedience. . . ."[76] In his own teaching, Jesus condensed the entire divine self-revelation in creation's history to the dual divine claim on human life: (1) for the human to love God with her or his entire self; and (2) for the human to love her or his neighbor as herself or himself.[77] As the complete fulfillment of this dual claim on human life, not only did Jesus disclose the very being of God as love, but Jesus represented, in his own complete love for God and the world, the image or model of authentic human life to which Christians gradually conform.

Furthermore, according to the pneumatology of the *BFM (1963)*, the Holy Spirit, "[t]hrough illumination, enables men to understand truth," "cultivates Christian character, comforts believers, and bestows the spiritual gifts by which they serve God through His church," and "enlightens and empowers the believer and the church in worship, evangelism, and service."[78] The Holy Spirit pours God's love into the hearts of all Christians, thereby empowering and guiding them to conform to Christ's image, toward which goal God nurtures and grows every Christian: "[s]anctification is the experience, beginning in regeneration, by which the believer is set apart to God's purposes, and is enabled to progress toward moral and spiritual perfection through the presence and power of the Holy Spirit dwelling in him."[79] I have described the divine encouragement and empowerment to fulfill this goal in the Christian's life as *conformative authority*. Nonetheless, with the goal of conformity to Christ, the *BFM (1963)* by no means seeks either to minimize or to deny the presence of diversity in the Christian community. The unity of conformity, for the *BFM (1963)*, does not require uni-formity of Christian experience for the many members of the body of Christ. Unity-in-diversity, however, does not imply chaotic pluralism in the Christian community, since that diversity gathers around the Christ to which it conforms.

4. Informative Authority

The concept of conformative authority tends to emphasize that living reality, Jesus Christ, to which the Holy Spirit encourages Christians to conform. In addition, however, as the source of truth for the Christian, the Holy Spirit grows, increases, and nurtures the living formation of Christlikeness in each disciple: "through the presence and power of the Holy Spirit," the Christian receives the empowerment "to progress toward moral and spiritual perfection."[80] The Holy Spirit actually in-forms each disciple with Christ. Furthermore, as the communicator of the truth about God revealed in Jesus Christ, the Holy Spirit corroborates the attestations about this God in the Christian scriptures to the convictions of the Christian's conscience and experience: "[t]hrough illumination He enables men to understand truth."[81] This pneumatological corroboration of the scripture's witness in the Christian's experience, then, enables the disciple of Jesus to perceive and to embrace the scriptures as both a human and a divine library of written testimonies to God's activity in and with creation: a collection "written by men divinely inspired," "a perfect treasure of divine instruction," a book with "God for its author, salvation for its end, and truth, without any mixture of error, for its matter." Insofar as the *BFM (1963)* extends the attestations in 2 Timothy about the Hebrew scriptures to the writings of the newer Christian canon as well, the SBC regards the Christian scriptures as "the sacred writings which are able to give you the wisdom that leads to salvation through faith which is in Christ Jesus," as "inspired by God, and profitable for teaching, for reproof, for correction, for training in righteousness," for the goal "that the man of God may be adequate, equipped for every good work."[82] Thus, in this way, the Holy Spirit employs the Christian Bible as the bedrock of the material dimension of informative authority, while the living Christ remains the formal dimension in this juncture of authority.

Most importantly, however, the Holy Spirit illumines the Christian's understanding of scripture's wisdom through a christological window into the scripture: "The criterion by which the Bible is to be interpreted is Jesus Christ."[83] Inasmuch as Jesus summarized the entire collection of scriptures as the divine effort to promote authentic human love for God and neighbor, interpreting the Bible through the christological criterion entails discerning various facets of this wisdom in the study of every biblical text. Augustine of Hippo long ago perceived this hermeneutical principle in the teaching of Jesus: "*Quisquis igitur scripturas diuinas uel quamlibet earum partem intellexisse sibi uidetur, ita ut eo intellectu non aedificet istam geminam caritatem dei et proximi, nondum intellexit*"; "[w]hoever, therefore, thinks that he understands the divine Scriptures or any part of them so that it does not build the double love of God and of our neighbor does not understand it at all."[84] The Holy Spirit enables the Christian to discover this ultimate intention at the basis of every biblical text. As a result, if an interpretation of scripture either fails to discern that wisdom or fails to promote the realization of the dual divine claim on human life, then that interpretation has missed the real point of the text under scrutiny, however accurate the historical, grammatical, literary, or philological studies of the text might have been. Thus, in this way, the Holy Spirit attests to the living Christ as the formal dimension of *informative authority*, while the Christian Bible remains the material dimension in this juncture of authority.

As a consequence, the *BFM (1963)* does not reduce informative authority to information as mere data, bits of knowledge, intellectual propositions, or cognitive constructs. The indwelling Holy Spirit attests to the authority of the Christian Bible, as the Spirit affirms the correlation of that written witness with the living Christ, to whom the Holy Spirit attests directly. This pattern repeats, in the Christian's personal experience, the order in the historical relationships between divine interactions with humanity and the origins of scripture. God discloses God's self in the events of human history—divine revelation. The scriptures comprise the primary or foundational witness to those past interactions between God and creation: the *BFM (1963)* describes the Christian Bible as "the record of God's revelation of Himself to man."[85] Thus, however one understands the first article of the *BFM (1963)*, and whether one construes it more strictly in terms of modern theories of biblical inerrancy or whether one interprets it more carefully in terms of the actual historical meaning of the confession's language itself, in the *BFM (1963)*, the Christian scriptures remain subservient to the living God of love. The scriptures receive their unquestionable authority functionally and practically, as the Holy Spirit attests to their veracity through the experience and conscience of each person who gratefully receives life from the living God through the Christ, Jesus of Nazareth.

5. Performative Authority

One may describe the extent to which conformation to Christ occurs in the Christian's life, through informative authority or in-formation with Christ, as *performative authority*. Literally, the word "perform" means "to form through," to complete, to fulfill, or to perfect. As the Johannine Christ reminds his disciples, "[b]y this all men will know that you are My disciples, if you have love for one another."[86] Insofar as the Christian genuinely claims a cognitive apprehension of the truth disclosed through the informative authority of the indwelling Holy Spirit, the Christian also enacts this truth in behavior as well as in thought. By the same token, if Christians do not love one another, then other humans will not recognize them as disciples of Jesus Christ. Without the extension or growth into loving behavior or activity among and toward others, conformation to Christ has not properly completed itself.

As warrants for this claim, the *BFM (1963)* cites texts from the book of James, the first Petrine epistle, and the first Johannine epistle. Christian faith actually suffers malformation, according to the book of James, to the extent that "faith, if it has no works, is dead, being by itself." The book of James construes the works of faith as the enactment or fulfillment of "the royal law, according to the Scripture, 'YOU SHALL LOVE YOUR NEIGHBOR AS YOURSELF.'" The first Petrine epistle develops its own understanding of the Christian's sanctification or growth in holiness as the fervent "love" of Christians for one another "from the heart." Even more forcefully from the Johannine perspective, on the one hand, without such performance in terms of love at least for Christian sisters and brothers, a Christian's claim to know the God of love becomes a lie. On the other hand, if the Christian loves as God has both called and empowered the Christian to love, then "in him the love of God has truly been perfected": "the one who says he abides in Him ought himself to walk in the same manner as He walked."[87]

Such increase or growth of the Christian's faith in or fidelity to God, as affirmed by the *BFM (1963)*, I have described as *performative authority*. In this respect, the Christian participates with God in the demonstration of God's message to a world in need. Confessional documents, as a consequence, *do not produce* such demonstrations of faith. Rather, doctrinal statements themselves *only cognitively represent* such fidelity to God. These cognitive expressions possess authority, however, only insofar as they rest upon practical expressions of that faithfulness to God in terms of love toward all neighbors, especially toward those neighbors who comprise the Christian community. Furthermore, and more radically, failure to perform or enact faith as love exposes the absence of genuine informative authority in all cognitively precise restatements of biblical claims, as Jesus himself boldly declared to his opponents:

> You search the Scriptures, because you think that in them you have eternal life; and it is these that bear witness of Me; and you are unwilling to come to Me, that you may have life. . . . but I know you, that you do not have the love of God in yourselves.[88]

6. Multiformative Authority

Genuine Christian life requires authentic or faithful performance or behavior from everyone who claims to be a disciple of Christ. Since all Christians participate in a universal priesthood, performative authority appears in multiple forms. Once again, the principle of the individual's competence before God affects the web of authority for Baptists. Rather than limiting the concept of performative authority as a reference to the individual Christian's behavior (in which behavior corresponds to, and thereby validates, both inner conformation to Christ and information by the Holy Spirit), however, the *BFM (1963)* expands its concept of performative authority to include a communal dimension. Among Baptists, multiple expressions of performative authority both produce, and interact as, the body of Christ or the Christian community. I have designated this juncture in the web of authority as *multiformative authority*.

The *BFM (1963)* refers to the community of Jesus Christ both as "*a local body* of baptized believers who are associated by covenant in the faith and fellowship of the gospel" and as "the body of Christ which includes *the redeemed of all the ages*."[89] Both forms of the Christian community figure into a Baptist vision of multiformative authority, yet both of them depend on "the historic Baptist principle": "The Soul's Competency in Religion under God," or "the soul's competency before God," realized in the Christian as "the priesthood of the believer."[90] This twofold concept of the Christian community yields both local and global expressions of multiformative authority.

(a) *Local Multiformative Authority*. In the Baptist vision, every new disciple receives from God the right, as well as the responsibility, voluntarily to associate with other Christians "by covenant" in the church as "a local body of baptized believers." The community originates as the voluntary assembly of the various persons whom God through Christ has already liberated. The verb "congregate," referring to this very activity, originates as a compound of two Latin words: *"com"*("with" or "together") and *"gregare"* ("to gather," "to assemble," "to flock").[91] The word "congregation," thus, literally refers to the voluntary gathering or assembly of those who resemble one another due to their willing reception of liberation from God through Christ. Because God ordains every Christian as a priest, all members of the Christian community exercise "the gifts, rights, and *privileges* invested in them by His [Christ's] Word" and "remain equally *responsible*" to one another and to God.[92]

Precisely on the previous basis, in the Baptist ecclesiological vision, the Christian community operates "through democratic processes under the Lordship of Jesus Christ."[93] With such statements, Baptists affirm the congregational polity of local Baptist churches, as radically distinct from episcopal (governance by a bishop or pastor) or presbyterial (governance by elders or even deacons) forms of polity. This perspective depends far more upon the Pauline concept of the Christian community as the body of Christ, a body in which all members remain necessary to the Christian community's fullest representation of Christ's real presence in the world than upon North American political theories about democracy.[94] Although all members of the local church participate in a common priesthood, the Holy Spirit has given to the diverse members of the body of Christ their own perspectives on the gospel of God, as well as different gifts of ministry, to produce a whole community and to benefit all participants in that community. Furthermore, these gifts to the various members of the body of Christ originate from the Holy Spirit's love for each Christian and the whole congregation. In addition, the Holy Spirit has empowered the members of the Christian community to employ these various gifts with love, in order for these gifts authentically to enhance or to benefit both the lives of the individual Christians and the life of their community.[95]

The priesthood of every Christian functions as the voluntary human source for each congregation as a *local* expression of the body of Christ. In this respect, individual Christians encouraged by and responsive to the Holy Spirit shape or form each local Christian community. For this reason, I have described this dynamic as local multiformative authority. Such interactions produce, increase, and nurture the growth of Christian understanding and behavior (faith and practice) in every specific Christian congregation.

(b) *Global Multiformative Authority*. Since the *BFM (1963)* also refers to the Christian community as "the body of Christ which includes *the redeemed of all the ages*," the ecclesiology of the *BFM (1963)* at its best also affirms a *global* multiformative authority. Local Christian communities or congregations participate in the larger Christian community or body of Christ. The SBC's historic ecclesiology, however, clearly describes the local Christian community as "an autonomous body."[96] In most of its history, the SBC has consistently discerned the origin of this ecclesiology in a commitment to the individual's competence before God, especially in terms of the individual's direct access and responsibility to God, freedom to respond positively to Christ, and freedom to associate voluntarily with other Christians.[97]

Nonetheless, also arising from commitment to the doctrine of the common Christian priesthood, the SBC has also consistently affirmed the local church's responsibility for interaction both with other Baptist Christian communities and with non-Baptist Christian congregations and organizations: "Christ's people *should*, as occasion requires, organize such associations and conventions as may best secure cooperation for the great objects of the kingdom of God"; "[c]o-operation is *desirable* between the various Christian denominations. . . ."[98] With such affirmations, whether always consciously or not, Baptists in the SBC at least implicitly have acknowledged both their own places within the larger history of Christianity and the value of perspectives from other historic Christian communions.

The SBC, however, has consistently qualified these affirmations in two major ways. First, all local Christian communities remain completely self-governing or autonomous with Christ's guidance: organizations, such as conventions or associations of churches, "have no authority over one another or over the churches." Second, Baptist Christian communities cooperate with other Christian denominations only on two major conditions: (1) "when the end to be attained is itself justified"; and (2) "when such cooperation involves no violation of conscience or compromise of loyalty to Christ and his Word as revealed in the New Testament."[99]

When individual Christians voluntarily gather or congregate with other Christians, thus forming Christian communities, they validate their claims to be disciples of Christ. In the way that performance actualizes or validates and nurtures the Christian's claim to a transformative experience with God, cooperation of Baptist congregations with one another and with other Christian organizations also demonstrates or validates claims to participation by the many different Christian congregations in the larger body of Christ. These modes of congregating literally cause the growth of the body of Christ. Producing and nurturing community both locally and globally constitute the dynamism of multiformative authority.

7. Interformative Authority

A final juncture in the web of authority presupposed by the *BFM (1963)*, *interformative authority*, originates from the dynamism of multiformative authority.[100] In the Christian community, Christians communicate with one another as priests to one another. The phrase, "interformative authority," designates the sources for growth, nurture, and increase originating from the communication and interaction among the members of the Christian community. Quite literally, this growth originates in the "between" of that communication.

For Baptists in the SBC, the doctrine of the common Christian priesthood emphasizes both the *privilege* and the *responsibility* of Christian freedom.[101] Even though this doctrine most certainly indicates every Christian's divine commission to minister to neighbors, both Christian neighbors and non-Christian neighbors (responsibility), the doctrine of the common Christian priesthood also affirms each Christian's liberated perspective as a divine gift (right or privilege). More importantly, the former dimension depends on the latter dimension.[102] The latter dimension, *liberation from* sin or distorted love, contains within itself the substance of the former dimension, *liberation for* faithfulness or authentic love toward both God and neighbor.

The person who has embraced the gospel of God receives and possesses a gift that invites the Christian to give it to others. The human's joy in the very reception of God's gospel of freedom motivates its holder to communicate this reality to her neighbors.[103] Each Christian can communicate (whether linguistically, morally, aesthetically, cognitively, or affectively) this experienced message with confidence that she or he offers the truth from God. Nonetheless, because such an experience also belongs to the neighbor who happily receives this good news, the neighbor also communicates God's gospel through his or her own perspective both to the disciple who originally communicated this truth and to other neighbors as well. Thus, the exercise of the Christian's common priesthood toward other Christians and toward those outside the Christian community discloses the incomplete character of each individual Christian's perspective.

The Christian who communicates her interpretation of the gospel, and yet also receives in response an interpretation of the gospel from a neighbor, discovers the relative adequacy of her own perspective. Hence, she realizes her own need for the neighbor's perspective, in order to increase an understanding of, more fully to realize, or more adequately to represent the gospel's truth. Although such a communicative experience prevents the individual Christian from legitimately promoting *absolute* human autonomy, insofar as this experience discloses the need for other - *individual* and *communal* Christian perspectives, neither does the communication of the gospel promote *absolute* human heteronomy. While the perspective of the other (oJ e{tero") always relativizes the perspective of the self (oJ ajutov"), the other always also shares the same experience of perspectival relativization. This mutual relativization of *individual* Christian perspectives continues to point both self and others beyond themselves as both individuals and community to the inexhaustible divine source of truth in and beyond the community (or to God or formative authority). Hence, interformative authority possesses a theonomous drive.[104] Even though each individual Christian both needs other Christians and cannot legitimately become an absolute rule in himself or herself, neither individual nor communal Christian alterities can legitimately become absolute rules unto themselves.[105] Even elevating a Christian community's perspective above the individual Christian's perspective as the norm for Christian life and understanding fails to answer every question about the gospel's truth, since every Christian community remains as much a fallible and sinful creature as does each Christian individual. A tensile dynamic functions between the Christian self and the Christian other, through which both can and must legitimately represent alternative perspectives and, therefore, questions for one another. A contemporary Christian hymn expresses this perspective well.

> We need each other's views to seeThe limits of the mind,
> That God in fact turns out to be Far more than we've defined,
> That God's one image shines in all, In every class and race,
> And every group receives the call To sing with faith and grace:
> We give our alleluias to the church's common chord:
> Alleluia! Alleluia! Praise: O praise, O praise the Lord![106]

Understanding the common priesthood essentially as ministry or service to the neighbor in need also implicitly emphasizes each Christian's privilege and ability to interpret biblical texts as aided by the Holy Spirit, interpretations that culminate not only in personal appropriations of meaning but also in the communication of that truth to others. In this respect, the communication of the gospel among members of the body of Christ shapes or forms both individual Christians and the Christian community itself. For this reason, I have described this dynamic as interformative authority. Such interactions produce, increase, and nurture the growth of Christian understanding and behavior (faith and practice) in every individual Christian and every local Christian congregation.

The process operating in the local Christian community among the various members operates also among the various Christian communities that both participate together in common tasks and share similar visions. Certainly, for entities such as communities, other factors affect this process. Nonetheless, the interactions between Christian communities also relativize every community's perspective. This experience, when it works most effectively, yields a similar double effect. First, perspectival relativization directs all communities to the need for one another, as resources to expand every community's experience and understanding of God's gospel. Second, this experienced relativity of every community's perspective directs all Christian communities always to look even beyond themselves in their collectivity to the inexhaustible divine source of truth. Hence, even global interformative authority discloses its theonomous drive. In this way, communities help to increase one another's appropriation and, thereby, communication of the inexhaustible wealth in the truth of God's loving relation with creation.

For the *BFM (1963)*, the goal of conformity to Christ by no means eliminates diversity from the Christian community. The unity of conformity, for the *BFM (1963)*, does not require uni-formity of Christian experience for the many members of the body of Christ in either local or global spheres. Although unity-in-diversity does not imply chaotic pluralism in the Christian community, it does imply the affirmation of genuine alterity, yet alterity often expressed in significant and severe differences or conflicts. In the Baptist vision of interformative authority, such diversity represents God's very own gift for the formation and nurture of Christian life and community.

The creative dissonance present within the concept of authority in the *BFM (1963)* suggests a concept of authority that differs drastically from authority understood as control, coercion, or domination. The SBC's historic, if not always consistent, avoidance of and resistance to the use of coercive measures for the attainment of common goals among Christians and their communities has invited this elaboration of the concept of authority at the basis of the *BFM (1963)*.[107]

I have referred to this document's concept of authority as a web rather than as a structure. The word "structure" originates from the Latin verb *"struere,"* which means to "heap up," "pile up," or "build." Even more significantly, *"struere"* appears to originate from the Indo-European root word, *"ster,"* which means to "spread, extend, stretch" or to "be rigid, stiff, thorny." In light of such etymological origins, the term "structure" tends to connote a concept of power as control, constraint, dominance, compulsion, or coercion. By contrast, the term "web" derives from the Old English verb *"wefan,"* related to the Old High German verb *"weban,"* both of which mean "to weave." Etymologists trace these words to another Indo-European root word, "*uebh*," which means to "weave" or to "move back and forth."[108]

The concept of authority in the *BFM (1963)* exhibits the characteristics of a web rather than the characteristics of a building's structure. As a web, the concept of authority possesses a pliability and a flexibility. The web of authority stretches, gives, and bounces under the weight of those who walk and live upon it. Whereas concrete foundations eventually disintegrate when cracks appear in them, a web's flexibility inhibits such disintegration even with the temporary relaxation or detachment of one strand.

A web has its own vulnerabilities, nonetheless, both in the delicate strands stretched between its various junctures and in the large spaces between the webbing itself. Hence, the web's vulnerability intensifies the vulnerabilities of those who depend upon it. A web's very weaknesses, however, also become its strengths. Through a web's spaces pass many objects without harm to the strands of the web. Although the strands of a web work only as they maintain their tensiveness, they can stretch and move into the spaces between themselves without damage. The tensile relationships between the different loci or junctures of authority may stretch into the spaces when jolted or assaulted by the pressures, oppositions, and ambiguities of life.

The verbal source of the metaphor "web," in the activity of weaving or moving back and forth between two points, also suggests other insights about the various junctures of authority. In the proper functioning of this concept, the various points or junctures remain connected, and the connections persist as tensile relationships. In other words, dialectical relationships among all of the junctures hold them together. Quite literally, the movement back and forth between the various junctures define those relationships or tensions.

Those who depend on this web of authority rely upon those dialectical relationships between the seven junctures. Without those relationships, the web dissolves. Unlike the rigid and abrasive structure of a building to which one can cling for security, a web, though flexible and smooth, with its stickiness also holds those who move and dwell upon it.

Dialectical relationships between seven major junctures define the web of authority in the *BFM (1963)*: formative, transformative, conformative, informative, performative, multiformative, and interformative authorities. More than simple interaction between these junctures, however, generates and maintains those tensions. One particular dynamic reality characterizes that interaction: the reciprocal relationships of love between God, self, and neighbor. This dynamic reality of love from both

God and humans weaves and reweaves (when circumstances necessitate repairs) the web of authority for personal and communal Baptist Christian life. In this light, even Baptists may confidently follow Augustine's profound advice: "*dilige, et quod vis fac*"; "love, and do what you will."[109]

VI. Purpose

The Preamble's sixth and final component concisely states the *purpose* of the report. Although statements of purpose usually appear somewhere near the beginning of a document, the authors of the *BFM (1963)* wisely located their statement of purpose in the final sentence of the Preamble. Despite the reminder, near the end of the Preamble, that Baptists in the SBC "most surely" hold "certain definite doctrines," as a qualification of the Baptist emphases on "the soul's competency before God, freedom in religion, and the priesthood of the believer," the placement of the statement of purpose definitely shapes an understanding of that purpose. According to the Preamble, then, "it is the purpose of this statement of faith and message to set forth certain teachings which we believe."[110]

The committee that produced the *BFM (1963)*, following the wisdom of the Committee on Baptist Faith and Message from 1925, perceived the need to issue an introductory statement that would prevent both the *attribution* of a credal character to its doctrinal statement and the *employment* of its doctrinal statement as a creed. With their introductory statements or preambles, both committees sought to qualify the nature, function, and use of confessional statements. Even though the doctrinal articles themselves remained very close to those in the *NHC (1833)*, a vast qualitative difference exists between that document and the two *BFMs*, especially the *BFM (1963)*. The *BFM (1963)* intensified that difference significantly, without denying the truth communicated through the doctrinal articles themselves.

While the doctrinal articles, or the "certain teachings which we believe," contain the genuine commitments held by the SBC in 1963, the Preamble prevents every reading, use, or understanding of those teachings that would seek to bypass the commitments also contained within the Preamble itself. Any interpretation of the doctrinal articles that elevates to an immutable status any doctrinal formulation contained in the *BFM (1963)* itself has misconstrued the very character of those doctrinal articles. In spite of their importance for describing historic Baptist beliefs, Baptists can legitimately read and affirm the articles of faith and practice only through the prism of the Preamble itself. Without that Preamble, those articles become elements of a creed—at least, in the sense specifically implied by the Preamble of the *BFM (1963)*. Hence, the physical location of the document's statement of purpose literally disallows any reading of either the statement of purpose or the doctrinal articles without passage through the previous components of the Preamble.

Conclusion

The contents of the Preamble to the *BFM (1963)*, as well as the Preamble's essential relationship to the doctrinal articles themselves, demonstrate the validity of the threefold hypothesis with which I began this study. The purpose's very placement within the Preamble demonstrates the necessary quality of that introductory statement. On the one hand, the Preamble's characterization of confessionalism supplies the legitimate conditions for the production and use of doctrinal statements among Baptists in the SBC. On the other hand, the implicit criteriology of credalism supplies the genuine limits for every confessional statement. Those previous conditions and limits arise from the basic Baptist principle, a principle woven into each component of this doctrinal document: *Every human finally stands invited and able to respond finally and only to the loving and beckoning triune God.*

*Portions of this chapter are adapted, with permission, from my recent essay: " 'Sacred Mandates of Conscience': A Criteriology of Credalism for Theological Method among Baptists," *Perspectives in Religous Studies 23* (Winter 1996). I especially thank Melissa Stewart, doctoral student in theology at the Divinity School of Vanderbilt University, for her helpful critical comments on an initial draft of this study.

Notes

[1]"Committee on Baptist Faith and Message," in *Annual of the Southern Baptist Convention: One Hundred Sixth Session in Kansas City, Missouri, 7-10 May 1963*, by the Executive Committee, Southern Baptist Convention (Nashville: Southern Baptist Convention, 1963) 63, 269-81 ("Proceedings," Thursday Morning, May 9, Items 112-124) (hereafter, cited as *BFM [1963]*). All references to the *BFM (1963)* will be to the text as it appears in *Annual SBC (1963)*.

[2]"Report of Committee on Baptist Faith and Message," in *Annual of the Southern Baptist Convention: Seventieth Session in Memphis, Tennessee, 13-17 May 1925*, by the Secretaries, Southern Baptist Convention (Nashville: Marshall and Bruce, 1925), 70-76 ("Proceedings," Second Day–Afternoon Session, May 14, Item 53) (hereafter, cited as *BFM [1925]*). All references to the *BFM (1925)* will be to the text as it appears in *Annual SBC (1925)*. My claim, of course, also applies to the *New Hampshire Confession* of 1833, which the Committee on Baptist Faith and Message substantially reproduced in its own

report in 1925. As illustrations of my claim, see various Baptist confessional documents from years prior to the formation of the SBC: "The New Hampshire Confession, 1833," in *Baptist Confessions of Faith*, rev. ed., William L. Lumpkin, ed. (Valley Forge PA: Judson Press, 1969), 360-367 (hereafter, cited as *NHC [1833]*); "The Philadelphia Confession, (1742)," in *Baptist Confessions, Covenants, and Catechisms*, vol. 11, Library of Baptist Classics, ed. Timothy George and Denise George (Nashville: Broadman and Holman, 1996) 56-93 (hereafter, cited as *PC [1742]*); "The Assembly or Second London Confession, 1677 and 1688," *Baptist Confessions of Faith*, Lumpkin, 235-95 (hereafter, cited as *SLC [1677, 1688]*); "Short Confession of Faith in XX Articles by John Smyth, 1609," in *Baptist Confessions of Faith*, Lumpkin, 97-101; and "A Short Confession of Faith, 1610," in *Baptist Confessions of Faith*, Lumpkin, 102-13. This claim also applies to the confessional statement of Southern Baptist Theological Seminary: "Abstract of Principles," from "Recommendation No. 3, Charter of the Southern Baptist Theological Seminary," in *Annual of the Southern Baptist Convention: Ninety-Seventh Session in St. Louis, Missouri, 2-5 June 1954*, by the Executive Committee, Southern Baptist Convention (Nashville: Southern Baptist Convention, 1954) 38 ("Proceedings," Wednesday Morning, June 2, Item 15) (hereafter, cited as *AP [1858]*).

³Often and in various ways, leaders of institutions in the SBC have failed to realize the Preamble's explicitly essential role in both the *BFM (1925)* and the *BFM (1963)*. For example, "Article I" from the "Bylaws" of Southwestern Baptist Theological Seminary (SWBTS), as included in the present *Faculty Manual* for the seminary, states the following about the seminary's articles of faith. "The Statement of Faith of the Seminary shall be the statement on the Baptist Faith and Message adopted by the Southern Baptist Convention in 1963. This Statement of Faith shall be published in the catalogue of the Seminary" ("Attachment 2: Bylaws," in *Faculty Manual, Southwestern Baptist Theological Seminary* [December 1995] 81). Nonetheless, while the seminary's present *Faculty Manual* reproduces the doctrinal articles from the *BFM (1963)*, the *Faculty Manual* does not include the preamble in its reproduction of that confessional document (see "Attachment 3: The Articles of Faith of Southwestern Baptist Theological Seminary," in *Faculty Manual [1995]* 101). Prior to the SBC's composition and adoption of the *BFM (1925)*, SWBTS employed the *NHC (1833)* as the seminary's confession of faith and published that document in the seminary's catalogue ("Articles of Faith of the Seminary," in *Second Annual Catalogue of the Southwestern Baptist Theological Seminary, 1908–1909*, vol. 1 [Waco TX: 1908] 42-45). Although the *NHC (1833)* supplied most of the articles of faith for the *BFM (1925)*, the *NHC (1833)* does not contain anything like the preambles of either the *BFM (1925)* or the *BFM (1963)*. SWBTS has not even consistently included its articles of faith in its catalogues or bulletins: a fairly large number of volumes omit the seminary's confessional statement. More importantly, although SWBTS later adopted the *BFM (1925)* as its confession of faith, the seminary's catalogues or bulletins consistently omitted that document's Preamble (e.g., *Bulletin of the Southwestern Baptist Theological Seminary, 1951–1952*, vol. 44 [Fort Worth TX: 1951] 26-31). During most of the seminary's history with the

BFM, even after SWBTS's adoption of the SBC's revised confession of faith, the *BFM (1963)*, the seminary's catalogues or bulletins continued to omit the Preamble to that document (e.g., *Bulletin of the Southwestern Baptist Theological Seminary, 1966–1967*, vol. 59 [Fort Worth TX: 1966] 40-42). In 1987, credalism had blossomed fully in the SBC with the report from the SBC's Peace Committee ("Special Reports: Southern Baptist Convention Peace Committee," in *Annual of the Southern Baptist Convention: One Hundred Thirtieth Session in St. Louis, Missouri, 16-18 June 1987*, ed. Executive Committee, Southern Baptist Convention [Nashville: Southern Baptist Convention, 1987] 56-57, 232-42 ["Proceedings," Tuesday Evening, June 16, Item 153]) (hereafter, cited as *RPC [1987]*). During the presidency of Russell H. Dilday, SWBTS prudently and finally began to publish the Preamble of the *BFM (1963)* at least in the seminary's bulletin or catalogue along with the doctrinal articles of the *BFM (1963)*. This prudent practice began in 1989 during the later years of Dilday's presidency of SWBTS and has inadvertently continued since Kenneth S. Hemphill began his own service as the seminary's president (e.g., *Bulletins of Southwestern Baptist Theological Seminary, 1989–1990, 1990–1991*, vols. 82-83 [Fort Worth TX: 1989] 131; *Bulletins of Southwestern Baptist Theological Seminary, 1991–1992, 1992–1993*, vols. 84-85 [Fort Worth TX: 1991] 132; *Catalogue of the Southwestern Baptist Theological Seminary, 1996–1997*, vol. 89 [Fort Worth TX: 1996] 153-54).

[4]During the annual meeting of the SBC in 1963, Herschel H. Hobbs, chairperson of the committee that revised the *BFM (1925)*, clarified the essential role of the Preamble for the *BFM (1963)*. The messengers to the Convention in 1963 concurred with Hobbs on this point: "By common consent, the Convention understood that the introductory material is a part of the committee's report and will be so included in the vote on adoption" (*Annual SBC [1963]* 63 ["Proceedings," Thursday Morning, May 9, Item 121]). Robert E. Naylor, in his own account of this event, noted the significance of this action by the SBC (Robert E. Naylor, *A Messenger's Memoirs: Sixty-One SOUTHERN BAPTIST CONVENTION Meetings* [Franklin TN: Providence House, 1995] 127). Hobbs reiterated this claim on more than one occasion. In his commentary on the *BFM (1963)*, Hobbs bluntly observed the following about the Preamble. "It should be noted that these statements are as much a part of the overall statement adopted in 1963 as are the various elements of faith found in the body of it. If this be denied or ignored, then the statement becomes a creed. Without this safeguard to the individual conscience it is highly doubtful that the Southern Baptist Convention would have voted its approval" (Herschel H. Hobbs, *The Baptist Faith and Message* [Nashville: Convention Press, 1971] 12). Even more recently, during an annual meeting of the SBC on its Tuesday afternoon session, 9 June 1981, Hobbs introduced the following motion: that "we reaffirm our historic Baptist position that the Holy Bible, which has truth without any mixture of error for its matter, is our adequate rule of faith and practice, and that we reaffirm our belief in ÔThe Baptist Faith and Message' adopted in 1963, including all seventeen articles, plus the preamble which protects the conscience of the individual and guards us from a credal faith." In the Wednesday morning session, 10 June 1981, when the

Convention considered scheduled motions, Hobbs discussed his motion. Hobbs began his explanation with the comments that follow. "This motion is designed to emphasize that the preamble is as much a part of the statement voted by the Convention as any other part. When the Convention voted to set up a committee to do the study that resulted in this statement, it said that the product *shall* serve as information to the churches and *may*—notice the difference—not shall, *may* serve as guidelines for agencies of the Convention" (*Annual of the Southern Baptist Convention: One Hundred Twenty-Fourth Session in Los Angeles, California, 9-11 June 1981*, by the Executive Committee, Southern Baptist Convention [Nashville: Southern Baptist Convention, 1981] 35, 45 ["Proceedings," Tuesday Afternoon, June 9, Item 53; Wednesday Morning, June 10, Item 118]). Hobbs had previously expressed this same perspective, even more forcefully, in an article. "The Preamble is as much a part of this statement adopted by the Southern Baptist Convention as any of the seventeen articles which follow. Without it the statement becomes a creed. And Baptists are not a credal people. Without this preamble the Convention would not have adopted it. Therefore, no one Southern Baptist or group of such has the right to seek to ignore the preamble in interpreting or applying it" (Herschel H. Hobbs, "Southern Baptists and Confessionalism: A Comparison of the Origins and Contents of the 1925 and 1963 Confessions," *Review and Expositor* 76 [Winter 1979]: 68). See an even earlier, though less developed, version of this statement by Hobbs (Herschel H. Hobbs, "The Baptist Faith and Message–Anchored but Free," *Baptist History and Heritage* 13 [July 1978]: 36).

[5]When Baptists of the South formed the SBC in 1845, they produced their first statement against credalism as the presupposition of the new organization: "We have constructed for our basis no new creed; acting in this matter upon a Baptist aversion for all creeds but the Bible" (William B. Johnson, et al., "The Southern Baptist Convention, To the Brethren in the United States; to the congregations connected with the respective Churches; and to all candid men," in *Proceedings of the Southern Baptist Convention in Augusta, Georgia, 8-12 May 1845* [Richmond VA: H. K. Ellyson Printer, 1845] 17-20; also see William Wright Barnes, "Why the Southern Baptist Convention Was Formed," *Review and Expositor*" 41 [January 1944]: 3-17; idem, *The Southern Baptist Convention: 1845–1953* [Nashville: Broadman Press, 1954] 12-32). While the Triennial Convention's Board rightly opposed slavery, it wrongly addressed the problem of missionaries as slaveholders. Similarly, however, while the Baptists of the South rightly resisted both the appearance of a non-congregational polity in the Convention and the imposition of a credal article, they wrongly continued to support slavery. Even more recently, since the beginning of the SBC's most recent political and theological conflicts in 1979, many faithful Baptist Christians in the SBC have warned about the impending danger of credalism in the SBC. I identify here only a few of those individuals. Very early in the SBC's most recent controversies, Grady C. Cothen boldly and carefully identified both the credal tendencies of the fundamentalist aggression in the SBC and the dangers of those tendencies for the SBC (Grady C. Cothen, "The Real Issue of Our Times," *Facts and Trends* 25 [February 1981]: 2; idem, "The Bottom Line of a Creed," *Facts and*

Trends 25 [April 1981]: 2; idem, "A Difference between Believing and a Creed," *Facts and Trends* 25 [May 1981]: 2; idem, "Now, I'm Scared," *Facts and Trends* 25 [June 1981]: 2; cf. Linda Lawson, "Cothen Underscores Ideals," *Facts and Trends* 27 [February 1983]: 5; "Cothen Recommends 'Ideals,' " *Facts and Trends* 27 [June 1983]: 11-13). Even in retirement, Cothen continues to alert Baptists to the danger of "creeping credalism" in the SBC (Grady C. Cothen, *What Happened to the Southern Baptist Convention? A Memoir of the Controversy* [Macon GA: Smyth & Helwys, 1993] 157-63; cf. idem, *The New SBC: Fundamentalism's Impact on the Southern Baptist Convention* [Macon GA: Smyth & Helwys, 1995] 65-85, 143-78). Similarly, also more than a decade ago, Slayden Yarbrough discussed the dangers of the SBC's drift into credalism for the Convention's historical commitments and self-definition, for its understanding of the production and use of theology, and for its concept of missions as cooperative not coerced endeavors (Slayden Yarbrough, "Is Credalism a Threat to Southern Baptists?" *Baptist History and Heritage* 18 [April 1983]: 21-33). Early in those controversies, Russell Dilday, former president of Southwestern Baptist Theological Seminary, also warned about the dangers of credalism, in a brief discussion of the historic Baptist principle of the individual human's competence in religion (Russell Dilday, "Individuals Must Respond to God Personally," *Facts and Trends* 25 [March 1981]: 5). See the following examples in which the distinction between confessions of faith and creeds operates: W. J. McGlothlin, ed., *Baptist Confessions of Faith* (Philadelphia: American Baptist Publication Society, 1911) xi-xii; Lumpkin, *Baptist Confessions of Faith*, 16-17; G. Keith Parker, *Baptists in Europe: History and Confessions of Faith* (Nashville: Broadman Press, 1982) 20; W. R. Estep, "Baptists and Authority: The Bible, Confessions, and Conscience in the Development of Baptist Identity," *Review and Expositor* 84 (Fall 1987): 600-601; idem, "Biblical Authority in Baptist Confessions of Faith, 1610–1963," in *The Unfettered Word: Southern Baptists Confront the Authority-Inerrancy Question*, ed. Robison B. James (Macon GA: Smyth & Helwys, 1994) 157; James E. Carter, "Southern Baptists' First Confession of Faith," *Baptist History and Heritage* 5 (January 1970): 24; idem, "Guest Editorial: The Bible and 20th-Century Southern Baptist Confessions of Faith," *Baptist History and Heritage* 19 (July 1984): 2-3; Walter B. Shurden, "Major Issues in the SBC Controversy," in *Amidst Babel, Speak the Truth: Reflections on the Southern Baptist Convention Struggle*, ed. Robert U. Ferguson, Jr. (Macon GA: Smyth & Helwys, 1993) 7-8; Claude L. Howe, Jr., "From Houston to Dallas: Recent Controversy in the Southern Baptist Convention," *Theological Educator* 41 (Spring 1990): 84-85; Edward B. Pollard, "What Shall We Think of Creeds?" *Review and Expositor* 12 (January 1915): 40-54; idem, "A Brief Study in Baptist Confessions of Faith," *The Chronicle* 7 (April 1944): 74-85; Harold W. Tribble, "Individual Competency and Use of Creeds," *The Chronicle* 7 (April 1944): 94-95; Yarbrough, "Is Credalism a Threat to Southern Baptists?" 21-33.

[6]In 1924, due to concerns about doctrine expressed during the Convention, the SBC's Committee on Resolutions recommended "that the following brethren be appointed to consider the advisability of issuing another statement of the Baptist faith and message and to report at the next Convention: E. Y. Mullins,

Chairman, L. R. Scarborough, C. P. Stealey, W. J. McGlothlin, S. M. Brown, E. C. Dargan, R. H. Pitt." The Convention adopted the Committee's recommendation (*Annual of the Southern Baptist Convention: Sixty-Ninth Session in Atlanta, Georgia, 14-18 May 1924*, by the Secretaries, Southern Baptist Convention [Nashville: Marshall and Bruce, 1924] 24, 49, 70-71, 80, 95 ["Proceedings," Wednesday–Afternoon Session, May 14, Item 22; Thursday–Afternoon Session, May 15, Items 50 and 51; Friday–Afternoon Session, May 16, Item 77; Saturday–Morning Session, May 17, Items 99 and 109]). E. Y. Mullins described "the historical significance of the Baptists" as their adherence to and promotion of the principle of "the competency of the soul in religion," the commitment from which all other distinctive Baptist interpretations of life in Christ derive as corollaries (E. Y. Mullins, *The Axioms of Religion: A New Interpretation of the Baptist Faith* [Philadelphia: Judson Press, 1908] 53). Even later in the SBC's history, following the SBC's annual meeting in 1936, the SBC met with the Northern Baptist Convention, specifically on the topic of the human individual's competency before God as the historic Baptist principle at the origin of every other major Baptist perspective ("The Soul's Competency in Religion under God: The Historic Baptist Principle for Today" [St. Louis MO: May 18-19, 1936], in *Annual of the Southern Baptist Convention: Eighty-First Session in Saint Louis, Missouri, 14-16 May 1936*, by the Executive Committee, Southern Baptist Convention [Nashville: Southern Baptist Convention, 1936] 108-15). Harold W. Tribble also reiterated this perspective (Harold W. Tribble, "The Competency of the Individual in Religion," *Review and Expositor* 41 [April 1944]: 142-49). Later still, in the mid-1940s, the SBC described its "distinctive belief" as its "Doctrine of Man in the personal order of life." The second point of this theological anthropology states the following: "Every man is endowed by the Creator with competence as a person to deal with God and with his fellowmen in all rightful relations." Additionally, according to this confessional document of the SBC, "[o]ut of this doctrine of the individual grows the Baptist conviction concerning all aspects of religious experience and life" ("Statement of Principles," in *Annual of the Southern Baptist Convention, 1945*, by the Executive Committee, Southern Baptist Convention [Nashville: Southern Baptist Convention, 1945] 59; "Statement of Principles," in *Annual of the Southern Baptist Convention: Eighty-Ninth Session in Miami, Florida, 15-19 May 1946* ["Proceedings," Thursday–Morning Session, May 16, Item 27], by the Executive Committee, Southern Baptist Convention [Nashville: Southern Baptist Convention, 1946] 38) (hereafter, cited respectively as *SP [1945]* and *SP [1946]*). Hobbs, later following Mullins virtually word for word, also described this principle as "the distinctive belief held by Baptists," "the source" of "all other elements of Baptist belief...," and even as "the rock whence they [Baptists] are hewn" (Hobbs, *Baptist Faith and Message*, 7, 9, 11).

[7]Mullins, *Axioms of Religion*, 58.

[8]"Recommendation No. 14," from the "Report of the Executive Committee," in *Annual of the Southern Baptist Convention: One Hundred Fifth Session in San Francisco, California, 5-8 June 1962*, by the Executive Committee, Southern

Baptist Convention (Nashville: Southern Baptist Convention, 1962) 64 ("Proceedings," Wednesday Morning, June 6, Item 44).

[9]Ralph H. Elliott, *The Message of Genesis* (Nashville: Broadman Press, 1961).

[10]K. Owen White, then pastor of First Baptist Church in Houston and a member of the SBC's Executive Committee, had launched a vicious public attack on Elliott's book, declaring it to be "poison," early in 1962 (K. Owen White, " '. . . Death in the Pot,' " *Baptist Standard* 74 [10 January 1962]: 6). Also, E. S. James, then editor of the *Baptist Standard*, campaigned vigorously in editorials against Elliott and his book (e.g., E. S. James, "Baptist Theologians and Their Books," *Baptist Standard* 74 [10 January 1962]: 4-5; idem, "Let Us Get Some Things Straight," *Baptist Standard* 74 [4 July 1962]: 4; idem, "The Dismissal of Professor Ralph H. Elliott," *Baptist Standard* 74 [14 November 1962]: 4-5; idem, "The Virginia Resolution Goes Too Far," *Baptist Standard* 74 [12 December 1962]: 4).

[11]K. Owen White delivered the first motion: "I move that the messengers to this Convention, by standing vote, reaffirm their faith in the *entire* Bible as the authoritative, authentic, infallible Word of God, that we express our abiding and unchanging objection to the dissemination of theological views in any of our seminaries which would undermine such faith in the historical accuracy and doctrinal integrity of the Bible, and that we kindly but firmly instruct the trustees and administrative officers of our institutions and [other] agencies to take such steps as shall be necessary to remedy at once those situations where such views now threaten our historic position." Herschel H. Hobbs, president of the SBC in 1962, later succeeded in dividing White's motion into two motions, both of which the SBC adopted anyway. The first motion retained the exact wording from the initial portion of White's original motion: "That the messengers to this Convention, by standing vote, reaffirm their faith in the *entire* Bible as the authoritative, authentic, infallible Word of God." The SBC adopted White's second motion after an "extended discussion," "an unsuccessful effort to refer the motion to the special committee appointed to prepare a statement of faith," and a minor yet significant amendment to the motion by White himself: "That we express our abiding and unchanging objection to the dissemination of theological views in any of our seminaries which would undermine such faith in the historical accuracy and doctrinal integrity of the Bible, and that we *courteously request* the trustees and administrative officers of our institutions and other agencies to take such steps as shall be necessary to remedy at once those situations where such views now threaten our historic position" (emphasis mine) (*Annual SBC [1962]* 65, 68 ["Proceedings," Wednesday Morning, June 6, Item 57; Thursday Morning, June 7, Items 83-86]). Ralph F. Powell introduced another motion: "I recommend that this Convention instruct the Sunday School Board to cease from publication and printing the book, *The Message of Genesis*, by Dr. Elliott, and that they furthermore recall from all sales this book which contradicts Baptist conviction." Although Powell ("upon request of Earl Harding" [then a trustee of Midwestern Baptist Theological Seminary and an opponent of Elliott]) withdrew his motion the next day, Ben D. Windham presented substantially the same motion later that same day: "That this

Convention instruct the Sunday School Board to cease publishing and to recall from all distribution channels, the book, *The Message of Genesis*, by Dr. Ralph Elliott." Later that same evening, however, the SBC refused to adopt Windham's motion (*Annual SBC [1962]* 65, 68, 71, 73 ["Proceedings," Wednesday Morning, June 6, Item 60; Thursday Morning, June 7, Item 91; Thursday Afternoon, June 7, Item 109; Thursday Night, June 7, Item 126]). From a slightly different perspective, Alvin O. West, also then a member of the SBC's Executive Committee, proposed one other motion in this connection: "That the Special Committee established by action of the Convention on Wednesday, June 6, 1962 (Item 44), be directed to include in its report a proposed definition of the words 'our historic position' as used in the motion of K. O. White, adopted at the morning Convention session on June 7, 1962." The SBC did not adopt West's motion (*Annual SBC [1962]* 71-72, 73 ["Proceedings," Thursday Afternoon, June 7, Item 114; Thursday Night, June 7, Item 127]). Acquiescing to the SBC's *courteous request*, Broadman Press later refused to reprint Elliott's book ("Broadman Press Says No Second Printing of Book," *Baptist Standard* 74 [18 July 1962]: 15). The trustees of Midwestern Baptist Theological Seminary (MBTS) made their own concession to the SBC's sentiments by terminating Elliott's employment with the seminary for his alleged insubordination: Elliott had sought another publisher for his book against the desire of MBTS's trustees. While the trustees asked Elliott voluntarily not to seek another publisher, they would not officially "request" of or instruct Elliott not to republish his book. The trustees feared the possible repercussions of any official efforts by them to ban the book itself, yet they had no qualms about taking Elliott's job from him ("Midwestern Trustees Vote to Dismiss Ralph Elliott," *Baptist Standard* 74 [31 October 1962]: 14). Elliott has recently written his own illuminating account of the events and issues surrounding this controversy (Ralph H. Elliott, *The "Genesis Controversy" and Continuity in Southern Baptist Chaos: A Eulogy for a Great Tradition* [Macon GA: Mercer University Press, 1992] 41-126).

[12]Baptist state papers certainly described the general public's perception of the situation in this way: for example, "[w]hile the committee [on Baptist faith and message] declined to point a finger in any direction, it is generally felt that the committee came into being because of the publication of *The Message of Genesis* by Ralph Elliott, a Midwestern Seminary professor" (" 'Guidelines' Subcommittee Named," *Baptist Standard* 74 [18 July 1962]: 15).

[13]*Annual SBC (1962)* 64; *BFM (1963)* 269 (1.1, 2) (emphasis mine).

[14]*Annual SBC (1962)* 64; *BFM (1963)* 269 (1.1, 2). The recommendation refers to a statement "as suggested in Section 2 of that report" (referring to the *BFM [1925]*). In its reference to "Section 2," presumably the recommendation refers to the second numbered paragraph among the numbered paragraphs of its introductory comments, since the only other portions of the *BFM (1925)* marked with the number "2" include two inapplicable sections: article 2 on the doctrine of God; and the second paragraph of the appended section, entitled "Science and Religion." In the paragraph to which I have referred among the introductory paragraphs of the *BFM (1925)*, the phrase appears that corresponds to the reference in the recommendation from 1962: "As in the past so in the future, Baptists should

hold themselves *free to revise their statements of faith* as may seem to them wise and expedient at any time" (*BFM [1925]* 71, 75-76) (emphasis mine).

[15]See the following examples: "Report on Interdenominational Relations," in *Annual of the Southern Baptist Convention: Eighty-Third Session in Richmond, Virginia, 12-15 May 1938* ("Proceedings," Thursday, Afternoon Session, May 12, Item 15), by the Southern Baptist Convention (Nashville: Southern Baptist Convention, 1938) 24-25 (hereafter, cited as *RIR [1938]*); "A Pronouncement upon Religious Liberty," in *Annual of the Southern Baptist Convention: Eighty-Fourth Session in Oklahoma City, Oklahoma, 17-21 May 1939* ("Proceedings," Saturday–Morning Session, May 20, Item 82), by the Executive Committee, Southern Baptist Convention (Nashville: Southern Baptist Convention, 1939) 114-16 (hereafter, cited as *PRL [1939]*); "Reply to World Council of Churches," in *Annual of the Southern Baptist Convention: Eighty-Fifth Session in Baltimore, Maryland, 12-16 June 1940* ("Proceedings," Friday–Afternoon Session, June 14, Item 66), by the Executive Committee, Southern Baptist Convention (Nashville: Southern Baptist Convention, 1940) 99 (hereafter, cited as *RWCC [1940]*); *SP (1945)* 59-60; *SP (1946)* 38-39. Also see notable confessional statements of the SBC prior to 1925: "Pronouncement on Christian Union and Denominational Efficiency," from "Report of Commission on Efficiency to the Southern Baptist Convention," in *Annual of the Southern Baptist Convention: Fifty-Ninth Session in Nashville, Tennessee, 13-18 May 1914* ("Proceedings," Fourth Day, Morning Session, May 16, Item 97), by the Secretaries, Southern Baptist Convention (Nashville: Marshall and Bruce, 1914) 73-78 (hereafter, cited as *PCU [1914]*); *Fraternal Address of Southern Baptists* (Southern Baptist Convention, 1920) (hereafter, cited as *FASB [1920]*); "Science and Religion," in *Annual of the Southern Baptist Convention: Sixty-Eighth Session in Kansas City, Missouri, 16-20 May 1923* ("Proceedings," Wednesday–Morning Session, May 16, Item 11), by the Secretaries, Southern Baptist Convention (Nashville: Marshall and Bruce, 1923) 19-20 (hereafter, cited as *SR [1923]*). In addition, see the concise yet comprehensive statement adopted only by the Foreign Mission Board: "A Statement of Belief," from "Appendix A: Seventy-Fifth Annual Report of the Foreign Mission Board," in *Annual of the Southern Baptist Convention: Sixty-Fifth Session in Washington, D. C., 12-17 May 1920*, by the Secretaries, Southern Baptist Convention (Nashville: Marshall and Bruce, 1920) 197-99 (hereafter, cited as *SB [1920]*).

[16]*Annual SBC (1962)* 64; *BFM (1963)* 269 (1.2) (emphasis mine). See the accounts by Hobbs of the committee's "Search for Counsel" from the SBC's broad constituencies, an effort that also solicited advice and suggestions from the SBC's seminaries (Hobbs, "Baptist Faith and Message—Anchored but Free," 37-38; idem, "Southern Baptists and Confessionalism," 59-61).

[17]Compare the efforts in this recommendation from 1962, both to adhere to the SBC's desire and to reflect the SBC's diversity, with the very different procedure behind the most recent doctrinal statement adopted, but not initially authorized, by the SBC in 1994: "The Report of the Presidential Theological Study Committee." In 1992, without authorization from the SBC itself, then president of the SBC, H. Edwin Young appointed a small, yet largely fundamentalist,

committee to produce a report on the doctrines of the SBC ("Report of the Presidential Theological Study Committee," in *Annual of the Southern Baptist Convention: One Hundred Thirty-Seventh Session in Orlando, Florida, 14-16 June 1994*, by the Executive Committee, Southern Baptist Convention [Nashville: Southern Baptist Convention, 1994] 102, 112-18 ["Proceedings," Wednesday Morning Session, June 15, Item 145]) (hereafter, cited as *RPTSC*). Furthermore, in 1962, the SBC rejected an amendment to "Recommendation No. 14," proposed from the floor of the Convention, "to include seminary presidents and faculty members on the committee" ("Committee of 24 Assigned to Study Statement of Baptist Faith," *Baptist Messenger* 51 [21 June 1962]: 2). By contrast, not only did the president of the SBC on his own initiative authorize the formation of the Presidential Theological Study Committee in 1992, but, with only a few exceptions, mainly academic personnel and seminary leaders held the few places on this committee. Consider the membership of the Presidential Theological Study Committee: Timothy F. George (co-chairperson); Roy L. Honeycutt (co-chairperson); William E. Bell; J. Walter Carpenter, Jr.; Mark T. Coppenger; Stephen D. C. Corts; Carl F. H. Henry; Herschel H. Hobbs; Richard D. Land; R. Albert Mohler, Jr.; and William B. Tolar. Furthermore, the committee as a whole most certainly did not adequately reflect the diversity still alive within the SBC.

[18]Herschel H. Hobbs, "The Committee on the Baptist Faith and Message," *Baptist Messenger* 52 (21 March 1963): 7.

[19]*Annual SBC (1962)* 64; *BFM (1963)* 269 (1.2) (emphasis mine).

[20]*BFM (1925)* 71; *BFM (1963)* 269.

[21]*BFM (1925)* 71.

[22]Hobbs, "Committee on the Baptist Faith and Message," 13.

[23]*BFM (1963)* 269; *BFM (1925)* 71.

[24]Although Edward Pollard did not distinguish explicitly between creeds and confessions of faith, he discerns characteristics in the historical functions and uses of creeds that resemble some of the criteria in the Preamble's implicit criteriology of credalism: "A twentieth-century creed should be individual, rather than *collective*; voluntary, rather than *compulsory*; educative, rather than *authoritative*; emotive, rather than *intellectual*; experimental, rather than *speculative*; practical, rather than *metaphysical*; fluid and not *fixed*" (Pollard, "What Shall We Think of Creeds?" 53-54) (emphasis mine). While creeds and confessions of faith share several characteristics, they differ from one another significantly enough that, especially when the SBC's confessional statements begin to function as creeds, the phenomenon of credalism itself has appeared. Despite a deep interdependence among the credal criteria, credalism itself can appear in varying degrees. Sometimes evidence will indicate only the *approach* of credalism or even *weak forms* of credalism: therefore, all of the following criteria may not necessarily apply to every specific object of analysis. Nonetheless, the applicability of one or more of these criteria to any doctrinal statement under scrutiny indicates the presence or approach of credalism to some degree, however slight that might be.

[25]About the five paragraphs of this component in the Preamble to the *BFM (1925)* (and, by implication, in the preamble to the *BFM [1963]*), Hobbs made

equally vehement observations. "Special notice should be taken of the words 'the adoption by the Convention.' This means that these five articles are a vital part of the overall statement of faith. The various doctrinal articles should not be interpreted without due recognition of these five statements" (Hobbs, "Southern Baptists and Confessionalism," 56). Shurden and Yarbrough emphasize the significance of this point as well (Walter B. Shurden, "Southern Baptist Responses to Their Confessional Statements," *Review and Expositor* 76 [Winter 1979]: 77-78; Yarbrough, "Is Credalism a Threat to Southern Baptists?" 25).

[26]In this section, I will frequently refer to the Preambles in the two confessions without repeated references to these few pages (*BFM [1925]* 71; *BFM [1963]* 269-70). I will also support the perspectives from the two *BFMs* with other documents from the SBC's confessional history, as well as with materials from other portions of the two *BFMs*.

[27]*BFM (1963)* 269-70. I have developed these characteristics and criteria a little differently elsewhere: Jeff B. Pool, " 'Sacred Mandates of Conscience': A Criteriology of Credalism for Theological Method among Baptists," *Perspectives in Religious Studies* 23 (Winter 1996).

[28] "Faith is the acceptance of Jesus Christ and commitment of the entire personality to Him as Lord and Saviour" (*BFM [1963]* 273 [Article 4]). The SBC has similarly described the human transformation in the re-establishment of right relations with God as "a radical renewal of the spiritual nature of man, due to the direct action of the Holy Spirit, and always in connection with conscious acceptance of Jesus Christ as Lord and Saviour. It is a spiritual transformation which results from the direct and immediate contact of the soul with the Spirit of God" (*PCU [1914]* 74). Again, according to the SBC, the Spirit's regeneration of sinful humans "is conditioned upon personal repentance towards God and faith in our Lord Jesus Christ. Repentance is a sincere renunciation of sin, and faith is genuine trust in the atoning Christ as Saviour and Lord" (*FASB [1920]* 8). "We hold that all people who believe in Christ as their personal Saviour are our brothers in the common salvation, whether they be in the Catholic communion, or in a Protestant communion, or in any other communion, or in no communion" (*RIR [1938]* 24; cf. *PRL [1939]* 115; *RWCC [1940]* 99; *SP [1946]* 38). "Salvation from sin is the free gift of God through Jesus Christ, conditioned only upon repentance toward God and trust in and commitment to Christ the Lord" (*Baptist Ideals* [Nashville: Sunday School Board of the Southern Baptist Convention, 1963] 12 [3.1]) (hereafter, cited as *BI [1963]*). W. T. Conner refused to define faith as the cognitive acceptance of certain propositions. "With Baptists, faith is the response of the whole person to God as revealed in Christ. Such a response is more than an intellectual matter. It is not just the acceptance of a doctrine or a dogma on the authority of the church, or the authority of the Bible, or on any other ground. It is the response of the whole man and establishes a personal, spiritual relation of the soul with God" (W. T. Conner, "Theology, A Practical Discipline," *Review and Expositor* 41 [October 1944]: 355). In its concept of faith, nonetheless, the more Reformed confessional statement for Southern Baptist Theological Seminary, the *Abstract of Principles*, tends to stress the cognitive and propositional quality of faith as primary: "saving faith is the belief, on

God's authority, of whatsoever is revealed in His Word concerning Christ; accepting and resting upon Him alone for justification and eternal life" (*AP [1858]* 38).

[29]See Augustine's formulation of this classic distinction (Augustine *De Trinitate* 13.2.5).

[30]*BFM (1963)* 270 (emphasis mine). As the Committee on Baptist Ideals stated about its own report in 1963, "one purpose of this report is to interpret ourselves." In addition, the human "is free to accept or reject religion; to choose or change his faith; to preach and teach the truth *as he sees it*, always with due regard for the rights and convictions of others" and so forth. Furthermore, as this confessional statement declares with regard to the relationship between faith and reason in Christian education, "genuine faith seeks intelligent understanding and expression" (*BI [1963]* 5, 11, 35 [2.3; 5.8]) (emphasis mine). The SBC has even perceived this same characteristic or impulse in the Christian scriptures themselves: "the one and only authority in faith and practice is the New Testament as the divinely inspired record and *interpretation of the supreme revelation of God through Jesus Christ* as Redeemer, Saviour, and Lord" (*SP [1946]* 38) (emphasis mine).

[31]Also see the following: *BFM (1963)* 275, 278, 279-80, 281 (especially, articles 6, 11, 12, 14, and 17); *PCU (1914)* 73-76; *FASB (1920)* 8-9, 11-15; *RIR (1938)* 24-25; *PRL (1939)* 115, 116; *SP (1946)* 38-39; *BI (1963)* 9-11, 14-15, 20-23 (2.1-3; 3.3; 4.4-5; 5.1). Also, see evidence of these claims even in the SBC's respectful though negative response to an invitation to join the World Council of Churches (WCC) in 1940. "Our Convention has no ecclesiological authority. It is in no sense the Southern Baptist Church. The thousands of churches to which our Convention looks for support of its missionary, benevolent, and educational program, cherish their independence and would disapprove of any attempted exercise of ecclesiastical authority over them" (*RWCC [1940]* 99). Both George W. Truett (as chairperson) and L. R. Scarborough participated on the committee that composed the SBC's reply to the WCC.

[32]John Leland, "The Virginia Chronicle," in *The Writings of John Leland*, ed. L. F. Greene, Religion in America Series, ed. Edwin S. Gaustad (New York: G. W. Wood, 1845; reprint, New York: Arno Press and *The New York Times*, 1969) 114n.* (page references are to the reprint edition). Fundamentalists in the SBC would benefit by heeding the wisdom in another observation by John Leland. "I have generally observed that when religion is lively among the people, no alienation of affection arises from a difference of judgment; and whoever considers that the Devil is orthodox in judgment, and that the Bible is not written in form of a system, will surely be moderate in dealing out hard speeches towards his heterodox brother" (Leland, "Letter of Valediction, on Leaving Virginia, in 1791," in *Writings of John Leland*, 172).

[33]"We must also refuse to accept or approve any form of proxy religion which puts priest or sacrament between the soul and God. In like manner, we are bound to disapprove of all ecclesiastical systems which set up human authorities over the consciences of those whom Christ has made free." "The equality of believers in the church is the necessary consequence of the equality of the status of men before God. That each local church is, and in the nature of the case should

be, self-governing and independent is a truth inseparable from the other truth that all men are directly responsible to God. The priesthood of all believers carries at its heart the necessity for self-government in church life" (*PCU [1914]* 74, 75). Similarly, according to the *FASB (1920)*, "[t]he members of a local church are spiritual equals. In the New Testament church there were no overlords or ecclesiastical superiors, to whom the members were under authority. This equality of believers in the church arises from the direct relation between each individual soul and the Lord Jesus Christ" (*FASB [1920]* 8). The SBC has produced a variety of similar statements. "We believe that a church of Jesus Christ is a pure democracy and cannot subject itself to any outside control, nor bend to a superior clergy" (*RIR [1938]* 24 [especially, point 3]). "The conception of the dignity of the individual as held by Baptists, is grounded in the conviction that every soul possesses the capacity and the inalienable right to deal with God for himself, and to deprive any soul of his right of direct access to God is to usurp the prerogatives of the individual and the function of God. . . . Standing as we do for the principle of voluntariness in religion, grounded upon the competency of the human soul, Baptists are essentially antagonistic to every form of religious coercion or persecution" (*PRL [1939]* 115). "Out of this doctrine of the individual grows the Baptist conviction concerning all aspects of religious experience and life." The local church "is a democratic body in which all the members are equally free and responsible participants" (*SP [1946]* 38 [emphasis mine]; also *SP [1945]* 59). J. B. Lawrence, a member of the Committee on Statement of Principles, later developing the principles of the confessional statement itself, considered "the primary and fundamental belief of Southern Baptists in the integrity of the individual as a person before God and man" to be "fundamental in Baptist denominational cooperation" (J. B. Lawrence, *Cooperating Southern Baptists* [Atlanta: Home Mission Board, Southern Baptist Convention, 1949] 12). "The priesthood of believers, therefore, means that all members serve as equals under God in the fellowship of a local church" (*BI [1963]* 15 [3.3]). Similarly, the Third Baptist World Congress issued a "statement of Baptist principles and purposes" in which this perspective also appears. E. Y. Mullins, then president of the Baptist World Alliance, wrote this statement: "There are various ways of stating *the fundamental Baptist principle*. . . . As to the nature of the Christian religion, we affirm that it is personal and spiritual. We believe in the *direct relation of each individual to God, and the right of every one to choose for himself in all matters of faith*. A Christian's religion begins in the soul when personal faith is exercised in Jesus Christ, the divine Redeemer and Lord" ("A Message of the Baptist World Alliance to the Baptist Brotherhood, to Other Christian Brethren, and to the World," in *Third Baptist World Congress, Stockholm, 21-27 July 1923: Record of Proceedings*, ed. W. T. Whitley [London: Kingsgate Press, 1923; Nashville: Baptist Sunday School Board, 1923; Philadelphia: American Baptist Publication Society, 1923] 223 [Friday, 27 July 1923]) (hereafter, cited as *MBWA [1923]*) (emphasis mine).

[34]Ignatius, *Epistle to the Smyrnaeans* 8.

[35]In its first confessional statement, the SBC indicated this in two of its explicit assumptions about Christian union: (1) "that all true disciples agree in

accepting the Lordship of Jesus Christ as supreme and final in all matters of faith and practice"; (2) "that in the New Testament alone do we find the sufficient, certain, and authoritative revelation of His will" (*PCU [1914]* 73-74). The SBC has produced several similar statements. As "the record of the messages" that inspired humans "received from God," the SBC declared that "the Scriptures are the sufficient, certain, and authoritative revelation of God in all matters of faith and practice, and that obedience to their teachings is binding upon all men" (*FASB [1920]* 6). "We here declare our unalterable belief in the universal, unchangeable, and undelegated sovereignty of Jesus Christ. We believe that he is the rightful and only head and sovereign of his churches; that his word and will, as revealed in the holy Scriptures, is the unchangeable and only law of his reign; that whatever is not found in the Scriptures, cannot be bound on the consciences of men" (*RIR [1938]* 24). "The ultimate source of Christian authority is Jesus Christ the Lord. . . . In its unique and unified disclosure of the will of God for mankind, the Bible is the final authority in pointing persons to Christ and in guiding them in all matters of Christian faith and moral duty" (*BI [1963]* 6, 7 [1.1-2]). According to the *BFM (1963)* as well, "therefore, the sole authority for faith and practice among Baptists is Jesus Christ whose will is revealed in the Holy Scriptures." Furthermore, although the Christian Bible is "the record of God's revelation of Himself to man," or "the supreme standard by which all human conduct, creeds, and religious opinions should be tried," Jesus Christ is "the criterion by which the Bible is to be interpreted" (*BFM [1963]* 270 [Preamble; and article 1]).

[36]Leland, "Virginia Chronicle," 114n.* Fundamentalist leaders in the SBC mistakenly and almost exclusively reduce credalism to this criterion alone, as did the SBC's Peace Committee in the first recommendation From its report in 1987: "Baptists are non-credal, in that they do not impose a man-made interpretation of Scripture on others" (*RPC [1987]* 240). Examples of this reductionism appear in numerous writings by some of these leaders. According to Timothy George, "Baptists have never been *credalistic* in the sense of placing manmade doctrinal constructs above Holy Scripture" (Timothy George, "The Priesthood of All Believers and the Quest for Theological Integrity," *Criswell Theological Review* 3 [Spring 1989]: 287; idem, "The Priesthood of All Believers," in *The People of God: Essays on the Believer's Church*, ed. Paul Basden and David S. Dockery [Nashville: Broadman Press, 1991] 88). Again, "the creeds and confessions of the church are not infallible artifacts of revelation" (Timothy George, "Dogma beyond Anathema: Historical Theology in the Service of the Church," *Review and Expositor* 84 [Fall 1987]: 700). Thomas Nettles similarly construes credalism. "Baptists have rejected credalism, and rightly so, since that word implies the elevation of a human document to the detriment of biblical authority" (Thomas J. Nettles, "Missions and Creeds: Part I," *Founders Journal* 17 [Summer 1994]: 21). "All concerned parties in the current crisis must be careful not to place any other entity, whether existential or written, above Scripture. Neither catechism, creed, or confession—nor reason, conscience, or current experience should be allowed to eclipse a clear and plain Scripture affirmation at any time. . . . If the wording of the Baptist Faith and Message permits agreement with the confession and a concurrent disagreement with the Scripture, then, just like the Athanasian correction

of the Eusebian Creed, unequivocal clarification is needed. To do less exalts the confession above the Scripture and gives it independent and idolatrous authority" (Thomas J. Nettles, "Credalism, Confessionalism, and the Baptist Faith and Message," in *Unfettered Word*, 144, 154).

37As an illustration of this claim, the SBC adopted a statement in 1923 in which it resisted the teaching of evolution as fact rather than as an unproven theory, yet in which the SBC expressed a positive attitude to unbiased scientific research. This statement came from the presidential address of E. Y. Mullins to the SBC in 1923 (entitled "Present Dangers and Duties"), the section entitled "Science and Religion," adopted by the Convention in 1923 "as the belief" of the SBC (*SR [1923]*), printed in the annual that year, as well as published and distributed by the Sunday School Board (*Annual SBC [1923]* 19-20 ["Proceedings," Wednesday–Morning Session, May 16, Items 11 and 12]). In 1925, the Committee on Baptist Faith and Message appended *SR (1923)* to the *BFM (1925)* with the following qualification: "Since matters of science have no proper place in a religious confession of faith, and since it is desirable that our attitude towards science be clearly understood, your committee deem [*sic*] it proper to submit the following statement on the relation between science and religion, adopted in 1923 by this Convention at Kansas City, and request [*sic*] that it be published in the minutes of the Convention" (*BFM [1925]* 75). In the *BFM (1963)*, the committee omitted this statement entirely.

381 Thess 5:19-22 (NRSV).

39This event commemorated the formation in 1814 of the Triennial Convention, the first national organization of Baptists in the United States. To fulfill its own role in this commemorative event, the SBC authorized and appointed its own Jubilee Advance Committee, functioning during the entire Baptist Jubilee Advance program (1959–1964), to coordinate the SBC's calendar and activities with those of other participating Baptist organizations (for example, see "Special Committees: Jubilee Advance Committee," in *Annual SBC (1963)* 263-66 [also see, "Proceedings," Thursday Night, May 9, Item 195]). The Committee on Baptist Ideals (chaired by Ralph A. Herring), a subcommittee of the SBC's Jubilee Advance Committee, interpreted its own assignment as an effort "to restate in relevant terms only those historic principles of Southern Baptists which with certain emphases serve to make clear their unique position and mission" (*BI [1963]* 3 [Introduction, 4]). In its last report to the SBC, this committee offered the following suggestion: "A copy of the pamphlet, 'Baptist Ideals,' produced by a committee of 17 dedicated scholars, with Ralph A. Herring as chairman, ought to be placed in the hands of every Southern Baptist" ("Special Committees: Jubilee Advance Committee," in *Annual of the Southern Baptist Convention: One Hundred Seventh Session in Atlantic City, New Jersey, 19-22 May 1964*, by the Executive Committee, Southern Baptist Convention [Nashville: Southern Baptist Convention, 1964] 261).

40*BI (1963)* 37 (5.9).

41See the qualification of this historic conviction by the Southern Baptist Convention Peace Committee, in the introduction to its first recommendation. "Although the Baptist Faith and Message Statement of 1963 is a statement of basic belief, it is not a creed. Baptists are non-credal, in that they do not impose a man-made interpretation of Scripture on others. Baptists, *however*, declare their commitment to commonly held interpretations which then become *parameters for cooperation*." Nonetheless, even there, the Peace Committee recommended the *BFM (1963)* as the guideline with the "parameters for cooperation" (*RPC [1987]* 240) (emphasis mine).

[42]Slayden Yarbrough astutely identifies the use of coercion to enforce conformity to confessional statements as the most necessary criterion with which to identify the phenomenon of credalism, even though he also notes other criteria. For example, borrowing elements from Philip Schaff's definition of the word "creed," Yarbrough primarily defines credalism through the criterion of coercion. "With emphasis on the phrases 'with authority' and 'necessary for salvation,' credalism . . . will be understood as the use of authoritative statements of faith as official bases of organization and as tests of orthodoxy. Such statements are considered to be binding upon adherents" (Yarbrough, "Is Credalism a Threat to Southern Baptists?" 23; similarly, Tribble, "Individual Competency and Use of Creeds," 94). By contrast, fundamentalist leaders who favor the employment of creeds, both as measures of orthodoxy and as devices to discipline divergent (morally, socially, politically, or doctrinally) members of Christian communities, refuse to identify such uses as coercive (see, as examples, George, "Priesthood of All Believers and the Quest for Theological Integrity," 287-91; idem, "Priesthood of All Believers," in *People of God*, ed. Basden and Dockery, 88-91; cf., idem, "Dogma beyond Anathema," 700-701, 703-706; Nettles, "Missions and Creeds: Part I," 23-26; idem, "Credalism, Confessionalism, and the Baptist Faith and Message," 148-51).

[43]Paul, the apostle, resisted such self-defeating Christian life (e.g., Gal 2:11-21; 3:1-7; 5:1-26).

[44]*BFM (1925)* 71; *BFM (1963)* 269.

[45]Besides the addition of numerous scriptural references below the article in 1963, only two insignificant differences occur between the two statements on "The Lord's Day." The *BFM (1925)* refers to "*works* of necessity and mercy only excepted," while the *BFM (1963)* refers to "*work* of necessity and mercy *being* only excepted" (*BFM [1925]* 73; *BFM [1963]* 276) (emphasis mine).

[46]As examples of alterations in meaning through changes in form, consider the following articles in the *BFM (1963)*: "I. The Scriptures," "II. God," "III. Man," "VI. The Church," "VII. Baptism and the Lord's Supper," "IX. The Kingdom," "XII. Education," "XIV. Cooperation," "XV. The Christian and the Social Order," and "XVI. Peace and War."

[47]For example, see the soteriological recombinations and reformulations in the *BFM (1963)*. The *BFM (1963)* contains one article with three major subpoints: article "IV. Salvation" (*BFM [1963]* 273-74). The committee combined and reduced six articles from the *BFM (1925)* to a single soteriological article: "4. The Way of Salvation," "5. Justification," "6. The Freeness of Salvation," "7. Regeneration," "8. Repentance and Faith," and "10. Sanctification" (*BFM [1925]* 72).

Chief Article of Faith 93

⁴⁸As an example, the *BFM (1963)* contains one article on eschatology ("X. Last Things"), an article representing the reduction of three articles from the *BFM (1925)* to a single paragraph: "15. The Righteous and the Wicked," "16. The Resurrection," "17. The Return of the Lord" (*BFM [1963]* 277; *BFM [1925]* 73).

⁴⁹See, for example, the anthropology of the *BFM (1963)*. According to the *BFM (1925)*, humans not only "inherit a nature corrupt and in bondage to sin" at conception, but "are under condemnation" for that sinful state even prior to becoming "actual transgressors" on the basis of moral capability (*BFM [1925]* 72). The reformulation of the doctrine of original sin in the *BFM (1963)*, however, although acknowledging the human biological and social inheritance of an inclination toward sin, describes humans as "under condemnation" for their sin only after becoming "transgressors" on the basis of their development of the capability for "moral action" (*BFM [1963]* 273). Hobbs notes this about the anthropology of the *BFM (1963)*. In the *BFM (1963)*, " 'condemnation' comes upon individuals following transgression 'as soon as they are capable of moral action.' This, of course, agrees with the position generally held by Baptists concerning God's grace in cases of those under the age of accountability and the mentally incompetent" (Hobbs, "Southern Baptists and Confessionalism," 63).

⁵⁰My use of the phrase, "the Baptist vision," significantly reflects the meaning attributed to it by James Wm. McClendon, Jr.: "the *guiding stimulus* by which a people (or as here, a combination of peoples) shape their life and thought as that people or that combination," or "the continually emerging *theme and tonic structure of their common life*" that serves "as *the touchstone* by which authentic Baptist life is discovered and described, and also as *the organizing principle* around which a genuine Baptist theology can take shape" (James Wm. McClendon, Jr., *Systematic Theology*, vol. 1, *Ethics* [Nashville: Abingdon Press, 1986] 27-28) (emphasis mine).

⁵¹*BFM (1925)* 71; *BFM (1963)* 269, 270 (emphasis mine).

⁵²*BFM (1925)* 73-74; *BFM (1963)* 281 (emphasis mine). Also, compare this concept to the doctrinal statement adopted by the Baptist World Alliance in 1923, through the presidential leadership of E. Y. Mullins. "A Christian's religion begins in the soul when personal faith is exercised in Jesus Christ, the divine Redeemer and Lord. As the Revealer of God to men and the Mediator of salvation, Jesus Christ is central for Christian faith. His will is the supreme law for the Christian. He is Lord of the conscience of the individual and of the Church. Hence, the Lordship of Jesus Christ is a cardinal teaching of Baptists. It excludes all merely human authorities in religion" (*MBWA [1923]* 223).

⁵³*BFM (1925)* 72-73; *BFM (1963)* 272.

⁵⁴*BFM (1963)* 270 (emphasis mine). Such an ordering occurs in both earlier and later statements by the SBC. In the SBC's statement on Christian union from 1914, the SBC declared that it assumes "[t]hat all true disciples agree in accepting the Lordship of Jesus Christ as supreme and final in all matters of faith and practice," even while also assuming "[t]hat in the New Testament alone do we find the sufficient, certain, and authoritative revelation of His will" (*PCU [1914]* 73, 74). In 1938, the SBC adopted a similar statement. "We here declare our unalterable belief in the universal, unchangeable, and undelegated sovereignty of Jesus Christ.

We believe that he is the rightful and only head and sovereign of his churches; that his word and will, as revealed in the holy Scriptures, is the unchangeable and only law of his reign; that whatever is not found in the Scriptures, cannot be bound on the consciences of men; and that the supreme test of true Christian discipleship is obedience to the will of Christ, as revealed in the Bible" (*RIR [1938]* 24). Similarly, in 1963, the SBC's Jubilee Advance Committee emphatically stated this order in its report: "The ultimate source of Christian authority is Jesus Christ the Lord"; the Bible "is the final rule for faith and practice because it is the inspired and trustworthy witness to the mighty acts of God in self-revelation and redemption, all brought to fulfilment [*sic*] in the life, teachings, and saving work of Jesus Christ" (*BI [1963]* 6, 7).

[55]*FASB (1920)* 5. Later, in 1945 and 1946, the SBC stated something similar in its elaboration of the SBC's "distinctive belief," "the Doctrine of Man in the personal order of life." According to that doctrinal statement, in order to enable the realization of God's purposes for human life, "God has provided in the gospel of Christ, through the power of the Holy Spirit, for the renewal of the individual soul by regeneration and for its response through the grace of God to the divine ideal" (*SP [1946]* 38; *SP [1945]* 59). H. W. Tribble expressed this perspective even more clearly. Accordingly, "that *final authority resides in Christ* and is mediated directly from Him to the Christian, for He is the Head of the church. The *Scriptures* are the inspired authority as the *record of God's revelation*, but they are to be *vitalized in Christian experience through the work of the Spirit of Christ* in the life of the Christian and through individual Christians in the life and work of the church" (Tribble, "Individual Competency and Use of Creeds," 94-95) (emphasis mine).

[56]*NHC (1833)*, in *Baptist Confessions of Faith*, Lumpkin, 361-62; "The Westminster Confession (1646)," in *Creeds of the Churches: A Reader in Christian Doctrine from the Bible to the Present*, 3d ed., ed. John H. Leith (Louisville KY: John Knox Press, 1982) 193-97; *SLC (1677, 1688)* 248-53; *PC (1742)*, in *Baptist Confessions of Faith*, Lumpkin, 348-53. This pattern also appears in the Calvinistic confessional statement of Southern Baptist Theological Seminary (*AP [1858]* 38).

[57]See the following examples: "A True Confession, 1596," in *Baptist Confessions of Faith*, Lumpkin, 82; "Short Confession of Faith in XX Articles by John Smyth, 1609," *Baptist Confessions of Faith*, Lumpkin, 100; "A Short Confession of Faith, 1610," in *Baptist Confessions of Faith*, Lumpkin, 102-103; "A Declaration of Faith of English People Remaining at Amsterdam in Holland, 1611," in *Baptist Confessions of Faith*, Lumpkin, 117-19; "Propositions and Conclusions concerning True Christian Religion, containing a Confession of Faith of certain English people, living at Amsterdam," in *Baptist Confessions of Faith*, Lumpkin, 125-42; "The London Confession, 1644," in *Baptist Confessions of Faith*, Lumpkin, 156-58; *FASB (1920)* 5-6.

[58]*BFM (1963)* 270. A similar concept, and sometimes a similar phrase, appears in some of the SBC's later confessional statements. For example, "the one and only authority in faith and practice is the New Testament as the divinely inspired *record and interpretation of* the supreme *revelation* of God through Jesus

Christ as Redeemer, Saviour, and Lord" (*SP [1945]* 59; *SP [1946]* 38) (emphasis mine). By the same token, the SBC's *FASB (1920)* largely continued to identify the Christian Bible itself with an event of divine revelation, despite its reference to the Christian Bible as "the record" of God's revelation. "We believe in the Scriptures of the Old and New Testaments as God's authoritative message to men concerning the way of salvation. Holy men of God spoke as they were moved by the Holy Spirit. The books of the Bible are the *record of* the *messages* which these inspired men *received from God*" (*FASB [1920]* 5-6) (emphasis mine).

[59]The authors of the *BFM (1963)* avoided adding, instead of this first addition, more widely-used older terms and phrases that appear in several of the SBC's confessional statements. Adopting a section from the presidential address of E. Y. Mullins to the SBC as the Convention's belief, the SBC affirmed the following formulation in 1923: "The Bible is God's revelation of Himself through man moved by the Holy Spirit, and is our *sufficient* [sic], *certain and authoritative guide* in religion" (*SR [1923]*, 19). In another message prepared by Mullins in 1923, as president of the Baptist World Alliance (BWA), the BWA affirmed an almost identical formulation: "If we indicate the source of our knowledge, we say the scriptures of the Old and New Testaments are divinely inspired, and are our *sufficient, certain and authoritative guide* in all matters of faith and practice" (*MBWA [1923]* 223). The SBC's Foreign Mission Board employed similar language in its own doctrinal articles in 1920: "I believe that the Holy Scriptures of the Old and New Testaments were written by men who were divinely inspired and that they are a *sufficient* and *final authority* in all matters of religious faith and practice" (*SB [1920]* 197). According to the *FASB (1920)*, the SBC held "that the Scriptures are the *sufficient, certain and authoritative revelation of God* in all matters of faith and practice . . ." (*FASB [1920]* 6). In the *PCU (1914)*, the SBC declared "[t]hat in the New Testament alone do we find the *sufficient, certain and authoritative revelation of His* [Christ's] *will*" (*PCU [1914]* 74). The previous and similar formulations originate from the doctrinal articles of Southern Baptist Theological Seminary, as formulated in 1858: "The Scriptures of the Old and New Testaments were given by inspiration of God, and are the only *sufficient, certain, and authoritative rule* of all saving knowledge, faith, and obedience" (*AP [1858]* 38). With one significant linguistic modification (trading the term "infallible" for the term "authoritative"), this phrase came from the *Philadelphia Confession* in 1742, which precisely followed the *Second London Confession* of 1677: "The Holy Scripture is the only *sufficient, certain and infallible rule* of all saving Knowledge, Faith and Obedience" (*PC [1742]*, in *Baptist Confessions of Faith*, Lumpkin, 56; *SLC [1677, 1688]* 248). Much of the language in the two previous confessions, of course, originated from the Calvinistic *Westminster Confession* of 1646 (see "Westminster Confession [1646]," in *Creeds of the Churches*, Leith, 193-96). Perhaps the avoidance of the older phrases and terms by the authors of the *BFM (1963)* resulted from their efforts to soften even further the mild Calvinistic elements still remaining in the *BFM (1925)* from the *NHC (1833)*. Thus, the committee in 1963 avoided using terms or phrases even about the Christian scriptures that recalled that Calvinistic dominance.

[60]*BFM (1963)* 270.

⁶¹Hobbs, "Southern Baptists and Confessionalism," 62.
⁶²See Heb 5:1–7:28 NRSV.
⁶³Hobbs, "Southern Baptists and Confessionalism," 62.
⁶⁴I especially thank my friend, Kip Ingram, for our many conversations about these issues. Although I have altered the model to some extent, he suggested the following linguistic pattern as one way to redescribe the web of authority presupposed by, yet detectable in, the *BFM (1963)*.
⁶⁵*BFM (1963)* 270.
⁶⁶See Joseph T. Shipley, *The Origins of English Words: A Discursive Dictionary of Indo-European Roots* (Baltimore MD: Johns Hopkins University Press, 1984) 22; Walter Bauer, *A Greek-English Lexicon of the New Testament and Other Early Christian Literature*, 4th rev. ed., trans. and ed. William F. Arndt and F. Wilbur Gingrich (Chicago: University of Chicago Press, 1957) 121.
⁶⁷Heb 12:2 (NAS). Although the Greek term translated as "author," "ajrchgo;n," has no etymological relationship to the root-word for the English word, "authority," it does convey a very similar network of meaning: such as, source, initiator, originator, founder. See alternative translations: "the *author* and *finisher* of our faith" (KJV); "the *pioneer* and *perfecter* of our faith" (RSV, NRSV) (emphasis mine). The *BFM (1963)* cites this verse as one of the biblical supports for its paragraph on "God the Son," in its second article, the doctrine of God (*BFM [1963]* 272).
⁶⁸1 John 4:8, 16. Unfortunately, the *BFM (1963)* does not cite these texts as support for the confession's article on the doctrine of God (see *BFM [1963]* 271-72).
⁶⁹The SBC has described the human transformation in the reestablishment of right relations with God as "a radical renewal of the spiritual nature of man, due to the direct action of the Holy Spirit, and always in connection with conscious acceptance of Jesus Christ as Lord and Saviour. It is a spiritual transformation which results from the direct and immediate contact of the soul with the Spirit of God" (*PCU [1914]* 74). Again, according to the SBC, the Spirit's regeneration of sinful humans "is conditioned upon personal repentance towards God and faith in our Lord Jesus Christ. Repentance is a sincere renunciation of sin, and faith is genuine trust in the atoning Christ as Saviour and Lord" (*FASB [1920]* 8). "We hold that all people who believe in Christ as their personal Saviour are our brothers in the common salvation, whether they be in the Catholic communion, or in a Protestant communion, or in any other communion, or in no communion" (*RIR [1938]* 24; cf. *PRL [1939]* 115; *RWCC [1940]* 99; *SP [1946]* 38). "Salvation from sin is the free gift of God through Jesus Christ, conditioned only upon repentance toward God and trust in and commitment to Christ the Lord" (*BI [1963]* 12 [3.1]). Again, see Conner's concept of faith (Conner, "Theology, A Practical Discipline," 355). In its concept of faith, nonetheless, the *AP (1858)* tends to stress the cognitive and propositional quality of faith as primary: "saving faith is *the belief*, on God's authority, *of whatsoever is revealed in His Word* concerning Christ; accepting and resting upon Him alone for justification and eternal life" (*AP [1858]* 38) (emphasis mine).
⁷⁰*BFM (1963)* 273.

[71] 1 John 4:9-10 NAS.

[72] 1 John 4:19 NAS.

[73] *BFM (1963)* 272, 273. Both of these dynamics appear in the Lucan narrative of Lydia's conversion: "And a certain woman named Lydia, from the city of Thyatira, a seller of purple fabrics, a worshiper of God, was listening; and *the Lord opened her heart to respond* to *the things spoken by Paul*" (Acts 16:14 NAS) (emphasis mine). This narrative demonstrates the inseparability of the two dynamics in transformative authority.

[74] *BFM (1963)* 269, 270.

[75] *BFM (1963)* 272, 273; 1 John 5:7. Also see John 14:26; 15:26; 16:7-14. The *BFM (1963)* cites these Johannine texts as some of its biblical support for the confession's paragraph, "God the Holy Spirit," in the second article of faith, the article on the doctrine of God (*BFM [1963]* 272).

[76] *BFM (1963)* 271.

[77] According to the Gospel of Matthew, Jesus used the phrase, "the Law and the Prophets," to describe the entire corpus of scriptures, even to refer to God's entire self-revelation in and to creation (Matt 7:12; 22:40; cf. Gal 5:14; Rom 13:8-10; 1 Cor 12:31–13:13). Although Jesus did not intend to abolish the divine revelation, he did reinterpret the scriptures on the basis of the authority he had received from his divine creator, with variations on the following formula: "You have heard that it was said, . . . but I say to you" (Matt 5:17-48). Despite the sincere desires and conscientious efforts of the scribes and Pharisees to obey the teachings of the scriptures, Jesus required the faithfulness of his own disciples to surpass the righteousness of the scribes and Pharisees, through living perfectly like their divine creator (Matt 5:20, 48). Furthermore, according to the Matthean evangelist, *Jesus* himself completely fulfilled the entire disclosure of God's purpose as attested by the scriptures. In this light, then, how did Jesus construe the content of the scriptures and their claims on or authority for human life? The synoptic Gospels supply a clear answer to this question. Jesus summarized the entire divine gift of scripture as dependent on God's double claim on human life: God created humans (1) to love God with their entire selves and (2) to love their neighbors as themselves (Matt 22:34-40; Mark 12:28-31; Luke 10:25-37; cf. John 13:34-35; 14:15-31; 15:1-17). Similarly, of course, Jesus also condensed "the Law and the Prophets" to the claim commonly designated as the "Golden Rule" (Matt 7:12; cf. Luke 6:31). See Eduard Schweizer's discussions of Jesus' summary and fulfillment of God's revelation to Israel (Eduard Schweizer, *The Good News According to Matthew*, trans. David E. Green [Atlanta: John Knox Press, 1975] 103-38, 174-75; also see Paul Ricoeur, "The Golden Rule: Exegetical and Theological Perplexities," *New Testament Studies* 36 [July 1990]: 392-97).

[78] *BFM (1963)* 272.

[79] *BFM (1963)* 273. As support for the second section of its soteriological article, the *BFM (1963)* cites Rom 8:29-39 and 1 John 1:6-2:11; also see Rom 5:5; 8:29; cf. 1 Cor 15:49; Phil 3:20-21; Col 3:8-17; Eph 3:14-19; 1 John 3:2.

[80] *BFM (1963)* 273.

[81] *BFM (1963)* 272.

⁸²2 Tim 3:15-17 NAS. The *BFM (1963)* cites 2 Tim 3:15-17 as one support for its article on the Christian scriptures; the confession also cites 2 Tim 3:16 as support for its section on God the Holy Spirit in its article on God (*BFM [1963]* 270, 272). Also, see William L. Hendricks, "The Difference between Substance (Matter) and Form in Relationship to Biblical Inerrancy," in *The Proceedings of the Conference on Biblical Inerrancy, 1987* (Nashville: Broadman Press, 1987) 481-89.

⁸³*BFM (1963)* 270.

⁸⁴Augustine *De Doctrina Christiana* 1.36.40; idem, *On Christian Doctrine*, trans. D. W. Robertson, Jr. Library of Liberal Arts (Upper Saddle River NJ: Prentice Hall, 1958) 30 (1.36.40).

⁸⁵*BFM (1963)* 270.

⁸⁶John 13:35 NAS; cf. Lev 19:18; Deut 6:5; Matt 19:16-22; 22:34-40; Mark 12:28-31; Luke 10:25-37; Rom 13:8-10; 1 Cor 13:1-13; Gal 5:13-14; Jas 2:8; 1 Pet 1:22-23; 1 John:3-11; 3:14-24; 4:7-21; 5:1-3.

⁸⁷Jas 2:8, 17; 1 Pet :22; 1 John 2:5, 6 NAS. The *BFM (1963)* cites Jas 2:14-26 in support of the confession's soteriology, in the second section of the fourth article, as well as Jas 2:8 and Jas 1:27, as backing for the confession's fifteenth article, "The Christian and the Social Order" (*BFM [1963]* 274, 280). The confessional statement also cites both 1 Pet 1:2-23 and 1 John 1:6-2:11 as supports for its section on sanctification in the soteriological article (*BFM [1963]* 274). I have borrowed the term "performative" from J. L. Austin, who used this term to identify one primary function of discourse (J. L. Austin, "Performative Utterances," in *Philosophical Papers*, by J. L. Austin [Oxford: Clarendon Press, 1961] 220-39). See a very similar approach by Mark I. Wallace, "Performative Truth and the Witness of the Spirit," *Southwestern Journal of Theology* 35 (Summer 1993): 29-36; idem, *Fragments of the Spirit: Nature, Violence, and the Renewal of Creation* (New York: Continuum, 1996) 63-87; cf. George Hunsinger, "Truth as Self-Involving: Barth and Lindbeck on the Cognitive and Performative Aspects of Truth in Theological Discourse," *Journal of the American Academy of Religion* 61 (Spring 1993): 41-56.

⁸⁸John 5:39-40, 42 NAS.

⁸⁹*BFM (1963)* 275 (emphasis mine); similarly, see the ninth article, "The Kingdom" (*BFM [1963]* 276-77).

⁹⁰*BFM (1963)* 270. Although Baptists often merely, and hence carelessly, equate the human's direct access to God with the priesthood of the believer, the latter concept actually differs from the former concept, inasmuch as the latter concept specifies the Christian actualization of the former concept. Elsewhere, I have discussed this distinction in a "conceptual genealogy of the principle of religious liberty" (see Jeff B. Pool, "Baptist Infidelity to the Principle of Religious Liberty," *Perspectives in Religious Studies* 17 [Spring 1990]: 14-22). Again, see Mullins, *Axioms of Religion*, 53; "The Soul's Competency in Religion under God: The Historic Baptist Principle for Today," in *Annual SBC (1936)* 108-15; Tribble, "Competency of the Individual in Religion," 142-49; *SP [1945]* 59; *SP [1946]* 38; and Hobbs, *Baptist Faith and Message*, 7, 9, 11).

[91] *Webster's Seventh New Collegiate Dictionary*, s.v. "flock," "congregate," and "gregarious."

[92] *BFM (1963)* 275 (emphasis mine).

[93] *BFM (1963)* 275; similarly, see *BI (1963)* 20-21.

[94] 1 Cor 12:1-14:40. According to the third section of the article on the doctrine of God in the *BFM (1963)*, the Holy Spirit "bestows the spiritual gifts by which they [believers] serve God through his church" (*BFM [1963]* 272). Although the *BFM (1963)* cites 1 Cor 12 as support for its ecclesiological article, the confession does not cite the thirteenth or fourteenth chapters of 1 Cor. In 1923, the Baptist World Alliance asserted that "Baptists stand for . . . the priesthood of all believers versus the priesthood of a class, democracy in the church versus autocracy or oligarchy or other forms of human authority" (*MBWA [1923]* 226).

[95] 1 Cor 13:1-13.

[96] *BFM (1963)* 275.

[97] Again, see *PCU (1914)* 74, 75; *FASB (1920)* 8; *RIR (1938)* 24 (especially, point 3); *PRL (1939)* 115; *SP (1946)* 38 (emphasis mine); also *SP (1945)* 59; Lawrence, *Cooperating Southern Baptists*, 12; *BI (1963)* 15 (3.3); and *MBWA (1923)* 223.

[98] *BFM (1963)* 279 (emphasis mine).

[99] Ibid.. The Baptist World Alliance had also emphasized this in 1923. "We hold fast to the freedom with which Christ has set us free, and this principle implies that we must be willing to love and to work with those who, agreeing with us on the main things and in loyalty to our distinctive Baptist principles, have their own personal convictions upon non-essentials. All Baptist organizations are formed on the voluntary principle. None of these possesses authority over any other. All enjoy equal rights and autonomy within the limits of their own purposes" (*MBWA [1923]* 223).

[100] I have coined and employed the term "interformative" in correspondence with the conceptual pattern developed through the previous junctures in the web of authority. With the concept "interformative authority," I have adapted Paul Ricoeur's concept of the "interlocutionary" or "allocutionary" act. For Ricoeur, the concept of the "interlocutionary or allocutionary act" signifies that discourse ". . . is addressed to someone" (Paul Ricoeur, *Interpretation Theory: Discourse and the Surplus of Meaning* [Fort Worth TX: Texas Christian University Press, 1976] 14-19; also see John R. Searle, *Speech Acts: An Essay in the Philosophy of Language* [Cambridge University Press, 1969]). As an alternative phrase, I could have used the equally strange word, "heteroformative," to convey a very similar meaning; this word conceptually would resemble Ricoeur's term, "allocutionary."

[101] The formal biblical basis for this doctrine principally includes the following texts: Exod 19:5-6; 1 Pet 2:4-10; Rev 1:5-6; 5:9-10. Martin Luther construed this doctrine in terms of a slightly different paradox, describing the freedom and bondage of the Christian's spirit as both lordship and servanthood. "A Christian is a perfectly free lord of all, subject to none. A Christian is a perfectly dutiful servant of all, subject to all" (Martin Luther, "The Freedom of a Christian, 1520," trans. W. A. Lambert and Harold J. Grimm, in *Luther's Works*, ed. Helmut T.

Lehmann, vol. 31, *Career of the Reformer: 1*, ed. Harold J. Grimm [Philadelphia: Muhlenberg Press, 1957] 344). According to the SBC's Committee on Baptist Ideals, the Christian "has entered into a royal priesthood and is privileged to minister for Christ to all men," and "is to share with them the faith he cherishes and to serve them in the name and spirit of his Lord" (*BI [1963]* 14-15). In their revisions of the *BFM (1925)*, the authors of the *BFM (1963)* added a section to the article on education that emphasized aspects of this polarity: "In Christian education there should be a proper balance between academic freedom and academic responsibility" (*BFM [1963]* 278). Unfortunately, this addition to the *BFM (1925)*, by originating as a fearful reaction against Ralph Elliott's commentary on Genesis, inscribed a false dichotomy between freedom and responsibility into the revised doctrinal statement for the SBC.

[102]Although the *BFM (1963)* does not contain a formulation of the universal Christian priesthood, the SBC's Committee on Baptist Ideals did produce and publish such a formulation in 1963. "Every man is competent to go directly to God for forgiveness through repentance and faith. He needs neither individual nor church to dispense salvation. There is but one mediator of God and man, Jesus Christ our Lord. After one has become a Christian, he has direct access to God through Christ. He has entered into a royal priesthood and is privileged to minister for Christ to all men. He is to share with them the faith he cherishes and to serve them in the name and spirit of his Lord. The priesthood of believers, therefore, means that all members serve as equals under God in the fellowship of a local church" (*BI [1963]* 14-15).

[103]See Augustine's classic formulation of this insight: "Everything which does not decrease on being given away is not properly owned when it is owned and not given" (Augustine, *On Christian Doctrine*, 8 [1.1.1]). On the basis of these organic factors, particularly in reference to the universal priesthood of all Christians, Auguste Sabatier contrasted the religion of the Spirit to religions of authority (e.g., Auguste Sabatier, *The Religions of Authority and the Religion of the Spirit*, vol. 16, Theological Translation Library [New York: Williams and Norgate, 1904] 255-79).

[104]Paul Tillich's insights into the "quest for theonomy," which originates from the conflict between autonomous reason and heteronomous reason, inform my analysis of the universal Christian priesthood (Paul Tillich, *Systematic Theology* [Chicago: University of Chicago Press, 1951] 1:83-86, 147-50; cf. idem, *Systematic Theology* [Chicago: University of Chicago Press, 1963] 3:249-68).

[105]The doctrine of the common Christian priesthood has certainly suffered among Baptists in the SBC from its construal as a warrant to render every private interpretation of biblical texts as equal to one another or valid. Obviously, such a perspective quite rightly emphasized the Christian's freedom from the imposition of creeds on the Christian conscience, whether secular or ecclesiastical impositions. Often, however, such construals of this doctrine have encouraged an irresponsible individualism. Taken to extremes, such construals can endanger the identity of the community itself, that is, the common message that the community endeavors to communicate. Nonetheless, although Timothy George properly notes the responsibility for ministry to neighbors as a central component in the doctrine

of the common Christian priesthood, by his uncritical application of Reformed and Lutheran construals of this doctrine to Baptist interpretations of the universal Christian priesthood, and by his virtual identification of "biblical authority and the dogmatic consensus of historic Christianity," George has almost completely reduced the doctrine of the universal Christian priesthood to the opposite extreme: *communal norms, as represented in binding Christian doctrinal documents or creeds* (Timothy George, "The Renewal of Baptist Theology," in *Baptist Theologians*, ed. Timothy George and David S. Dockery [Nashville: Broadman Press, 1990] 13-25; idem, "The Reformation Roots of the Baptist Tradition," *Review and Expositor* 86 [Winter 1989]: 16-18; idem, "Priesthood of All Believers," in *People of God*, 85-95; idem, "Priesthood of All Believers and the Quest for Theological Integrity," 283-94). This second offense constitutes an even more serious danger than the first misrepresentation of this doctrine.

[106] "We Need Each Other's Voice to Sing," lyrics by Thomas H. Troeger, tune ("Wedding Gift") by Carol Doran, in *New Hymns for the Life of the Church* (Oxford: Oxford University Press, 1992) 10 (no. 5, verse 3).

[107] In 1923, the SBC's Executive Committee stated this most pointedly in its report to the Convention: "We co-operate, not by coercion, but by mutual consent" ("Defining the Work of the Convention," from "Report of Executive Committee," in *Annual SBC [1923]* 74 ["Proceedings," Friday–Evening Session, May 18, Item 86]). Given the SBC's situation at the time, the Executive Committee considered this statement important enough to repeat to the Convention in the following year ("Report of Executive Committee," in *Annual SBC [1924]* 25 ["Proceedings," Wednesday-Afternoon Session, May 14, Item 25]). See other similar statements by the SBC: *PCU (1914)* 75-76; *FASB (1920)* 8-9, 14-15; *BFM (1925)* 74; *PRL (1939)* 115; *RWCC (1940)* 99; *SP (1946)* 39; *BFM (1963)* 275, 279; *BI (1963)* 20-21, 30-31.

[108] Shipley, *Origins of English Words*, 387, 424-25; *Webster's Seventh New Collegiate Dictionary*, s.v. "structure," "weave," and "web." My choice of this metaphor to describe the concept of religious authority among Baptists signals a holistic and nonfoundationalist approach to interpreting the relationships among the various Christian doctrinal loci, a perspective similar to Nancey Murphy's description of the "web-like structure of systematic theology": "while theology may be systematic in the sense of being interconnected, it is not systematic in the sense that we can make the connections by means of a single linear argument" (Nancey C. Murphy, *Reasoning and Rhetoric in Religion* [Valley Forge PA: Trinity Press, 1994] 199, 200; cf. W. V. O. Quine, "Two Dogmas of Empiricism," in *From a Logical Point of View* [Cambridge MA: Harvard University Press, 1953] 43-44; W. V. O. Quine and J. S. Ullian, *The Web of Belief*, 2d ed. [New York: Random House, 1978]).

[109] Augustine *Tractatus in epistolam Joannis* 7.8; idem, "Seventh Homily: 1 John 4:4-12," from "Ten Homilies on the First Epistle General of St. John," in *Augustine: Later Works*, ed. John Burnaby, Library of Christian Classics: Ichthus Edition, ed. John Baillie, John T. McNeill, and Henry P. Van Dusen (Philadelphia: Westminster Press, 1955) 316 (7.8).

[110] *BFM (1963)* 270.

Chapter 2

God, the Bible, and Authority in
The Baptist Faith and Message (1963)

William L. Hendricks

Introduction

In this chapter, I will consider the topics of God, the Bible, and authority, as reflected in *The Baptist Faith and Message (BFM)*.[1] Candid and critical evaluation as well as fresh exegesis and explanation of the *BFM* are long overdue. This is so because denominational leaders have shifted their usage of the *BFM*. The use of the *BFM* as a definitive credal statement reflects this shift, despite the Preamble of the document itself. Especially is this the case in matters of employment and discharge from employment throughout all denominational agencies. In the absence of an agreed-upon interpretation of the *BFM's* content and in the light of its ambiguous hermeneutical statement, "[t]he criterion by which the Bible is to be interpreted is Jesus Christ," this restrictive use of the document seems incongruous with its avowed purpose. On the one hand, the document is being used too restrictively. On the other hand, there seems to be a prevailing opinion, by those using the document as a litmus test for denominational employment, that the *BFM* is not restrictive enough or specific enough in certain areas, so as to be able to state precisely and verbally what seems desirable in the prevailing political milieu. Several specific ideas are not included in the *BFM*: the inerrancy of the scriptures (in that exact wording), the restriction of women from the role of pastor, an absolutist position against abortion, a statement concerning pastoral authority, and a strong statement against homosexuality, among other issues.

In light of these tensions, use of the *BFM* as a policy-document for employment, and the growing dissatisfaction that the *BFM* does not address several contemporary issues, Baptists may expect both a mounting pressure for a reexamination of the *BFM* and perhaps a call for a new or revised statement of faith for the SBC. In such a case, it is highly desirable to remember the important distinction between a confession of faith, dealing with matters of belief, and a covenant among the faithful dealing with matters of conduct.[2] A re-examination of the *BFM*, the historical context of its birthing, and its revisions is imporant. One particular concern of this article is the broader ecumenical and historical context in which creeds and confessions have informed the Church universal.

I. Where to Begin?

In 1962, one of the presidents of a Baptist state convention, who participated on the committee to revise the *BFM (1925)*, assured me that it was not necessary to go behind 1845 (the date of the SBC's formation) to explore any sources or reasons for reevaluation. That was an uninformed and shortsighted view, since the *BFM* owes much of its substance to the *New Hampshire Confession* of 1833.[3]

In this chapter, I contend that any reexamination of the *BFM* must be explored in the wider venue of confessions and belief-statements in both scripture and tradition. Only by this approach will Baptists be able to find an integral relationship between biblical and historical practices and provide a principle of biblical validation for the later widespread practice throughout Christendom of confessing faith through written statements of faith, confessions, and creeds.

It is axiomatic that worship and experience precede doctrine and reflection on belief (*lex orandi; lex credendi*). Worship and the formation of doctrine must work in tandem. Nevertheless, the experience of God, which God's own self makes possible, is *primus inter pares* in relating God to confessions about God. Therefore, any revision of a confessional statement should be preceded by and accompanied by spiritual awakening and a surcharge of worship and ethical action.

I will address the topics of this chapter with the following approach. (1) This chapter explores biblical confessions and the earliest confessions of the ancient Christian community to 450 A.D., in order to establish a pattern of confession. (2) I challenge the ideological perspective that a formal principle of authority must precede the vital elements (or doctrinal articles) of a confession. (3) I also both explicate why statements of biblical authority have taken priority of place over the confession of belief in God, Christ, and Spirit and ask if such an order is appropriate. (4) In addition, I examine antecedent Baptist confessions and circumstances leading to the present order of the *BFM's* articles. (5) I explicate the stated content of the *BFM's* articles on the scriptures and God. (6) Finally, I propose to revise the order of the *BFM's* first two articles of faith.

II. "Wee beleeve with our hearts & confes with our mouths"[4]

The brief Pauline injunction about confessing and believing (Rom 10:9-10) is a platform that the Christian community as a whole adopted from its earliest days. The practice of repeating a brief statement of belief began in the Old Testament with the Hebrew *shema* (Deut 6:4-9; 11:13-21; Num 15:37-41). The Deuteronomic confession is predicated on Exodus 20:2-3 and is restated in various ways in the Hebrew scriptures.[5] This earliest of the biblical confessions is still the confessional thread binding ancient and modern Judaism. Throughout the centuries of Western civilization, the Jewish witness (*marturia*) has often been martyrdom, indeed, even for millions of Jews in the twentieth century. Confession is serious business, born out of a life of commitment to a statement of belief.

The New Testament also reports many confessions and has embedded credal formulations. *Maranatha* (1 Cor 16:21), meaning "the Lord is coming" or "come Lord," is possibly one of the earliest Christian confessions.[6] It is noteworthy that the Christian scriptures close with a version of this Aramaic confession-prayer (Rev 22:20b).

Closely related is the simple confession, "Jesus is Lord," which is the basis of such later confessional statements as the confession in Acts 8:37. That confession may be a later interpolation reflecting a much earlier baptismal confession.[7]

The Petrine confession in Matthew 16:16 has been both defining and, in another sense, divisive for Christian ecclesiology. Matthew 28:19 is another early baptismal confession. The Johannine confessions are predictably and unanimously christological: Nathaniel's confession (John 20:28), the second Petrine confession (John 6:68-69), and Thomas' confession (John 20:28). 1 John 4:2 posits the confession of the incarnation as the dividing line between true belief and heretical docetism.

The Pauline confessions contain what will later be styled tenets of the faith, doctrines, or articles of belief. 1 Corinthians 8:6 and 15:3-4 are the earliest of these statements. 1 Corinthians 8:6 ties the confession of Israel to Christian belief and, in its second clause, ties Christ to God in an equivalent way. 2 Timothy 3:16 is, perhaps, the most developed list of christological actions in the New Testament.[8] Closely related are hymnic elements such as Colossians 1–2.

The lines between confessions, prayers, and hymns were not as clearly drawn in the New Testament era as in later centuries. Biblical faith is always first a believing and then a verbal digest of what is "most surely" believed. New Testament expressions of belief are principally christological and are expressed in polemical contexts.

The "Jesus Prayer," "Lord Jesus Christ, Son of God, have mercy upon us," is a wedding of confession and devotion that occurred early in the Christian community.[9] This pattern of confession persisted into the formative period of Christianity until Chalcedon (450 A.D.). Ignatius of Antioch (ca. 107 A.D.) expressed a confession in opposition to the Gnostic heresies emerging early in the second century. Ignatius's confession is christological, moving from the Davidic ancestry of Jesus Christ to Christ's session and eschatological anticipation.[10]

Irenaeus of Lyons (f. 175–202 A.D.), with three expressions of early Christian belief, was the forefather of the *Apostles Creed*.[11] All three of his statements are tripartite (trinitarian). His are the first statements referring to scriptures as normative and suggesting the importance of apostolic tradition. Both the second and third forms of his confession have fulsome statements about the blessings of affirming and the consequences of denying these basic beliefs. Tertullian (f. 200–220 A.D.), champion of the Holy Spirit as a Montanist, suggests in his second statement of faith (*Adversus Praxeam* 2) a fuller explication of the triune God, giving stress to the work of the Paraclete, which he felt could be expressed by faithful women and men. Novatian (ca. 250 A.D.) expressed belief in the Father and the Son, and introduced the Spirit with an interesting proto-authority principle: "Moreover, the order of reason and the authority of faith, in due consideration of the words and Scriptures of the Lord, admonishes us, after this, to believe also in the Holy Ghost."[12]

Origen, in *De Principiis* (ca. 230 A.D.), acknowleded in the preface to his confession of faith that "all believers in Christ accepted the books of the Old and New Testaments as a full revelation of the divine truth . . . ."[13] Then, Origen proceeded to give his statement of faith, adding that God is the "God of the Old and New Testaments." The historical progression of the canon cautions against understanding Origen's canon as equivalent with the Protestant canon of today.[14] Lucian of Antioch (ca. 300 A.D.), as reported by Athanasius, wrote a lengthy christological section, concluding with an appeal to biblical authority: "For we truly and clearly both believe and follow all things from the Holy Scriptures that have been transmitted to us by the Prophets and Apostles."[15]

From the brief biblical and historical survey of confessions, the following pattern appears. (1) The earliest confessions are brief and experientially based statements of faith, the *shema*: "Jesus is Lord." (2) Significant statements of faith in the Christian community are basically christological. (3) Early in Christian history, trinitarian statements of faith based on the acts of the threefold God became the norm. (4) Appeals to scripture and biblical authority emerged in tandem. (5) Confessions grew and expanded in a context of dissenting opinions and as challenges to heretical beliefs. This developmental look at how confessions emerge leads to this question: *Does authority precede confession?*

III. Do Formal Statements of Authority Necessarily Precede or Take Primary Place in Confessions of Faith?

People are products of their education or the lack of it. The question, "Do formal statements of authority necessarily precede or take primary place in confessions?" is unsettling. One instinctive response is "of course they do!" Certainly, this has been the case since the Protestant Reformation, especially among the followers of the so-called magisterial reformation. Numerous subsequent Reformed and Lutheran creeds begin by establishing the authority of scripture before speaking about God.[16] Biblical confessions and the early Christians did not speak of biblical authority much. The authority of scripture was acknowledged in other sections of the confessions implicitly, not explicitly: in a material way, not a formal way. Following the magisterial reformers, many Protestant confessions have begun with an article on scripture rather than with an article on God.

In Lumpkin's collection of Baptist confessions, however, only two contain an article on scripture, per se, prior to the *Second London Confession* of 1677, which was based on the Presbyterian *Westminster Confession* of 1646. Both of those early Baptist confessions place their articles on scripture after their articles on God: the *First London Confession* of 1644 (articles 7 and 8), the *Midland Confession* of 1655 (based on the *First London Confession* of 1644) (article 3).[17] With the *Second London Confession* in 1677, Baptists most fully meet and mix in form and substance with the Calvinist, classical Reformed tradition. The *New Hampshire Confession* of 1833 retained a truncated order of the *Second London Confession*, retaining the statement on scripture as its first article.[18] In turn, the *New Hampshire Confession* became the basis for the *Baptist Faith and Message* in both 1925 and 1963.[19]

The point in rehearsing the previous litany is not to denigrate the early Anabaptist and early English Baptist associational confessions as not supporting belief in a strong view of biblical authority. On the contrary, their articles are liberally laced with biblical quotations and allusions. Their uses of scripture were not predicated on a prior statement of authority; rather, their uses of scripture were organic, integral, referring to specific biblical quotations as illustrations of the substance they were confessing. Anabaptist and early English Baptist confessions are quite biblicist without first establishing a formal principle of authority. The answer to the question, "Do formal statements of authority necessarily precede or take primary place in confessions of faith?" is "No!" Moreover, there are no well-established Baptist confessions that do so until 1677.

It was a twist of fate or a direct stroke of providence, according to one's interpretation, as to how the *New Hampshire Confession*, with its article on scripture preceding its statements on God, was preserved, propagated, and adopted by the Southern Baptist Convention. Much of the credit lies in the life and times of J. Newton Brown, a principal framer of the *New Hampshire Confession*. Two decades later, Brown became the editorial secretary of the American Baptist Publication Society. Brown, "on his own authority," published the confession in his influential work, *The Baptist Church Manual*, from which it was taken and used by J. M. Pendleton in his *Church Manual*.[20] The rest is history. Before the SBC adopted the *BFM* in 1925, a committee of prominent leaders in the SBC added ten sections to the *New Hampshire Confession*.

IV. Were There Alternatives?

There were alternatives in the SBC to the order in which the committee placed the articles on scripture and God in the *BFM*. In 1920, the SBC published the *Fraternal Address of Southern Baptists*. This document contains an eight-point doctrinal formula that, doubtless, was written as a long conscience and interpreting baptist tradition to the main purpose of the article, namely, to express Baptist autonomy in the face of movements toward Christian union that had eventuated in the founding of the Federal Council of Churches in 1908 (later, the National Council of Churches in 1950). This address contains a traditional, trinitarian, article on God as its first article. The second article is quoted here at length:

> We believe in the Scriptures of the Old and New Testaments as God's authoritative message to men concerning the way of salvation. Holy men of God spoke as they were moved by the Holy Spirit. The books of the Bible are the record of the messages which these inspired men received from God. The Old Testament is the preliminary and the New Testament is the completed revelation of the Gospel of our redemption. In our study of the Scriptures we are constantly impressed with the unity and progress of the revelation of divine truth. This truth was imparted to men by slow degrees as they were able to receive it. The earlier books of the Old Testament give us the beginnings and the books of the New Testament the endings of the saving truths of God's revelation. The wonderful unity and harmony of the various parts of Scriptures show with great clearness the presence of an overruling and guiding divine mind. The center of the entire revelation is Jesus Christ and His eternal Kingdom. All the earlier stages lead up to the crowning revelation in Jesus Christ. Thus the incarnation of the Son of God is the key to the meaning of all history. From the above setting forth of our view, it clearly follows that we hold that the Scriptures are the sufficient, certain

and authoritative revelation of God in all matters of faith and practice, and that obedience to their teachings is binding upon all men.[21]

This article on scripture is marked by several items: (1) recognition of scripture as "the record of the messages" that "inspired men received from God"; (2) recognition of progressive revelation; (3) christological centering; and (4) acknowledgment of scripture as sufficient in "all matters of faith and practice." This brief confession was signed by the members of the committee who drafted it: E. Y. Mullins, president of Southern Baptist Theological Seminary; J. B. Gambrell, president of the Baptist General Convention of Texas; Z. T. Cody, editor of the *Baptist Courier*; L. R. Scarborough, president of Southwestern Baptist Theological Seminary; and William Ellyson, president of the SBC's Foreign Mission Board.

There was the option of this brief statement from 1920. The *Fraternal Address of Southern Baptists* should be given careful consideration by contemporary Baptists who might be considering an updated yet classical statement of Baptist beliefs. Especially noteworthy is the placement of the article on scripture after the article on God.

In 1923, the SBC adopted as its belief a portion of E. Y. Mullins's presidential address to the Convention. The SBC entitled this statement *Science and Religion*.[22] The statement on scripture in Mullins's speech is important for the progression of this chapter. "The Bible is God's revelation of Himself through man moved by the Holy Spirit, and is our sufficient [,] [*sic*] certain, and authoritative guide in religion."[23] This statement on scripture was another option, available to the SBC prior to the adoption of the *BFM* in 1925. This statement reflects a high view of scripture and rightly consigns its sphere of authority to religious matters.

Both the *Fraternal Address of Southern Baptists* and the statement on *Science and Religion* contain strong statements on scripture. What is needed is a fresh examination of the *BFM* and the possibility of its revision and replacement, an option left open by the *BFM's* Preamble itself. There *were* other options, and there *are* other options. Before identifying those options, however, a look at the *BFM's* first two articles is required.

V. Holy Bible, Book Divine

This section examines the first article of the *BFM (1963)*. The following interpretation of this article mentions several considerations and raises questions about each sentence.

"The Holy Bible was written by men divinely inspired and is the record of God's revelation of Himself to man."[24] This also is a strong declaration on scripture. Many object to it, however, because it contains the term "record." Such protesters feel that the phrase "record of revelation" does not suggest that the Bible is revelation. The problem is one of definition and authority. If one states boldly that the Bible is the totality of revelation, then the Bible has displaced both the acts of God that preceded the written accounts and the subsequent acts of the Spirit in scripture's canonization and interpretation. The latter activity of God's Spirit make God's presence known in the church today.

Moreover, God comes before scripture both temporally and as authority. In confessing the faith, should Baptists start with God or scripture? One circular argument says that, without the witness of scripture, humans would not know God. Furthermore, the matters of tradition and experience enter the discussion. Without the Christian community, the scriptures would not have been preserved. Without contemporary Christian experience, there would be no point in raising or discussing the issue of authority.

Such circular argumentation could be avoided by clarifying statements in a confession's preface that would resolve both the issue of divine priority and the desire to affirm scripture as a vital part of revelation. A statement on authority that should clarify Baptist priorities might resemble the following affirmation: The authority of the Christian faith is (1) the Triune God, (2) as revealed in scripture, (3) as expressed in heritage, (4) and as made real in experience, corporate and individual. God, Bible, Christian heritage, and Christian experience, placed in that order, would clarify the matter of priorities. The sections of a Baptist confession of faith should reflect this order of authority.

To incorporate scripture as a part of revelation, Baptists might define revelation as divine manifestation, inspiration, and illumination as guided by God's Spirit. Manifestation is composed of God's original acts of self-disclosure in history; inspiration is human perceiving, recording, and interpreting of these divine acts; illumination is God making clear the acts of divine manifestation as recorded in scripture in a redemptive experience. In this definition, the original actions of God, their subsequent inscripturation, and the appropriations all have a place in descending order.

The God of the Bible comes before the Bible, not after it. Orders of being precede orders of knowing. The scriptures are significant means of revelation. Jesus Christ is God's living Word (John 1:1); the scriptures contain written words from and about God. Christian experience is the Word and words of and about God finding expression in and through God's community.

Another issue in the *BFM's* statement on scripture concerns gender-inclusiveness. This issue is one of the most persistent in contemporary

American culture. Does "man" mean all of humankind, or is it irredeemably masculine? There are powerful and numerous arguments for the use of gender-neutral terms.[25]

Even more sensitive are the issues of gender and language as these pertain to God. For many Baptists in the SBC, it would be of small consequence if the confession were to read as follows: "The Holy Bible was written by *persons* divinely inspired." What response should Baptists make, however, to the phrase, "revelation of *Himself* to man" (humans!)? For many Baptists, this is a moot question. Their response is that God is referred to as masculine in scripture and God is referred to as Father by Jesus. Therefore, this language must be retained.[26] I should note, however, that the attribution of masculinity to God is not the issue of the *BFM's* article on scripture, although it will become an issue in the *BFM's* second article. An alternative to the last clause of the first sentence in the *BFM's* article on scripture might read as follows: "and is the record of God's own Self-revelation to humans."

About the Bible, the next sentence of the *BFM's* first article states the following: "It is a perfect treasure of divine instruction." This sentence is more of an encomium, rather than additional information. In the *New Hampshire Confession*, from which this and the next sentence are borrowed *in toto*, this short sentence is part of one long sentence whose cadence and coherence read more easily than they do in the *BFM's* disjunctive formulation.

The *BFM's* article on the Bible continues: "It has God for its author, salvation for its end, and truth, without any mixture of error, for its matter."[27] The battle has raged as to whether the phrase, "without any mixture of error," means the same as the term "inerrant" in current discussions.[28] The word "inerrancy" is a seventeenth-century mathematical concept. It holds the biblical materials accountable to modern scientific concepts of truth that were unknown and, doubtless, of no consequence to the biblical authors.

The *BFM's* phrase, "salvation for its end," reinforces a narrow inerrantist position (applicable to spiritual matters), rather than the broad inerrantist position (referring to all areas: science, geography, history, and so on) I agree with Dewey Beegle, Jack Rogers, and others who assert that the concept of inerrancy sets up a mathematical model of truth, a model that has more to do with physical and scientific models than it does with psychological and relational models of truth.[29] The fact that "truth," by definition, contains no error heightens the ambiguity. Moreover, discussions of postmodernism have called into question the absolutist conceptions of truth that were a part of modernism.[30]

The next sentence of the *BFM's* article on the Bible also raises critical concerns for Baptists in the SBC. Referring to the Bible, the *BFM* affirms the following: "It reveals the principles by which God judges us; and therefore is, and will remain to the end of the world, the true center of Christian union, and the supreme standard by which all human conduct, creeds, and religious opinions should be tried."[31] Recent discussions about religious pluralism may deserve consultation, however, in order to broaden or to define and to defend this exclusivist position on the Christian scriptures.[32] It is one thing to affirm that scripture works for all persons. It is another to expect that all of humanity is aware of, willing to abide by, and acknowledges these claims. Although these statements are easily affirmed by Christians, the problems for contemporary religious dialogue and the Christian commitment to missions are how to interpret and to apply this sentiment. On the one hand, it poses a theological problem to deny this sentence in the *BFM's* article on the scriptures: Are not biblical ethics the code for all human conduct? On the other hand, it poses an ethical problem to affirm this sentence without discussion and clarification about the status of the irreligious and those of other religious beliefs. This, like all confessions, is an in-house affirmation. This particular confession on behalf of all persons requires education, discussion, mission, and exemplification, if those beyond the adherents to the confession are to be informed and convinced.

The final sentence of the *BFM's* first article reads as follows: "The criterion by which the Bible is to be interpreted is Jesus Christ." This sentence presumably represents an attempt to reformulate the Reformation's slogan: *Christus est Rex et Dominus Scripturae*, Christ is king and lord of scripture. (1) This may mean that the teaching of Jesus found in the Synoptic Gospels is the touchstone by which all other canonical scriptures are to be interpreted. (2) This sentence may mean that the risen Christ by the Holy Spirit will guide the church. (3) This affirmation may mean that, in the event of competing interpretations, a phrase or act from the accounts about Jesus' ministry is to be decisive.[33] The sentence may mean all three of these insights. The ambiguity gives full rein of interpretation to the individual. This is precisely what the *BFM's* Preamble indicates should be the case. I will plead in the next section for a more christocentric reading of the entire *BFM*. The ambiguity of the final sentence in the *BFM's* first article may be felicitous, but it is no less ambiguous regardless of one's interpretation.[34]

VI. Only God, God Only, Fully God

The *BFM (1963)* has three large sections in its second article that the *BFM (1925)* does not contain.[35] Incredible as it may seem, and even with the christological and experiential predilection of E. Y. Mullins, in the *BFM (1925)*, there were no separate sections on God as Father, Christ, and Holy Spirit.[36] In this respect, the *BFM (1963)* is a much stronger theological document. I recall spirited discussion in seminary faculty meetings urging these fully trinitarian statements.[37] These additions to the *BFM* in 1963 explain why only the document's second article contains subset additions.

In the sentences of the first paragraph on the doctrine of God proper, the following insights may be noted. The *BFM (1963)* breaks apart the long sentences of the *BFM (1925)* and the *New Hampshire Confession*, which it loosely resembles. This breaking up of the descriptive terms ascribed to God eventuates in a proliferation of masculine pronominal references to God.[38] Incidentally, whereas the *BFM (1925)* confesses in the passive voice, "He [God] is revealed to us," the *BFM (1963)* uses the active voice: "The eternal God reveals Himself to us."[39] The active voice is decidedly preferable. The first sentences establish a firm monotheism, in keeping with classical confessions, going back at least to Irenaeus (180 A.D.), but doubtless incorporated from earlier Baptist confessions, especially the *New Hampshire Confession*.[40] The second sentence could be strengthened, at least from a modern God-who-acts, God-is-known-by-what-God-does perspective, by placing the acts of God (Creator, Redeemer, Preserver, and Ruler) before the perfections of God - (intelligent, spiritual, personal Being).

With the phrase, "God is infinite in holiness and all other perfections," the scholastic language continues. What else could one say besides "Yes, indeed" or "Yea, verily"? When asked what this sentence means, one would have to admit that it would require a short course in theology and several carefully crafted paragraphs to explicate that simple sentence. This correct but unexplained wording is so far removed in understanding from the beginning of the *Fraternal Address of Southern Baptists*. That document from 1920 is filled with staccato statements that relate humanity to God in warm and welcome ways: "God is a personal and spiritual and holy Being who loves men with an everlasting love."[41] The brief, inclusive, trinitarian confession in the *Fraternal Address of Southern Baptists* is preferable to the more scholastic treatment of the doctrine of God in the *BFM (1963)*.

"To Him we owe the hightest love, reverence, and obedience." With this sentence, the *BFM (1963)* makes the turn to the subject. The subject is "we." The *New Hampshire Confession* begins with the subject in its "We believe." Each article of the *New Hampshire Confession* has supplied or gives the explicit words "We believe."[42] One may argue, of course, that the "we believe" of the *BFM* is understood and taken for granted. The Preamble of the *BFM (1963)* sets the context for the *BFM* and concludes with the sentence: "It is the purpose of this statement of faith and message to set forth certain teachings which we believe."[43] The names of the members of the drafting committee are appended. Then, the *BFM* begins with Article One on the scriptures. It would be a stronger statement if each section of the *BFM* began with the words "We believe." The "we" is not defined. It is assumed that, not only the drafters of the *BFM*, but also all who accept it is the "we" who believe it. Another question arises: Are the "we" the only ones who owe God "the highest love, reverence, and obedience?" Or, is it the case that "that God whom we acknowledge, ought to be worshiped by all?"[44] The argument may seem scholastic and immaterial. I prefer the *BFM's* statement. On the one hand, Baptists surely live in an age that is willing for them to confess their own obligations, but not the obligations of others. On the other hand, that which Baptists confess about humanity in general is also important.[45]

The *BFM* continues with the following affirmation: "The eternal God reveals Himself to us as Father, Son, and Holy Spirit, with distinct personal attributes, but without division of nature, essence, or being."[46] This is a straightforward confession of the trinitarian nature of God. As mentioned earlier, the *BFM (1963)* speaks of *God revealing Godself*, rather than *God being revealed* as in the *BFM (1925)*. The language of nature, essence, and being entails all of the classical scholastic discussion. It is important and necessary to incorporate a trinitarian discussion, but is still possible to do so in more dynamic and relational categories.

The *BFM (1925)* concluded its short article on the doctrine of God with references from both the Old and New Testaments in such fashion that no discernible order can be readily observed. The *BFM (1963)* contains no references to scripture at the end of its first paragraph on the doctrine of God, but includes extensive biblical references after its entire second article. The references of the *BFM (1963)* are generally and appropriately in canonical order.

VII. *Pater Noster*, Our Father, the Divine Parent

The term "father," as a designation for God, has recently received criticism by those who observe that this patriarchal word and its associations have overshadowed feminine and inclusive biblical words for God.[47] Moreover, a pastoral concern for women and men who have been physically abused by their fathers lends gravity to the situation. Because the term "father" as a designation for God is both biblical and classical, it would be very difficult to erase it from Christian vocabulary. Some argue that the gender-inclusive term "parent" is a more helpful designation. While this may be true, there are strong counterarguments based on the biblical materials, especially Jesus' own use of the term "father" to refer to God. Additionally, the designation "father" is universally repeated by Christianity in its prayers and liturgy. Particularly is this the instance in the Lord's Prayer, the *Pater Noster*. The issue is hotly debated today.

Three insights could ameliorate this situation. (1) Male Christians need to use language about God that includes carefully-nuanced insights about God, cognizant of the numerous feminine metaphors for God. (2) Christian understanding of God needs to make it clear that God is beyond sexuality. (3) In understanding God as father, Baptists need to interpret the fatherhood of God christologically. Baptists must not read "father" from a reference or understanding of human fatherhood. A Christian frame of reference sees the term "father" through the experience of Christ. Such a christological interpretation would include strength and suffering, tenderness and severity, passion and presence.

In the *BFM (1963)*, the section on God as father begins with an active description: "God as Father reigns with providential care . . . ." This care extends to the "universe" and "human history," to all of God's creatures "according to the purposes of His grace." This classic, comforting statement is a good beginning. It states what God does. The second sentence, however, descends to adjectives. God is "all powerful, all loving, and all wise."[48] Certainly! Nevertheless, would not a continuation of the verbal statements be more appropriate? *By God's power, God made the world. By God's love, God redeems the world. By God's wisdom, God guides the world.*

Those who know God through Christ claim a special sense of God as divine parent. This is an understandable and essential confession for the "we" who frame and affirm the document. According to this section's concluding sentence, "He is fatherly in his attitude toward all men."[49] The substance of this sentence should be maintained because of its biblical correctness, its irenic attitude, and its evangelical intentions. Once more, I would call for a critical and constructive exploration of all biblical citations in the *BFM (1963)*. Might not a parallel, marginal placement of biblical references (as in the *Second London Confession*) add clarity and more precision to the fewer references that refer specifically to the insights of each article in the *BFM (1963)*?[50]

VIII. What to Do?

What remains is to draw together the constructive suggestions made throughout this chapter toward any possible revision or restructuring of the *BFM*. I hope that the studies in this book will be a catalyst for Baptists in the SBC to reexamine the *BFM*. Herschel H. Hobbs recalls that the Committee on Baptist Faith and Message in 1963 had three choices: (1) "to write a new statement"; (2) "to study and recommend reaffirmation of the 1925 statement"; or (3) "to present a revised form of the 1925 statement."[51] With a change of date from 1925 to 1963 in the previous choices, those are the options that face Baptists in the SBC today. My sentiments, like those of the committee in 1963, would be to take the third option. To that end, I offer the following suggestions.

First, Baptists should review the classical expressions of Christian belief to discover their ancient, ecumenical connections to the Church universal. The *Orthodox Creed*, printed in London in 1679 and representing General Baptists of the Midlands, contains an extensive affirmation of the *Nicene Creed*, the *Athanasian Creed*, and the *Apostle's Creed*. According to the framers of that Baptist confession, these three creeds "ought thoroughly to be received, and believed. For we believe, they may be proved, by most undoubted authority of holy scripture, and are necessary to be understood of all christians [sic]."[52]

Second, Baptists should review the Anabaptist expressions of faith and practice with their christological, New Testament, and warm-hearted experiential bases. Robert Friedmann asserts that the Anabaptists, while not formally and overtly interested in creeds or even in formal confessions, nevertheless, were orthodox in their confessional statements on their views of trinity and christology. In Thomas *Müntzer's* christology, one finds an emphasis singularly absent in the *BFM (1963)*, an emphasis that Baptists might well find apropos to the suffering of the contemporary world. That idea *Müntzer* called "the bitter Christ," a strong emphasis on Jesus' sufferings as a pattern for Christian living.[53]

Third, Baptists in the SBC should explore again the christocentric emphasis, the emphasis on the Lordship of Christ, made by Mullins and other framers of fraternal and irenic Baptist expressions of faith.[54]

> There are various ways of stating the fundamental Baptist principle. If we indicate the source of our knowledge, we say the scriptures of the Old and New Testaments are divinely inspired, and are our sufficient, certain, and authoritative guide in all matters of faith and practice. As to the nature of the Christian religion, we affirm that it is personal and spiritual. We believe in the direct relation of each individual to God, and the right of everyone to choose for himself in all matters of faith. A Christian's religion begins in the soul when personal faith is exercised in

Jesus Christ, the divine Redeemer and Lord. As the Revealer of God to men and the Mediator of salvation, Jesus Christ is central for Christian faith. His will is the supreme law for the Christian. He is Lord of the conscience of the individual and of the Church. Hence, the Lordship of Jesus Christ is a cardinal teaching of Baptists. It excludes all merely human authorities in religion.[55]

Also, the SBC published a statement in 1964 entitled *Baptist Ideals*. This statement contains the following strong christological affirmation: "*The ultimate source of authority is Jesus Christ the Lord, and every area of life is to be subject to his lordship.*"[56]

As apparent in the previous examples, Baptists possess a rich confessional heritage. Hence, while reexploring the Baptist confessional heritage, Baptists should search further, earlier, and more widely than the *Second London Confession* of 1677, the *Philadelphia Confession* of 1742, and the *New Hampshire Confession* of 1833.

Fourth, Baptists in the SBC should take to heart another suggestion in any reexamination of the *BFM*: this suggestion concerns the wording of the document. Where possible, Baptists should use contemporary, gender-neutral language. The expression of Baptist beliefs should be in active, unambiguous terms—classical statements made in simple, forthright ways, as, for example, in the *BFM's* fifth article, on "God's Purpose of Grace." When the *BFM (1963)* says of election, "[i]t excludes boasting and promotes humility," Baptists in the SBC should retain such expressions and remember them.[57] Any confession of Baptists should be inclusive. A Baptist confession should be verbal and active, rather than adjectival and passive. For example, the short powerful verbs in the third section of the *BFM's* article on the doctrine of God, describing the Holy Spirit, are laudatory. The penultimate sentence of that article, which sentence is not parallel with the other declarations, might read as follows: "The Spirit brings the assurance of God by conveying God's presence and uniting the believer with Christ."[58] That which Baptists confess, or the content, matters. The way in which Baptists confess something, or the form, also matters.

Fifth, I strongly recommend that Baptists in the SBC reverse the first and second articles of the *BFM (1963)*. I recommend this change, because theologically it is appropriate to give God priority in all things. The authority of scripture comes from God's authority. It is God whom Baptists confess, first and foremost. It is axiomatic that Baptists know about God principally, primarily, and most clearly through scripture. It is systematically wrong, however, to place belief in scripture prior to belief in God. There is certainly strong precedent in Baptist confessions for placing God first in a contemporary Baptist confession of faith. The *True*

Confession of 1596 contains a strong statement on biblical authority: the seventh article, which supplies a bridge from the confession's affirmations about God and humanity (in the first six articles) to the confession's affirmations about the person and work of Christ (in articles eight through seventeen). The *London Confession* of 1644 also holds its statement on biblical authority as the seventh article. The English *True Gospel-Faith Declared According to the Scriptures* of 1654 handled the scriptures as the *a priori* authority and simply stated its affirmation of the Bible in the superscript to the confession. A most ironic reversal of the doctrines of God and the Bible occurs in the *Doctrinal Statement of the North American Baptist Association*. Belief in the "Trinity of God" is followed by the extremely conservative second affirmation about the "infallibility and plenary-verbal inspiration of the Scriptures."[59] My inclination is first things first, and this means that confession of God (Father, Son, and Holy Spirit) should come before Baptist confessions about the Bible.

Sixth, Baptists should remember the distinction between a confession of faith and a covenant. They are complementary, but they are not identical. A confession affirms what one believes; a covenant gives agreement as to how one acts. True, Baptists act out of their beliefs. The several issues mentioned in my introduction, however, should not be placed in a statement of faith. Rather, if deemed necessary, they should be in a covenantal agreement. A covenantal agreement is only in effect so long as all parties to the covenant abide by it. Covenants should be positive rather than proscriptive. Church covenants have hit rocky shoals when they itemize sins to be avoided. Inevitably, some sins are missed (for example, child pornography); some sins are indigenous to the human person (such as tattling, backbiting, and excessive anger); still other sins are socially and culturally conditioned (for example, the use of alcohol as a beverage). Rather, covenants should accentuate positive, general principles of Christian conduct.

Seventh, preeminently, last but not least, those who think in terms of a revised confession of faith must remember the purpose of such a statement according to the Baptist heritage. Inscribed before and within all Baptist confessions must be the explicit and implicit affirmations of the priesthood of all believers and the autonomy of each local church.

Notes

[1]"Report of Committee on Baptist Faith and Message," in *Annual of the Southern Baptist Convention: Seventieth Session in Memphis, Tennessee, 13-17 May 1925*, by the Secretaries, Southern Baptist Convention (Nashville: Marshall and Bruce, 1925) 70-76 ("Proceedings," Second Day–Afternoon Session, May 14, Item 53) (hereafter, cited as *BFM [1925]*). In 1963, the SBC

revised this statement, publishing both the original and the revised versions parallel to one another: "Committee on Baptist Faith and Message," in *Annual of the Southern Baptist Convention: One Hundred Sixth Session in Kansas City, Missouri, 7-10 May 1963*, by the Executive Committee, Southern Baptist Convention (Nashville: Southern Baptist Convention, 1963) 63, 269-81 ("Proceedings," Thursday Morning, May 9, Items 112-124) (hereafter, cited as *BFM [1963]*).

[2] See Charles W. Deweese, *Baptist Church Covenants* (Nashville: Broadman Press, 1990), especially the Foreword.

[3] "The New Hampshire Confession, 1833," in *Baptist Confessions of Faith*, rev. ed., ed. William L. Lumpkin (Valley Forge PA: Judson Press, 1969) 360-67 (hereafter, cited as *NHC [1833]*).

[4] From "A True Confession, 1596," in *Baptist Confessions of Faith*, Lumpkin, 82.

[5] See 2 Sam 7:22, 1 Kgs 8:60, Ps 18:31, Ps 86:10, Isa 43:10-12, Zech 14:9. I am indebted for the materials in this section to Philip Schaff and David S. Schaff, eds., *The Creeds of Christendom*, vol. 2, *The Greek and Latin Creeds*, 6th ed. (New York: Harper & Row, 1931; Grand Rapids: Baker Book House, 1990).

[6] See Gerhard Kittel, ed. *Theological Dictionary of the New Testament*, vol. 4, *L-N*, trans. and ed. Geoffrey W. Bromiley (Grand Rapids: Eerdmans, 1967) s.v. "maranaqav," by K. G. Kuhn.

[7] See Oscar Cullman, *The Earliest Christian Confessions*, trans. J. K. S. Reid (London: Lutterworth Press, 1949).

[8] My point, that New Testament confessions are eminently christological and expressed in polemical contexts, does not hinge on the date or authorship of the materials.

[9] See Per-Olaf Sjgran, *The Jesus Prayer*, trans. Sydney Linton (Philadelphia: Fortress Press, 1975).

[10] On these early Christian confessions, see Schaff, *Creeds*, 2:11-39.

[11] See Irenaeus *Contra Haereses* 1.10.1; *Adversus Haereses* 3.4.1-2; 4.33.7.

[12] Schaff, *Creeds*, 2:21.

[13] Ibid.., 2:22.

[14] See Hans von Campenhausen, *The Formation of the Christian Bible*, trans. J. A. Baker (Philadelphia: Fortress Press, 1972).

[15] Schaff, *Creeds*, 2:28.

[16] As examples, see the following: "The Formula of Concord, A.D. 1576 (1584)" and "Confessio Helvetica Posterior, A.D. 1566," in *The Creeds of Christendom*, vol. 3, *The Evangelical Protestant Creeds*, 6th ed., eds. Philip Schaff and David S. Schaff (New York: Harper & Row, 1931; reprint, Grand Rapids: Baker Book House, 1990) 93-94, 237-38 (831-33).

[17] "The London Confession, 1644" and "The Midland Confession, 1655," in *Baptist Confessions of Faith*, Lumpkin, 158, 198.

[18] *NHC (1833)* 361-62.

[19] See "The Assembly or Second London Confession, 1677 and 1688," *NHC (1833)*, and "Statements of Faith of the Southern Baptist Convention, 1925 and 1963," in *Baptist Confessions of Faith*, Lumpkin, 235-96, 360-67, 390-400.

[20]Lumpkin, *Baptist Confessions of Faith*, 360-61. Also see J. M. Pendleton, *Church Manual: Designed for the Use of Baptist Churches* (Philadelphia: American Baptist Publication Society, 1867) 41-61.

[21]"Fraternal Address of Southern Baptists," *Baptist Standard* 32 (26 February 1920): 5.

[22]"Science and Religion," in *Annual of the Southern Baptist Convention: Sixty-Eighth Session in Kansas City, Missouri, 16-20 May 1923*, ed. Secretaries, Southern Baptist Convention (Nashville: Marshall and Bruce, 1923), 19-20 ("Proceedings," Wednesday Morning Session, May 16, Item 11) (hereafter, cited as *SR [1923]*).

[23]*SR (1923)* 19.

[24]*BFM (1963)* 270.

[25]See, for example, Molly Marshall, *What It Means to Be Human* (Macon GA: Smyth & Helwys, 1995).

[26]Elizabeth Johnson carefully considers and rebuts this argument (Elizabeth A. Johnson, *She Who Is: The Mystery of God in Feminist Theological Discourse* [New York: Crossroad, 1992]). Also see the following: Joan Chamberlin Engelsman, *The Feminine Dimension of the Divine* (Philadelphia: Westminster Press, 1979); Mary McClintock Fulkerson, *Changing the Subject: Women's Discourses and Feminist Theology* (Minneapolis MN: Fortress Press, 1994); Ursula King, ed., *Feminist Theology from the Third World* (New York: Orbis Books, 1994); Rosemary Radford Ruether, *Sexism and God-Talk* (Boston: Beacon Press, 1983).

[27]*BFM (1963)* 270.

[28]For a claim of equivalency, see Harold Lindsell, *The Battle for the Bible* (Grand Rapids: Zondervan, 1976). For a more carefully nuanced and qualified view, see Dwight A. Moody, "The Bible," in *Has Our Theology Changed? Southern Baptist Thought Since 1845*, ed. Paul A. Basden (Nashville: Broadman and Holman, 1994) 7-40.

[29]See the following: Dewey Beegle, *The Inspiration of the Scriptures* (Philadelphia: Westminster Press, 1963); Jack Bartlett Rogers and Donald K. McKim, *The Authority and Interpretation of the Bible: An Historical Approach* (San Francisco: Harper, 1991).

[30]See Walter Anderson, *Reality Is Not What It Used To Be* (San Francisco: Harper, 1990).

[31]*BFM (1963)* 270.

[32]See Huston Smith, *The World's Religions* (San Francisco: Harper, 1991).

[33]It is used this way by Herschel Hobbs in his comments on the Elliott controversy (see Herschel H. Hobbs, "Southern Baptists and Confessionalism: A Comparison of the Origins and Contents of the 1925 and 1963 Confessions," *Review and Expositor* 62 [Winter 1979]: 68; idem, *The Baptist Faith and Message* [Nashville: Convention Press, 1971] 30). Such an application may well be a contravention of other more widely accepted hermeneutical principles.

[34]Someone should devote a doctoral dissertation to a careful study of the biblical references given as support for this first article of the *BFM (1963)*. It is surely the case that these texts should be considered as illustrative and not that each one is a prooftext for all that the article portends.

[35] *BFM (1963)* 271-72.
[36] *BFM (1925)* 71; cf. *BFM (1963)* 271-72.
[37] See Hobbs, "Southern Baptists and Confessionalism," 59-60.
[38] Again, see the following works: Johnson, *She Who Is*; Engelsman, *Feminine Dimension of the Divine*; Fulkerson, *Changing the Subject*; King, *Feminist Theology from the Third World*; Ruether, *Sexism and God-Talk*.
[39] *BFM (1925)* 71; *BFM (1963)* 271.
[40] Irenaeus *Contra Haereses* 1.10.1, in Schaff, *Creeds*, 2:13; *NHC (1833)*, article 2, in *Baptist Confessions of Faith*, Lumpkin, 362.
[41] "Fraternal Address of Southern Baptists," 5.
[42] *NHC (1833)* 361-67.
[43] *BFM (1963)* 270.
[44] See James Wm. McClendon, Jr., *Systematic Theology*, vol. 2, *Doctrine* (Nashville: Abingdon Press, 1994) 122ff. McClendon speaks of sin only in the light of grace, not as a necessary acknowledgment of all persons before grace.
[45] For example, see Molly Marshall's exposition of the *BFM's* anthropology in this book's third chapter.
[46] *BFM (1963)* 271.
[47] For example, see Johnson, *She Who Is*.
[48] *BFM (1963)* 271.
[49] Ibid..
[50] Both the doctrine of God the Son and the doctrine of God the Holy Spirit are included in the article on the doctrine of God in the *BFM (1963)*. Other chapters in this volume, however, address aspects of those sections in this second article of that doctrinal confession.
[51] Hobbs, "Southern Baptists and Confessionalism," 60.
[52] "The 'Orthodox Creed,' 1678," article 38, in *Baptist Confessions of Faith*, Lumpkin, 326.
[53] Robert Friedmann, *The Theology of Anabaptism*, vol. 13, *Studies in Anabaptist and Mennonite History* (Scottdale PA: Herald Press, 1973) 50-53.
[54] For example, see again the "Fraternal Address of Southern Baptists."
[55] "A Message of the Baptist World Alliance to the Baptist Brotherhood, to Other Christian Brethren, and to the World," in *Third Baptist World Congress, Stockholm, 21-27 July 1923: Record of Proceedings*, ed. W. T. Whitley (London: Kingsgate Press, 1923; Nashville: Baptist Sunday School Board, 1923; Philadelphia: American Baptist Publication Society, 1923) 223. E. Y. Mullins, then president of the Baptist World Alliance, delivered this message.
[56] *Baptist Ideals* (Nashville: Sunday School Board of the Southern Baptist Convention, 1963) 6.
[57] *BFM (1963)*, 275; also in *BFM (1925)* 72.
[58] Cf. *BFM (1963)* 272.
[59] "A True Confession, 1596," "The London Confession, 1644," "The True Gospel-Faith, 1654," and "Doctrinal Statement of the North American Baptist Association," in *Baptist Confessions of Faith*, Lumpkin, 82-87, 158, 192, 380.

Chapter 3

God's Way with Wayward Humanity
Protology, Anthropology, and Hamartiology in
*The Baptist Faith and Message (1963)**

Molly T. Marshall

It is a well-documented fact that the status of confessions and creeds has been heightened during these recent years of internecine warfare among Baptists of the Southern Baptist Convention (SBC). Drafted "to define doctrine in terms general enough to incorporate diverse segments of the convention," the *Baptist Faith and Message* has become a veritable battleground for competing perspectives.[1] Lacking in these forays is a wider theological perspective that critically reflects on these articles in terms of the streams of influence that flow into this confession.[2] The purpose of this brief essay is to interpret and evaluate the protology, anthropology, and hamartiology of the *BFM (1963)*, as found, respectively, in three of that confession's articles: the second article, particularly its first section, "God the Father"; the third article, "Man"; and the seventeenth article, "Religious Liberty."[3]

Overture

It is appropriate to begin any analysis of this document with a review of the Preamble.[4] As Leon McBeth judiciously reminds Baptists, this introductory statement "was attached both in 1925 and again in 1963 and specifically adopted as part of the confession."[5] The wisdom of these forebears is evident: they wanted to preserve the statement's confessional nature and stave off the credalist usage, a usage, nevertheless, that has been inexorably growing since 1973, when the Baptist Faith and Message Fellowship was formed—a self-appointed watchdog group bent on enforcing compliance with the confession.[6]

The phrase, "Baptists are not a credal people," has almost become an axiom within the SBC's tradition, and yet its meaning is not at all as univocal as some would imply.[7] Certainly, it means that Baptists have resisted religious conformity, from whatever source; it means that Baptists have retained the Bible as the *norma normans* for all their teaching and instruction; and it means that to no creed has infallibility ever been ascribed. None was seen to be beyond revision—witness William Lumpkin's anthology that contains forty-five separate confessional documents.[8] This seems to indicate that all confessional documents are provisional; none can say it all without distortion. The ecclesial work of writing confessions is never finished.

The Preamble sets the tone for what is to follow. It declares that confessions "are only guides in interpretation, having no authority over the conscience." Further, "Baptists emphasize the soul's competency before God, freedom in religion, and the priesthood of the believer."[9] Clearly sounded at the outset are these distinctive Baptist notes of responsible freedom before God accorded to all persons. In this introduction, Baptists in the SBC can hear echoes of the sustained theme of E. Y. Mullins, one of the original revisers of the *New Hampshire Confession* of 1833, in the statement from 1925.[10] Mullins accentuated the primacy of the personal, particularly in religious experience, helping to move Baptists of the SBC beyond the rigidity of Calvinist theology.[11] Both neo-Calvinists and non-Calvinists agree that no one seriously challenged the predominance of Calvinistic theology as did he. After Mullins assumed the presidency of The Southern Baptist Theological Seminary (SBTS) in 1899, the Calvinistic perspective of Boyce, which had prevailed since the founding of the seminary, diminished rapidly.

The Preamble also instructs Baptists about the nature of Christian doctrine. It is a "living faith" that "must experience a growing understanding of truth and must be continually interpreted and related to the needs of each new generation."[12] Of the many percipient cautions in the Preamble to the *BFM (1963)*, this is the one that is perhaps most often ignored. Whereas the impulse that drove the original and revised statements had to do with engaging contemporary scientific and hermeneutical concerns, the more recent use of the document has been as a *regula fidei*, a measure for determining who is outside the faith. No longer a catechetical instrument for teaching Christian faith, it has become a cudgel for dividing the SBC's Baptist family.[13] Ideally, the confession simply articulates the contours of Baptist affirmations that give identity and coherence to this particular ecclesiastical tradition within the Body of Christ.

I. Theology of Creation

In appropriate recognition of the primacy of the doctrine of God (theology proper), the *BFM (1963)* greatly expands the statement on God in the *BFM (1925)*. Following an introductory statement that offers general affirmations about the deity, the first section of the article on God focuses attention on "God the Father."[14] Here, in compact form, is a description of God as "intelligent, spiritual, and personal Being," one who is knowable and incomprehensible, relational and intentional toward the beloved creation. Further, the confession delineates the foundational functions of God as "Creator, Redeemer, Preserver, and Ruler of the universe." The confession is thoroughly biblical in its perception of the ongoing relationship between God and the creation; God does not simply set in motion the grand, groaning project of creation, but tenderly attends its need for sovereign direction and parental nurture.

The introductory statement to the second article also speaks of the fundamental relationship humans are to have with God: "To Him we owe the highest love, reverence, and obedience." Human lives are inescapably before God, *coram Deo*, as Martin Luther never tired of proclaiming. Humans have been made for communion with the One who addresses them; their natural response to their Maker should be worship, self-giving, and responsible stewardship. This comprises humanity's "reasonable service."

The first section of this article, "God the Father," moves more specifically into the work of the primordial being, the first person of the Trinity, who "reigns with providential care over His universe, His creatures, and the flow of the stream of human history according to the purposes of His grace."[15] This is an encompassing depiction of the sweep of God's care for what the divine activity of "letting be" has wrought. God has not left the creation, neither untoward creatures and their machinations, nor the ultimate outcome of finite reality, to its own devices. There is a large measure of inscrutability in the phrase "according to the purposes of His Grace." It gives both comfort and concern: the purposes of God's grace are both trustworthy and, at times, unknown in the daily textures of human life. God's intention to redeem and preserve seem almost imperceptible in a world hell-bent in its presumed self-determination. The function of God as "Ruler," a familiar ascription in the confessional history of the wider Christian tradition, has a measure of hiddenness about it.[16] Yet, these forthright declarations buttress the confidence of Baptist Christians, and rightly so, for Christian faith is "not yet sight."

Again, this section puts forward statements that can be made only of God: "all powerful, all loving, all wise." I am not persuaded that any particular logic drives the order of these affirmations; this language is not included in the *NHC (1933)* or the *BFM (1925)*. Here it functions as an explication of the being of God as "father." Power without wisdom could seem capricious; wisdom and power without love could be autocratic or impersonal. That these three attributes are joined together speaks of the compassionate mode of God's way with humanity.

This reality is extended by the subsequent statements: "God is Father in truth to those who become children of God through Jesus Christ. He is fatherly in His attitude toward all men." A shift occurs with this language; earlier, this section of the article evinced an anthropological relation to God that all persons enjoy by virtue of being creations of God. The focus in these further statements is the christological relation with God, which is a possibility for all humankind. While God relates to all humanity as the sovereign God who makes "rain to fall on the just and the unjust" (Matt 5:45), there is a qualitative difference in the relation to those who "become children of God through Jesus Christ." The appellation, "Father in truth," is a significant distinctive; it describes a new filial identity for those who are in Christ. It seems to suggest that the unredeemed have only a tangential relationship to God, largely unconscious and presumptive. It is this genial general providence that goes unrecognized by the vast majority of humanity. People who confess their faith in Jesus Christ, however, are adopted as persons whom God claims as beloved daughters and sons. Although all are created in the image of God, not all will be "conformed to the image of God's Son."

The next section of the confession's second article addresses "God the Son." It is a robust christology that does not neglect the real humanity of the Lord. He is portrayed as "taking upon Himself the demands and necessities of human nature and identifying Himself completely with mankind yet without sin."[17] In terms of theological method, it is significant to place christology before anthropology, for this sketches out true humanity, that is, how God intended human life to be. This has been accomplished only in the Christ. Only in light of the full faithfulness of Jesus do humans see their humanity for what it is and begin to understand their sin.[18]

The third and final section of the confession's second article, "God the Holy Spirit," anticipates the following article on humanity, when it affirms that the work of the Spirit "convicts of sin, of righteousness and of judgment."[19] It would be helpful if the relationship of the Spirit to the believer and the nonbeliever were more clearly demarcated at this juncture. Indeed, the reality of God as *Creator Spiritus* has seldom been sufficiently accentuated in Baptist confessions; the primary accent has been soteriological, rather than protological or anthropological. This has led, in my judgment, to a truncated understanding of the encompassing role of God's Spirit, the One who vivifies all of creation and sustains it for God's purposes.

II. Theology of Humanity

The third article of the *BFM (1963)* guides the entire confessional statement's understanding of humanity. The declaration, that humanity "was created by a special act of God, in his own image, and is the crowning work of His creation," is specifically directed toward the evolutionary crisis of the 1920s and the controversies over the interpretation of Genesis in the 1960s.[20] The statement is open enough, however, to permit an interpretation of theistic evolution; it does not require that one be a "scientific creationist" to claim fidelity to this general affirmation.

Properly, humanity is described as created in the image of God, before confessing the reality of humanity as sinful beings. As the "crowning work of creation," humanity has a special dignity and close relationship to the One who shares the divine image with the creatures. It is very important for the contemporary interpreter to note that the generic use of "man" surely includes women as equal bearers of the image of God.[21] Presently, the church is undergoing critical reflection on the proper role of women as ecclesiastical leaders. Stressing the fundamental God-given equality of the sexes is foundational to the further theological construction of God's calling and gifting of women for ministry—in the same manner that God has called and gifted men—through Christ Jesus. Clearly, then, God gives to both male and female the mandate for responsible stewarding of the good creation; both share in "original righteousness" and subsequent culpability for rebelling against the divine prohibitions.[22]

The theme of humanity's responsibility before God is taken up later in the confessional statement. The seventeenth article, "Religious Liberty," develops the idea of the liberty of conscience, outlined already in the Preamble. There is a clear qualification to this freedom: "God alone is Lord of the conscience . . . ."[23] God grants to the individual or gathered community the right to dissent from "the doctrines and commandments of men which are contrary to His Word or not contained in it." This ministry of dissent seems no longer to be perceived as a key expression of Baptist identity. Prophetic insight and truth telling have suffered ineluctably, because of the SBC's departure from this Baptist principle. Once again, the *BFM (1963)* bespeaks its heritage from the Reformation, by returning to its center of gravity: the scriptures and the living Word of God retain a higher authority than temporal human contrivances. Sadly, in recent years, Baptists in the SBC have been more content to debate the nature of the scriptures than to do the hard work of interpreting their message for people today.

Christian women and men do have civil obligations that must not be neglected, but these obligations are once again relativized by adhering to the higher demand of "the revealed will of God." Concomitant to this principle is the forthright statement of religious freedom, which entails the separation of church and state.[24]

III. Theology of Sin

The statement of humanity's willful turning away from intimate fellowship with the Creator is put in stark Augustinian terms: "In the beginning man was innocent of sin and was endowed by his Creator with freedom of choice." The statement further underscores that it was the misuse of this remarkable and fearful gift that precipitated human sin against God and the introduction of sin into the human race. While not ameliorating human responsibility, the statement notes that through "the temptation of Satan man transgressed the command of God . . . ."[25] Sin, thus, is deliberate rebellion against what has been clearly prohibited by God. It is not *felix culpa*, the Irenaean intuition, that makes the Edenic story a tragic accident or immature expression of developing identity. The intentional refusal to live within limits set by God renders a profound estrangement of humans from their Creator.

The Christian is not exempt from struggling with sin; the doctrine of sin cannot be relegated to the trespass at the beginning of the human story. The confession's fifth article, "God's purpose of Grace," details the consequences of sin for those who have already trusted Christ as their savior: "Believers may fall into sin through neglect and temptation, whereby they grieve the Spirit, impair their graces and comforts, bring reproach on the cause of Christ, and temporal judgments upon themselves . . . ."[26] Obviously, the *BFM (1963)* does not affirm sinless perfection nor the idea of sanctification as completed prior to death. This statement suggests that the punishment for sin is built into the sin: that is, the punishment for sin is sinning. Grieving the Spirit, defaming the cause of Christ, bringing temporal judgments on themselves, each of these consequences suggests that Christian persons are inescapably bound up with the life of God and the lives of others. Indeed, there is a direct rejection of any notion that one's sin concerns only him or her. This note must be repeatedly sounded for our day in which individualism is given ultimate priority.

To the credit of those who drafted the *NHC (1833)* and the subsequent *BFM (1925)*, some dimensions of the Augustinian vision have been moderated. While "original innocence" of humanity at the time of creation is assumed, this confessional document does not ascribe *super donum additum* (supernatural gifts) that lessen the significance of Jesus Christ as the true model of humanity. When the perfection of "Adam" is overly stressed (Augustine's view), the eschatological orientation of Christian faith is neglected, and more seriously, the christocentric shaping of true humanity is abandoned. Furthermore, the confession departs from classic Augustinianism by eschewing any notion of seminal transmission of sin, the view that remains at the heart of orthodox Catholicism and governs its baptismal theology. The confession formulates the concept of original sin as follows: "whereby his posterity inherits a nature and an environment inclined toward sin, and as soon as they are capable of moral action become transgressors and are under condemnation."[27] In this phrase occurs a careful delineation between inherited *guilt* (as in the classic definition of "original sin") and an inherited *nature* and environment inclined toward sin. This careful nuancing articulates a Baptist principle of voluntarism: that is, each individual is responsible for his or her decisions before God, while at the same time acknowledging his or her solidarity and complicity with corporate sinful humanity.[28] Humans are sinners because they sin; humans are also sinners because their environment seduces them to sin. Human guilt comes from the human's own wrongdoing; the human's context makes habitual sinning its primary mode. The statement also suggests that God discerns when one is "capable of moral action," or "the age of accountability" as Baptists are fond of saying. In this caveat, there is a tacit indication of God's graciousness to those who do not easily fit into our categories of moral development. With so many children being born into homes marked by violence and amoral instruction, Baptists would do well to remember that "conviction of sin," the work of the Holy Spirit, must be abetted by the patient guidance of those whose consciences have been numbed to the righteousness of God.[29] The idea of personal accountability before God is greatly diminished by a culture marked by the goal of self-fulfillment.

Because of the sinful state of all humanity, it is not possible for people to live as God intends. It requires a work of grace to "enable man to fulfill the creative purpose of God." Part of that purpose is to live in "holy fellowship" with the One for whom humans are made; another part is to bear God's image in the world as those marked by communing love. God's tenacious grace makes possible the continuation of God's creative purpose; human rebellion will not ultimately thwart God's preserving and ruling over the good creation.

Once again, the confession's third article returns to a general affirmation of all persons. Human personality is deemed sacred by virtue of being God's own creation and because of Christ's death for all humanity: "therefore every man possesses dignity and is worthy of respect and Christian love."[30] While the SBC's missionary efforts have certainly attested to the foundational belief that Christ died for all, Baptists's cavalier treatment of those in the Christian family and beyond who have differed from them has often failed to demonstrate respect and Christian love. Baptists in the SBC have been too provincial in their understanding of the extent of grace.

Significantly, there is no hint in this confessional statement of a "limited atonement" that views Christ's self-giving on the cross as offered only for the "elect."[31] Rather, there is the indication that the significance and dignity of all persons is heightened by the Word being made flesh and his obedience unto death. This section is marked by the Anabaptist influence that offered the possibility of wider inclusion of persons among the redeemed than the tradition flowing out of Geneva.[32] Presently, Baptists in the SBC are attempting to integrate this disparate strand of theological influence into their self-understanding and ecclesial praxis.[33]

Reprise

This brief review of the statement's teaching on creation, humanity, and sin reveals the confluence of different streams of Baptist theology. The *BFM (1963)* has stood the tests of three quarters of the twentieth century because it is a good statement, clear, and carefully nuanced. It bears the marks of several theological skirmishes, as did the earliest conciliar statements of the church. Perspectives are framed in particular fashion because of the specificity of the challenges they have undergone.

The confession is forthrightly Baptist, which may be its greatest strength. It moves away from the *Second London Confession* of 1677 in expressing its doctrinal stance.[34] It is not considered to be (as was the later *Abstract of Principles*) a faithful repetition of the central truths found in the *Westminster Confession* of 1646.[35] Following the *NHC (1833)*, it grounds itself in the voluntarist principles of Baptist identity.

When the Separate Baptists in the South, following the strong leadership of Richard Furman (one strongly influenced by the revivalist efforts of George Whitefield), agreed to use the Regular Baptists's statement, the *Philadelphia Confession* of 1742, they did so on certain conditions.[36] After considerable debate as to the propriety of having any confession of faith at all, the report of the committee was received with the following explanation:

> To prevent the confession of faith from usurping a tyrannical power over the conscience of any, we do not mean, that every person is bound to the strict observance of everything therein contained; yet that it hold forth the essential truths of the gospel. . . . Upon these terms we are united, and desire hereafter, that the names Regular and Separate be buried in oblivion. . . .[37]

This kind of caution must be preserved as Baptists in the SBC attempt to find a way to bridge current theological divides. Baptists can concur with the logic of having confessions, provided they are seen as provisional and are not used as weapons to drive other Christians out of the fold. The impulse currently at work among Baptists of the Southern Baptist Convention equates confessions with the "faith once delivered to the saints."[38] Propositions, no matter how carefully framed and nuanced, can never fully represent the personal aspect of the Christian's faith, that is, the Word become flesh, and the continuing incarnation of the Lord in the church. Doctrine has to do with the "essential practices of the church," as James McClendon puts it. Doctrine is what the church must teach *now* in order to be the church. Thus, dynamism, rather than fixity, must be the character of Baptist doctrine expressed in the confessions of faith.

*I dedicate this chapter both to Roy L. Honeycutt, Jr., former president ot the Southern Baptist Thelogical Seminary, who gave me my first job teaching theology among Southern Baptists, and to Thomas E. Clifton, president of Central Baptist Theological Seminary, who gave me another opportunity within the larger Baptist family.

Notes

[1] Bill J. Leonard, *God's Last and Only Hope: The Fragmentation of the Southern Baptist Convention* (Grand Rapids: Eerdmans, 1990) 69. See "Committee on Baptist Faith and Message," in *Annual of the Southern Baptist Convention: One Hundred Sixth Session in Kansas City, Missouri, 7-10 May 1963*, by the Executive Committee, Southern Baptist Convention (Nashville: Southern Baptist Convention, 1963) 63, 269-81 ("Proceedings," Thursday Morning, May 9, Items 112-124) (hereafter, cited as *BFM [1963]*).

[2] An interesting enterprise would be to examine in detail how the scriptural texts listed under each of the articles actually informs their affirmations. It would be a daunting task to glean an overarching hermeneutical perspective on the selection of the disparate texts cited.

[3] Written in 1925 and revised in 1963, the *Baptist Faith and Message* cannot be expected to conform to contemporary linguistic conventions. Hence, when citing the confession I will not use [sic] to note the presence of exclusivist language, albeit reading its affirmations put forward in this language further reinforces my supposition that the SBC's controversy has been driven more by masculine will-to-power than has been acknowledged. See my essay "Setting Our Feet in a Large Room," in *Beyond the Impasse? Scripture, Interpretation, and Theology in Baptist Life*, eds. Robison B. James and David S. Dockery (Nashville: Broadman Press, 1992) 189, n. 1.

[4] Robison James reminds Baptists that, because the Preamble "subordinates the ensuing confession of faith *to the Bible*, it provides a new kind of protection against the possibility that the confession might gain enough status to usurp the authority of the Bible itself" (Robison B. James, "Credalism, Confessionalism, and the Baptist Faith," in *The Unfettered Word: Southern Baptists Confront the Authority-Inerrancy Question*, ed. Robison B. James [Macon GA: Smyth & Helwys, 1994] 140). His analysis remains a helpful resource for the often vexed question of the authority of confessions in light of the Bible.

[5] H. Leon McBeth, ed., *A Sourcebook for Baptist Heritage* (Nashville: Broadman Press, 1990) 503.

[6] David T. Morgan offers a careful historical overview of the formation and activity of the Baptist Faith and Message Fellowship (David T. Morgan, *The New*

Crusades, The New Holy Land: Conflict in the Southern Baptist Convention, 1969–1991 [Tuscaloosa AL: University of Alabama Press, 1996]).

[7]Although concurring that Baptists have never been *credalistic*, Timothy George argues that "the idea that voluntary, conscientious adherence to an explicit doctrinal standard is somehow foreign to the Baptist tradition is a peculiar notion not borne out by a careful examination of our heritage" (Timothy George, "Conflict and Identity in the SBC: The Quest for a New Consensus," in *Beyond the Impasse*, 203).

[8]William L. Lumpkin, ed., *Baptist Confessions of Faith*, rev. ed. (Valley Forge PA: Judson Press, 1969).

[9]*BFM (1963)* 269, 270.

[10]See the following: "The New Hampshire Confession, 1833," in *Baptist Confessions of Faith*, Lumpkin, 360-67 (hereafter, cited as *NHC [1833]*); and "Report of Committee on Baptist Faith and Message," in *Annual of the Southern Baptist Convention: Seventieth Session in Memphis, Tennessee, 13-17 May 1925*, by the Secretaries, Southern Baptist Convention (Nashville: Marshall and Bruce, 1925) 70-76 ("Proceedings," Second Day–Afternoon Session, May 14, Item 53) (hereafter, cited as *BFM [1925]*).

[11]In his magisterial systematic theology, Mullins wrote: "It is only after the Christian knows God in redemptive experience through Christ that he is in a position to understand God . . . whom Jesus Christ revealed" (E. Y. Mullins, *The Christian Religion in its Doctrinal Expression* [Valley Forge PA: Judson Press, 1917] 32). According to Paul Basden, this approach to Christian doctrine "departed drastically from the high Calvinistic approach of Boyce, which started with the doctrine of God and then reached conclusions based largely on philosophical deductions" (Paul A. Basden, "Predestination," in *Has Our Theology Changed? Southern Baptist Thought Since 1845*, ed. Paul A. Basden [Nashville: Broadman and Holman, 1994] 51).

[12]*BFM (1963)* 270.

[13]See Nancy Tatom Ammerman's description of how the confessional statement became an instrument to force persons from the fold (Nancy Tatom Ammerman, *Baptist Battles: Social Change and Religious Conflict in the Southern Baptist Convention* [New Brunswick NJ: Rutgers University Press, 1990] 255-56).

[14]*BFM (1963)* 271; cf. *BFM (1925)* 71. Gender-specific language for God is surely one of the most contested areas in contemporary theological construction. This article replicates the language of the confession, yet I want to note my personal discomfort with the confession's exclusively masculine language for God. A fully-orbed biblical theology must take into account other metaphors for God, both feminine and transpersonal (cf. Jann Aldredge Clanton, *In Whose Image? God and Gender* [New York: Crossroad, 1990]; and Ruth Duck, *Gender and the Name of God* [New York: Pilgrim Press, 1991]). Baptists must heed Rosemary Radford Ruether's warning against "linguistic idolatry"—making graven images through using only one image for God, the male (for example, Rosemary Radford Reuther, *Sexism and God-Talk: Toward a Feminist Theology* [Boston: Beacon Press, 1983] 66-68).

¹⁵Although John MacQuarrie's language for God is somewhat dated, it still provides a helpful way to describe the dynamic trinitarian being of God (see John MacQuarrie, *Principles of Christian Theology,* 2d ed. [New York: Charles Scribner's Sons, 1977] 199f.).

¹⁶For constructive guidance, I commend the recent work of my former teacher and colleague, which offers sustained reflection on the difficulty that the doctrine of providence presents amidst the extremities of human suffering across the ages (see E. Frank Tupper, *A Scandalous Providence: The Jesus Story of the Compassion of God* [Macon GA: Mercer University Press, 1995]).

¹⁷*BFM (1963)* 271.

¹⁸I am indebted to James Wm. McClendon, Jr. for this insight (see James Wm. McClendon, Jr., *Systematic Theology*, vol. 2, *Doctrine* [Nashville: Abingdon Press, 1994] 123).

¹⁹*BFM (1963)* 272.

²⁰*BFM (1963)* 272. James Leo Garrett, Jr. handles the latter controversy in an even-handed manner (James Leo Garrett, Jr., "Are Southern Baptists 'Evangelicals'?" in *Are Southern Baptists "Evangelicals"?* by James Leo Garrett, Jr., E. Glenn Hinson, and James E. Tull [Macon GA: Mercer University Press, 1983] 112ff.).

²¹The theological concept, "image of God," has been the subject of lively debate throughout Christian history. Rather than a possession, it is the "capacity to respond freely in love to the creative one who calls." It is more a goal than an intrinsic faculty; it is relational and becomes clearer as we are "conformed to the image of God's Son" (cf. my treatment of this significant aspect of humanity in *What It Means to Be Human* [Macon GA: Smyth & Helwys, 1995] 41f.).

²²Cf. also the thirteenth article, "Stewardship" (*BFM [1963]* 279).

²³*BFM (1963)* 281.

²⁴Because William R. Estep addresses these issues at length in this book's last chapter, I note them only briefly here.

²⁵*BFM (1963)*, 272-273 (article 3). Paul Ricoeur suggests that an anthropocentric locus of evil is one-sided; the serpent in the temptation story reminds people that evil "had to be whispered" to the humans. Sin comes both from within and without (Paul Ricoeur, *The Symbolism of Evil*, trans. Emerson Buchanan [New York: Harper & Row, 1976] 257ff.).

²⁶*BFM (1963)* 275.

²⁷*BFM (1963)* 273 (article 3). Herschel Hobbs goes beyond the language of the confession in his statement, "the image was destroyed" (Herschel H. Hobbs, *The Baptist Faith and Message* [Nashville: Convention Press, 1971] 53). Indeed, the very fact that God continues to hold "fallen" humanity accountable suggests that the capacity to respond to the address of God has not been eradicated.

²⁸I have been helped by the distinction drawn by Thomas Finger between an *extensive* and *intensive* view of humanity's sinfulness or depravity. An intensive view accents *total* depravity, viz., humanity is as bad as can be, hardly remaining human. An extensive view, while no less serious about the reality of sin, suggests that there is no part of us that remains untouched by sin, although God continues

to keep us in "common grace" (see Thomas Finger, *Christian Theology: An Eschatological Approach*, vol. 2 [Scottdale PA: Herald Press, 1989] 143).

[29]Conscience cannot be considered an unfailingly reliable moral guide, Dale Moody warns: "Conscience without conditioning does not tell what is right" (Dale Moody, *The Word of Truth: A Summary of Christian Doctrine Based on Biblical Revelation* [Grand Rapids: Eerdmans, 1981] 241).

[30]*BFM (1963)* 273.

[31]In my unpublished Hoover Lectures offered at Baptist Theological Seminary at Richmond, April 1995, I noted how hymnody had contributed to the diminution of the Calvinist hold on Baptist theology. Hugh McElrath and others have argued that the chief modification of Calvinist theology among Baptists occurred when they began to sing the hymns of Wesley. Not only did the Wesleyan influence encourage congregational singing, but the notions of free will and wideness in God's mercy characteristic of these hymns began to modify the exclusivistic parameters of Calvinism.

[32]In Geneva, Calvin showed an intolerance toward nonconformists. Glenn Hinson has likened this quest for doctrinal purity to that of the Roman Catholic inquisitors. "Although Geneva became a haven for harassed Protestants, it also expelled many others who did not agree with Calvin's views . . ." (see E. Glenn Hinson, *Soul Liberty: The Doctrine of Religious Liberty* [Nashville: Convention Press, 1975] 77; cf. Glen H. Stassen, "Anabaptist Influence in the Origin of the Particular Baptists," *Mennonite Quarterly Review* 36 [October 1962]: No. 4).

[33]See W. R. Estep, "Southern Baptists in Search of an Identity," in *The Lord's Free People in a Free Land*, ed. W. R. Estep (Fort Worth TX: Faculty of the School of Theology, Southwestern Baptist Theological Seminary, 1976) 145-70.

[34]See "The Assembly or Second London Confession, 1677 and 1688," in *Baptist Confessions of Faith*, Lumpkin, 235-95.

[35]See "Abstract of Principles," from "Recommendation No. 3, Charter of the Southern Baptist Theological Seminary," in *Annual of the Southern Baptist Convention: Ninety-Seventh Session in St. Louis, Missouri, 2-5 June 1954*, by the Executive Committee, Southern Baptist Convention (Nashville: Southern Baptist Convention, 1954) 38 ("Proceedings," Wednesday Morning, June 2, Item 15) 38-39; "The Westminster Confession (1646)," in *Creeds of the Churches: A Reader in Christian Doctrine from the Bible to the Present*, 3d ed., ed. John H. Leith (Louisville KY: John Knox Press, 1982) 192-230.

[36]See "The Philadelphia Confession, (1742)," in *Baptist Confessions, Covenants, and Catechisms*, vol. 11, Library of Baptist Classics, ed. Timothy George and Denise George (Nashville: Broadman and Holman, 1996) 56-93.

[37]McBeth, *Sourcebook for Baptist Heritage*, 166.

[38]As one of the SBC's most significant and recent examples of this impulse toward credalism, see the "Report of the Presidential Theological Study Committee," in *Annual of the Southern Baptist Convention: One Hundred Thirty-Seventh Session in Orlando, Florida, 14-16 June 1994*, by the Executive Committee, Southern Baptist Convention (Nashville: Southern Baptist Convention, 1994) 102, 112-18 ("Proceedings," Wednesday Morning Session, June 15, Item 145).

Chapter 4

"Rooted and Grounded in Jesus Christ"
Christology and Soteriology in
The Baptist Faith and Message (1963)

Warren McWilliams

Introduction

The Baptist Faith and Message of 1963 is extremely christocentric, with every article explicitly referring to Christ. The Preamble sets the tone for the document by suggesting that our faith is "rooted and grounded in Jesus Christ," who is "the sole authority for faith and practice among Baptists."[1] The aim of this essay will be to interpret and evaluate the christology and soteriology of the *BFM (1963)*, focusing especially on its soteriology. The discussion will center primarily on the relevant sections from the articles on the doctrines of "God," "Salvation," "God's Purpose of Grace," "Baptism and the Lord's Supper," "The Kingdom," and "Last Things."

Academic theologians often distinguish christology, or the person of Christ, from soteriology, or the work of Christ. Although the authors of the *BFM (1963)* did not organize their discussion of Jesus under those two rubrics, they addressed many of the typical concerns of theologians. Spread throughout the articles are discussions of Jesus' deity, humanity, atonement, and return. The document devotes considerably more attention to soteriology than christology, reflecting a typical Baptist concern with salvation.

I. Christology

On christology, the *BFM (1963)* initially follows the pattern of christology from above. The article on "God" as the Trinity identifies Christ as "the eternal Son of God" and moves on to the incarnation in Jesus.[2] The interpretation of Christ is set firmly within the context of the three persons of the Trinity. Although the emphasis on Jesus throughout the document might lead some observers to accuse the *BFM (1963)* of being dangerously close to christomonism, the trinitarian context for its christological discussion guards against such a misunderstanding.

In the section on "God the Son," the authors briefly identify several important topics: the virginal conception and birth of Jesus, his obedience of God's will, his humanity, his impeccability, his death, his resurrection, his ascension, and his eventual return. These doctrines are common Baptist doctrinal statements, mentioned, for example, in the Foreign Mission Board's "Statement of Belief" from 1920.[3] Working within the general context of a Chalcedonian understanding of christology, the *BFM (1963)* affirms Christ's deity and humanity. Although soteriology is addressed in other articles as well, this article clearly affirms that Jesus' death is the basis for the reconciliation between God and sinful humanity. Although Jesus "will return in power and glory," he now dwells spiritually in believers.[4]

Even though the *BFM (1963)* generally follows the pattern of "christology from above," starting with the deity of the eternal Son and moving to his incarnation in Jesus, the majority of this article follows a narrative approach to christology that is compatible with the model of "christology from below." The "from above" model often leaves theologians open to the charge that they neglect the earthly ministry of Jesus, including his teaching, miracles, and table fellowship. The *BFM (1963)* does not address these issues explicitly, dealing instead with issues related to the beginning of Jesus' earthly life (incarnation, virgin birth), his passion, resurrection, and return.

Although the section on "God the Son" neglects Jesus' earthly ministry, an entire article is devoted to the major theme of his teaching and preaching in the synoptic Gospels: the ninth article, on the kingdom of God. The ninth article supplements the lean treatment of Jesus' teaching ministry by highlighting this rich theme. The article begins by distinguishing two aspects of the kingdom of God: God's "general sovereignty over the universe and His particular kingship" over those who voluntarily acknowledge God's rule. The kingdom of God is further identified as "the realm of salvation." People enter this realm by committing themselves to Jesus. Entrance into the kingdom of God is so closely tied to Jesus that it is called the "kingdom of Christ," in the article on "Education," and "Christ's kingdom," in the article on "Cooperation."[5]

A confession of faith is not designed or intended to wrestle with all of the details of biblical interpretation, and the article on "The Kingdom" clearly avoids debates about interpretations such as consistent eschatology or realized eschatology. The article's perspective is closest to the consensus view, sometimes called inaugurated eschatology, which mediates between the present reality of the kingdom and the future completion of the kingdom.[6] Believers are in the kingdom now, but the "full consummation of the Kingdom" awaits Jesus' return. While Christians await Jesus' *parousia*, they can actively do God's will on earth.[7] Larry Baker's chapter in this volume of studies addresses the Christian's moral obligations in this regard.

The article on the kingdom of God balances the present and future aspects of the kingdom as well as the divine and human work to establish the kingdom. Without implying that believers can create the kingdom on earth, believers are encouraged "to pray and to labor" for the coming of the kingdom.

The inclusion of a major article on the kingdom of God also reminds Baptists that their relation to Christ has corporate as well as individual dimensions. Many Baptists understand salvation in a highly individualistic fashion. The kingdom of God, however, is clearly a social or corporate image. The emphasis on the kingdom, rooted in Jesus' teaching, is a helpful corrective to the individualistic view of Christianity prevalent at times in Southern Baptist life.

The christology of the section on God the Son also neglects the problematic issue of the exact relationship of Christ's deity and humanity. For example, the article does not use the Pauline image of *kenosis* (Phil. 2:7) and does not articulate a detailed position on how Jesus "emptied" himself in the incarnation. Also, the article does not explicitly refute the christological heresies of the early centuries, even though it affirms the essential deity and humanity of Christ. Although several Baptists in the SBC have addressed christological issues in their writings, one scholar suggested that there has been no significant change in the SBC's thinking about Jesus since 1845.[8]

Although the *BFM (1963)* falls firmly in the orthodox tradition of the early councils and creeds, it neglects some themes important to christological reflection. For example, although it affirms the deity of Christ, the confession does not highlight the cosmic Christ in a significant way.[9] Traditional concerns such as *logos* christology are overlooked, and the newer interest in "green" or ecological christology is not anticipated.[10] Issues such as christophany, the appearance of the preincarnate Christ, are not raised. The preaching of Christ to the dead (1 Pet 3:18-20; 4:6), mentioned in early creeds, is also ignored.

The *BFM (1963)* does not use the traditional Reformed typology of Jesus as prophet, priest, and king in its christology. The *Baptist Faith and Message* from 1925 briefly refers to this scheme in its article on "Repentance and Faith," but that language was dropped in the revision of 1963.[11] This threefold typology has the advantage of providing a balanced perspective on Jesus' mission. A heavy concentration on Jesus as priest, for example, usually signals a preoccupation with soteriological concerns. Jesus certainly transcends and perfects all of these Old Testament categories. Focusing on Jesus as king or prophet enables a theologian to introduce Jesus' teaching ministry, especially his announcement of the kingdom's arrival. The *BFM (1963)* does not identify Jesus as prophet, priest, and king, but does dedicate a significant article to the kingdom of God.

II. Soteriology

The *BFM (1963)* devotes significantly more attention to soteriology than to christology. Soteriology can refer to the doctrine of the savior (the work of Christ) or to the doctrine of salvation. Both dimensions of soteriology are addressed in this confession of faith.

That Jesus is the basis for human salvation is noted several times in the *BFM (1963)*. The Preamble refers to "the simple conditions of salvation revealed in the New Testament, viz. repentance towards God and faith in Jesus Christ as Saviour and Lord." The section on "God the Son" indicates that Jesus' death provides redemption from sin for humanity.[12]

The brevity and simplicity of a confession of faith naturally rule out extended discussion of the nature of Christ's work or mission. Although the document does not explicitly endorse a specific theory of atonement, for example, the article on "Man" suggests that Christ "died for man." Many Southern Baptists interpret Jesus' death in sacrificial, substitutionary terms, but the confession does not stress those categories. Jesus is described as "the One Mediator" in the section on "God the Son," and his blood is mentioned explicitly in the article on "Salvation."[13]

Many Baptists in the SBC seem satisfied to affirm that Jesus provided salvation, without worrying about the details of atonement-theory. A recent study of writing theologians in the SBC suggests that they have explored a number of the traditional atonement theories. W. T. Conner, for example, is linked to the Christus Victor theory popularized by Gustaf Aulén. Dale Moody supported the use of sacrificial imagery.[14] Fisher Humphreys proposed "cruciform forgiveness" as an innovative model.[15] Many Baptist pastors and lay Christians feel more comfortable with Anselm's satisfaction theory or Calvin's penal theory.

Although the *BFM (1963)* is surprisingly brief on the work of Christ, it devotes more attention to the nature of salvation. The fourth and fifth articles develop the details of the temporal process of salvation and the eternal context for salvation.

The article on the doctrine of salvation uses several biblical images to delineate aspects and stages of salvation. The term "redemption," used twice in the introduction to the article, seems to serve as an umbrella term for the discussion. The terms "redemption" and "redemptive mission" were also used in the discussion of "God the Son." Jesus' death provided the basis for redemption, but the Holy Spirit "seals the believer unto the day of final redemption," thus suggesting that the concept of "redemption" serves as the rubric for the entire process of salvation.[16]

Although the root meaning of "redemption" is liberation, Jesus is not depicted as a liberator in a significant way in the confession.[17] The emergence of multiple forms of liberation theology primarily postdated the *BFM (1963)*. Yet, Jaroslav Pelikan has argued that Jesus as liberator has been the dominant image of Jesus in the nineteenth and twentieth centuries.[18] Much of the ferment in contemporary christology and soteriology revolves around the image of Jesus as liberator. One wonders how a strong emphasis on Jesus as redeemer/liberator could or should affect Southern Baptist thinking on the status of minority groups, including African-Americans and women.

The article on "Salvation" in the *BFM (1963)* synthesizes several articles from the *BFM (1925)* but retains the discussion of election and perseverance in a separate article.[19] Salvation is presented as a process composed of three stages or phases. The first stage receives the most attention, reflecting the evangelistic heritage of Baptists. Viewing salvation as a process has been a major emphasis of the SBC's recent writing theologians. Yet, the *BFM (1963)* does not develop a detailed *ordo salutis*, or order of salvation.[20] Besides a general presentation of the three stages, the document does not deal with the exact sequence of faith, regeneration, election, calling, and other components of salvation.[21]

The discussion of salvation draws on a number of biblical images, although much of the language is distinctively Pauline. For example, the Johannine imagery of abundant life or eternal life is neglected, and Paul's emphasis on salvation as adoption is ignored. Paul's comprehensive image of the Christian life "in Christ" is not highlighted.

The first stage of salvation, called regeneration or the new birth, involves God's grace and the work of the Holy Spirit. The human response includes repentance and faith. This first stage is also identified with "justification," which is defined as acquittal. The confession does not address the traditional issue of whether justification is exclusively forensic, meaning that humans are *declared righteous* because of Jesus' righteousness, or whether humans are *made righteous*. Humans become new creatures, and human hearts are changed, but moral perfection is a goal rather than an immediate gift. Terms such as "propitiation" and "expiation," which have prompted heated debate among scholars, are not employed in the article.

The nature of justification was addressed by the Southern Baptist Convention at its annual meeting in 1994. The signing of the document "Evangelicals and Catholics Together" led to the passage of a resolution reaffirming "the historic Baptist doctrine of justification, namely, that the righteousness of Christ is imputed to us by grace alone through faith in Christ alone without any addition of good works or human efforts. . . ."[22] Some Baptists feared that the accord with Roman Catholics compromised the Baptist understanding of justification.

The second phase of salvation, sanctification, has sometimes been neglected in Baptist theology in comparison with regeneration. Baptists, however, have had strong interests in Christian education, discipleship, and moral concerns that are related to sanctification. The SBC's pamphlet from 1964, *Baptist Ideals*, includes "Salvation by Grace" as the first topic under the heading, "The Christian Life." Other topics in that section, all related to sanctification, are discipleship, the priesthood of believers, the home, and citizenship.[23]

Sanctification involves striving for "moral and spiritual perfection." The SBC's confession, however, does not advocate the possibility of sinless perfection in this life. Perfection is only achieved at glorification, the final stage of salvation. Baptists generally are closer to Luther's emphasis on the Christian life: *simul justus et peccator*. Christians can and do occasionally sin, but they should strive for the ideal of perfection. The discussion of perseverance in the article on "God's Purpose of Grace" suggests that believers may "fall into sin," but that they will persevere unto the end: "All true believers endure to the end."[24]

One of the striking phrases in the article on "Salvation" is "redemption of the whole man" in the article's first sentence. Although that phrase seems to promise a holistic notion of salvation and its consequences, the article highlights the spiritual or vertical dimensions of salvation. Salvation results in "a change of heart" and "a relationship of peace and favor with God." No attention is paid at this point to the impact of salvation on one's relations with other people or the natural world. In a later article, "Evangelism and Missions," the *BFM (1963)* declares that the new birth "means the birth of love for others." The article on "The Christian and the Social Order" also notes that the transformation of society is "rooted in the regeneration of the individual by the saving grace of God in Christ Jesus."[25] Baptists in the SBC, only in recent years, have gained a deeper interest in the consequences of sin and salvation for the natural world.

Another neglected aspect of this salvation of "the whole man" is any interaction with the charismatic view that Jesus saves us from sin and sickness. Although Baptists generally believe in the possibility of miracles and divine healing today, the article on "Salvation" does not suggest that Jesus liberates humans automatically from physical disease. Texts such as Matthew 8:17 (quoting Isaiah 53:4) have been cited by some charismatics as support for the elimination of sin and sickness through salvation.[26] The *BFM (1925)* added the phrases, "and every other needed blessing" along with "peace and favor with God," to its description of the benefits of justification.[27] The *BFM (1963)* highlights the spiritual dimensions of salvation and ignores or implicitly rejects other dimensions of salvation.

One issue that is introduced briefly in the *BFM (1963)* has become a major topic in recent evangelical discussions. The Lordship of Christ is basic to Baptist theology, but the "Lordship Salvation" controversy has surfaced with new urgency in recent years. According to the *BFM 1963)*, becoming a Christian involves accepting "Jesus Christ as Lord and Saviour." The first stage of salvation involves the "commitment of the entire personality to Him as Lord and Saviour."[28] The general principle of the Lordship of Christ is explicit several times in the rest of the document. For example, Jesus is the "criterion by which the Bible is to be interpreted."[29] Church government is also guided by the Lordship of Christ. This emphasis on the Lordship of Christ has been a frequent theme in Baptist life. George Truett once said that, for Baptists, the absolute Lordship of Christ is "the dominant fact in all their Christian experience, the nerve center of all their Christian life, the bedrock of all their church polity, the sheet anchor of all their hopes, the climax and crown of all their rejoicings."[30]

The Lordship-Salvation controversy focuses on the question, "Can you accept Jesus as Saviour without accepting him as Lord?"[31] Some theologians answer "Yes," arguing that linking salvation and Lordship borders on a new legalism. Most Baptists in the SBC seem closer to the view that accepting Jesus as Lord of all of life is essential to an informed decision for Christ as Savior.

Historically, one of the most problematic issues for Baptists has been election or predestination. Both Calvinist and Arminian themes appear in Baptist history. Although some observers see a decline in Calvinist influence on the SBC in recent decades, others see a resurgence of Calvinism.[32] The *BFM's* article on "God's Purpose of Grace" handles the issue of election judiciously. Salvation is ultimately the work of God, but that divine initiative is compatible with human freedom and the use of "means." One practical result of election is that salvation "excludes boasting and promotes humility."[33]

The article on the doctrine of election does not explicitly promote double-predestination or extreme Calvinism. The article on "The Freeness of Salvation" in the *BFM (1925)*, which sounds more Arminian, was not incorporated into the *BFM (1963)*. The *BFM (1925)* insists that "[t]he blessings of salvation are made free to all by the Gospel. . . . Nothing prevents the salvation of the greatest sinner except his own voluntary refusal to accept Jesus Christ as teacher, Saviour, and Lord."[34] The SBC's *Baptist Ideals* says that "Christ died for all men," suggesting support for general atonement rather than limited atonement. That document adds that "God is graciously disposed toward all men in spite of their moral corruption and spiritual rebellion."[35]

Baptists in the SBC, like other evangelicals, often debate the issues of general and limited atonement and divine sovereignty and human freedom. The *BFM (1963)* does not totally ignore these issues, but it supplies some general affirmations that are acceptable to a wide range of interpretations.

The Baptist understanding of salvation impacts the concept of the ordinances, especially the ordinance of baptism. The article on "Baptism and Lord's Supper" stresses that baptism is "an act of obedience symbolizing the believer's faith in a crucified, buried, and risen Saviour, the believer's death to sin, the burial of the old life, and the resurrection to walk in newness of life in Christ Jesus."[36] Views such as the baptism of infants and baptismal regeneration are clearly eliminated by this statement. Methods such as aspersion and affusion are also rejected in the article by the affirmation of immersion. Believer's baptism and a regenerate church membership have been hallmarks of the Baptist heritage and are assumed rather than argued in the *BFM (1963)*.[37]

Another major component of the christology of the *BFM (1963)* is its treatment of eschatology. The return of Christ will usher in the consummation of the kingdom of God. The article on "Last Things" focuses on a few basic events, such as the resurrection of the dead and final judgment, rather than developing a detailed chronology. Baptists in the SBC have advocated all of the major millennial schemes in their history, and the *BFM (1963)* does not explicitly endorse or critique any of these millennial views. Writers of curriculum material for the Baptist Sunday School Board are regularly instructed on how to handle sensitive eschatological issues. Broadman Press also has published major commentaries on Revelation from dispensational, historic premillennial, and amillennial perspectives.

One of the obvious consequences of the strong statements on christology and soteriology in the *BFM (1963)* is an emphasis on evangelism and missions. The increasing pluralism in American society has prompted renewed discussion of the issue of salvation in many denominations. Baptists such as Clark Pinnock have encouraged a wider hope for the salvation of the unevangelized, those who have never heard the gospel.[38] Baptists of the SBC have passed two resolutions in recent years that reaffirm an exclusivistic understanding of salvation. In 1988, messengers approved the resolution, "On the Necessity of Salvation." The resolution responded to those who argue for "a plurality of mediators," universalists, those who believe salvation is based on good works, and those who deny the reality of hell. The resolution reaffirmed the article of the *BFM (1963)* on salvation, quoting the fourth article, section (A) in particular.[39]

In 1993, the messengers adopted a resolution on "The Finality of Jesus Christ as Sole and Sufficient Savior." Although the *BFM (1925)* was not cited, the phrase "all-sufficient Saviour" is used twice in that document.[40] The SBC's resolution in 1993 rejected "universalism, radical pluralism, theological inclusivism, and religious relativism, all of which call into question the clear teaching of Holy Scripture and historic Baptist belief in the particularity and finality of the revelation and salvific work of Jesus Christ. . . ."[41]

The exclusivistic language of the two resolutions mentioned previously reflects the SBC's concern to maintain an emphasis on the need for a personal relationship with Jesus. Views such as universalism are clearly rejected. The resolutions, however, do not address some of the troublesome issues related to salvation. For example, the eternal destiny of infants is not dealt with explicitly in the *BFM (1963)*. Salvation is a necessity because all humans are sinners. The status of infants and young children, however, is often treated with the notion of the age of accountability, a term not found in the *BFM (1963)*. The confession's article on "Man" indicates that "his posterity inherits a nature and an environment inclined toward sin and as soon as they are capable of moral action become transgressors and are under condemnation."[42] Many Baptists believe that infants who die are accepted into heaven, yet they had no opportunity to establish an informed, personal relationship with Jesus. The same condition might apply to those with severe mental limitations.[43]

Both of these resolutions are concerned to encourage vigorous evangelistic and missionary activity. Any deviation from an exclusivistic understanding of christology and soteriology is seen as an undermining of the traditional Baptist emphasis on evangelism and missions.

Interpreting and evaluating a confessional statement is difficult, even when one does not try to read the minds of the original authors. In its articles on christology and soteriology, the *BFM (1963)* highlights some traditional Baptist affirmations. The document does not explicitly reject alternative views, letting the positive statements provide the focus. Some early creeds, such as the declaration of the council of Chalcedon in 451 A.D., carefully balanced affirmations and denials. The *BFM (1963)*, however, does not explicitly deal with traditional heresies such as Nestorianism or Arianism.

The *BFM (1963)* also neglects some issues important to a full-blown christology. The earthly ministry of Jesus is deemphasized, except for the significant article on the kingdom of God, which treats a major theme in Jesus' teaching. The neglect of Jesus' miracles, or of miracles in any article, is surprising in light of the strong stress on the supernatural elements of Christianity in the Preamble. The question of Jesus' descent into hell was included in some of the early creeds, but it is omitted in the *BFM (1963)*.

That the *BFM (1963)* ignores some issues could be explained in a number ways, besides the obvious brevity of the document. One explanation is that these issues are not essential to orthodoxy. As long as a Baptist affirms the basics, such as the deity and humanity of Jesus and the necessity of salvation, these other issues, such as Jesus' descent into hell, can be ignored. Another explanation is that these omissions are acknowledgments of diverse opinions among Baptists in the SBC on these issues. The article on "Last Things," for example, does not specify any millennial scheme for Baptists. Baptists have in fact held all of the major views on the millennium and the tribulation.

The christology of the confession is properly placed in the context of the article on the Trinity. The document avoids any hint of subordinationism of the Son, common in early heresies. The *BFM (1963)*, nevertheless, might be criticized by some for being too preoccupied with the Son. Father and Spirit are clearly affirmed in the article on the doctrine of God, but the references to Jesus dominate the rest of the document. Baptists may not be in danger of a unitarianism of the second person, but their interests clearly lie in the revelation and activity of God in the Son.

The confession has a stronger interest in soteriology than in christology in the narrow sense of the person of Christ. Knowing about Jesus is not enough; sinners need personal relationships with Jesus. Most of the document's attention is focused, however, on the first stage of salvation. In interpreting the beginning of salvation, the authors drew from Paul's analysis more than Jesus' own way of describing his followers. Following Jesus, or discipleship, is not the primary way that the *BFM (1963)* describes salvation.

Sanctification and glorification are mentioned briefly, but these topics are relatively undeveloped in the confession. The minimal attention to sanctification is surprising in light of the strong emphasis in Baptist life on the Lordship of Christ. Baptists have been accused of paying more attention to the prenatal care of Christians than to their postnatal care. The emergence of the Lordship-Salvation controversy partially is due to a renewed concern with expressing the Lordship of Christ throughout the Christian's experience.

Baptists will continue to debate the exclusivism of salvation. The popularity of evangelical writers, such as Clark Pinnock, will likely trigger ongoing discussions about the salvation of the unevangelized. The traditional doctrine of the age of accountability will probably undergo further study. The age of accountability seems to imply that someone can reach heaven without a full knowledge of Jesus. Baptists will need to clarify how the status of an unevangelized adult differs from the status of an infant.

Confessions of faith are "only guides in interpretation, having no authority over the conscience," according to the Preamble. The *BFM (1963)* presents a valuable summary of the major affirmations of faith held by Baptists. This confession's sections on christology and soteriology deserve serious attention by Baptists.

Notes

[1] *The Baptist Faith and Message* (Nashville: Sunday School Board of the Southern Baptist Convention, 1963) 5; also, see "Committee on Baptist Faith and Message," in *Annual of the Southern Baptist Convention: One Hundred Sixth Session in Kansas City, Missouri, 7-10 May 1963*, by the Executive Committee, Southern Baptist Convention (Nashville: Southern Baptist Convention, 1963) 270 (hereafter, cited as *BFM [1963]*). Other quotations from this confession will be given in the text by identifying the article as well.

[2] *Baptist Faith and Message*, 8 (article 2, section B); also, *BFM (1963)* 271.

[3] "Statement of Faith, Foreign Mission Board, SBC, 1920," in *A Sourcebook for Baptist Heritage*, ed. H. Leon McBeth (Nashville: Broadman Press, 1990) 485; originally as, "A Statement of Belief," from "Appendix A: Seventy-Fifth Annual Report of the Foreign Mission Board," in *Annual of the Southern Baptist Convention: Sixty-Fifth Session in Washington, D. C., 12-17 May 1920*, ed. Secretaries, Southern Baptist Convention (Nashville: Marshall and Bruce, 1920) 197.

[4] *Baptist Faith and Message*, 8-9 (article 2, section B); *BFM (1963)* 271.

[5] *Baptist Faith and Message*, 14, 16, 17 (articles 9, 12, 14); *BFM (1963)* 276, 278, 279.

[6] For examples, see Bert Dominy, *God's Work of Salvation*, Layman's Library of Christian Doctrine (Nashville: Broadman Press, 1986) 67, 155; John Newport, *What Is Christian Doctrine?* Layman's Library of Christian Doctrine (Nashville: Broadman Press, 1984) 34-42.

[7] *Baptist Faith and Message*, 14 (article 9); *BFM (1963)* 276.

[8] Paul Basden, "Introduction," in *Has Our Theology Changed? Southern Baptist Thought Since 1845*, ed. Paul Basden (Nashville: Broadman and Holman, 1994) 3.

[9] For a brief discussion of the cosmic Christ, see William L. Hendricks, *Who Is Jesus Christ?* Layman's Library of Christian Doctrine (Nashville: Broadman Press, 1985) 63-64.

[10] See, for example, Steven Bouma-Prediger, *The Greening of Theology: The Ecological Models of Rosemary Radford Ruether, Joseph Sittler, and Jürgen Moltmann* (Atlanta: Scholars Press, 1995).

[11] "Report of Committee on Baptist Faith and Message," in *Annual of the Southern Baptist Convention: Seventieth Session in Memphis, Tennessee, 13-17 May 1925*, ed. Secretaries, Southern Baptist Convention (Nashville: Marshall

and Bruce, 1925) 72 (article 8) (hereafter, cited as *BFM [1925]*); cf. *BFM (1963)* 273 (article 4, section 1); also in McBeth, *Sourcebook for Baptist Heritage*, 510.

[12]*BFM (1963)* 269, 271 (Preamble, article 2, section 2).

[13]*BFM (1963)* 271, 273 (articles 2.2, 3, 4).

[14]Walter D. Draughon III, "Atonement," in *Has Our Theology Changed?* 96-110.

[15]Fisher Humphreys, *The Death of Christ* (Nashville: Broadman Press, 1978) 116-35.

[16]See the *BFM (1963)* 271, 273-274 (articles 2.2, 4).

[17]William E. Hull, *The Christian Experience of Salvation*, Layman's Library of Christian Doctrine (Nashville: Broadman Press, 1987) 101-109.

[18]Jaroslav Pelikan, *Jesus Through the Centuries* (New Haven: Yale University Press, 1985) 206-19.

[19]*BFM (1963)* 273-75 (articles 4 and 5).

[20]As examples, see Dominy, God's Work of Salvation; 120-24; and Hull, Christian Experience of Salvation, 12-15.

[21]For a recent discussion, see Stanley J. Grenz, *Theology for the Community of God* (Nashville: Broadman and Holman, 1994) 594-99.

[22]See the following: "Evangelicals and Catholics Together: The Christian Mission in the Third Millennium," *First Things* no. 43 (May 1994): 15-22; "Resolution No. 5–On Southern Baptists and Roman Catholics," in *Annual of the Southern Baptist Convention: One Hundred Thirty-Seventh Session in Orlando, Florida, 14-16 June 1994*, ed. the Executive Committee, Southern Baptist Convention (Nashville: Southern Baptist Convention, 1994) 107.

[23]*Baptist Ideals* (Nashville: Sunday School Board of the Southern Baptist Convention, 1964) 5-8.

[24]*BFM (1963)* 275 (article 5, ¶ 2).

[25]*BFM (1963)* 273, 278, 280 (articles 4, 11, 15).

[26]For a clear treatment of this issue, see Millard J. Erickson, *Christian Theology* (Grand Rapids: Baker Book House, 1984) 2:836-41.

[27]*BFM (1925)* 72 (article 5); McBeth, *Sourcebook for Baptist Heritage*, 509.

[28]*BFM (1963)* 273 (article 4, section 1, ¶ 2).

[29]*BFM (1963)* 270 (article 1).

[30]George W. Truett, *Baptists and Religious Liberty* (Nashville: Sunday School Board of the Southern Baptist Convention, 1920) 10; also in McBeth, *Sourcebook for Baptist Heritage*, 470.

[31]For a helpful overview of the discussion, see Millard J. Erickson, "Lordship Theology: The Current Controversy," *Southwestern Journal of Theology* 33 (Spring 1991): 5-15.

[32]See the following perspectives: Paul Basden, "Predestination," in *Has Our Theology Changed?* 68-72; and Jesse C. Fletcher, *The Southern Baptist Convention: A Sesquicentennial History* (Nashville: Broadman and Holman, 1994) 372-74.

[33]*BFM (1963)* 275 (article 5, ¶1).

[34]*BFM (1925)* 72 (article 6); also in McBeth, *Sourcebook for Baptist Heritage*, 509.

[35]*Baptist Ideals*, 4-5.

[36]*BFM (1963)* 276 (article 7, ¶ 1).

[37]See Warren McWilliams, "The Church Seeks to Be Regenerate," in *Defining Baptist Convictions: Guidelines for the Twenty-First Century*, ed. Charles W. Deweese (Franklin TN: Providence House, 1996) 121-29.

[38]See, for example, Clark H. Pinnock, *A Wideness in God's Mercy: The Finality of Jesus Christ in a World of Religions* (Grand Rapids: Zondervan, 1992); and Henry N. Smith, "Salvation in the Face of Many Faiths: Toward a Hermeneutic of Optimism," *Southwestern Journal of Theology* 35 (Spring 1993): 26-31.

[39]"Resolution No. 3–On the Necessity of Salvation," in *Annual of the Southern Baptist Convention: One Hundred Thirty-First Session in San Antonio, Texas, 14-16 June 1988*, ed. the Executive Committee, Southern Baptist Convention (Nashville: Southern Baptist Convention, 1988) 67-68 ("Proceedings," Wednesday Morning, June 15, Item 170); see *Baptist Faith and Message*, 11; *BFM (1963)* 273.

[40]*BFM (1925)* 72 (articles 4 and 8); also in McBeth, *Sourcebook for Baptist Heritage*, 508, 510.

[41]"Resolution No. 1–The Finality of Jesus Christ as Sole and Sufficient Savior," in *Annual of the Southern Baptist Convention: One Hundred Thirty-Sixth Session in Houston, Texas, 15-17 June 1993*, ed. the Executive Committee, Southern Baptist Convention (Nashville: Southern Baptist Convention, 1993) 94 ("Proceedings," Wednesday Morning, June 16, Item 141).

[42]*BFM (1963)* 273 (article 3).

[43]For good discussions, see William L. Hendricks, *A Theology for Children* (Nashville: Broadman Press, 1980) 238-51; John Sanders, *No Other Name: An Investigation into the Destiny of the Unevangelized* (Grand Rapids: Eerdmans, 1992) 287-305.

Chapter 5

Mirror of Doctrine
Personal Morality and Social Ethics in
The Baptist Faith and Message (1963)

N. Larry Baker

Introduction

The confession of faith that stands among Baptists of the Southern Baptist Convention (SBC) as the touchstone for doctrine has much to say about the moral life of believers as well. The *Baptist Faith and Message* of 1963 (*BFM [1963]*) weaves belief and behavior together in a single document.[1] Framers of the confession knew that beliefs matter, because life must have foundations and beliefs shape lives. The authors, however, also knew that correct doctrine is no substitute for Godlike living.

The *BFM (1963)* opens with an article on the Bible and anchors each of its seventeen articles with biblical references. Neither an insistent claim to be biblical nor verses pulled out of the Bible as prooftexts, however, can make a position biblical. In order to be biblical, the confession of faith must accord with the biblical message.

Measure the vision of the Christian life in the *BFM (1963)*, and its biblical birthright becomes clear. The starting point and the underlying assumption of the *BFM (1963)* are biblical. The *BFM (1963)*, like biblical religion, links God and self and neighbor. The document from 1963 expresses the message that personal faith cannot be private. Important as it is to have a firsthand relationship with God, both biblical religion and the *BFM (1963)* declare that true faith is not a religion of two.

The message of the *BFM (1963)* is clear: To be valid, Christian piety must be put into practice and connect with life. Here the confession is true to Old and New Testaments alike.

Baptists in the SBC have kept this confessional statement at the center of the denomination's doctrinal debate for more than three decades. Nevertheless, Baptists in the SBC have focused their attention primarily on the first article, "The Scriptures." They have given scant attention to the moral and ethical vision embodied in the document. The following paragraphs will address the neglected understanding of the Christian moral life embodied in the *BFM (1963)*.

I. Confessional Heritage

Baptists were little more than three centuries old, and the SBC only eight decades old, when the latter body adopted its first confessional statement. Thus, Baptists of the SBC had neither a long confessional history nor a great number of statements that shaped their life. Nevertheless, in the

United States, two confessions, the *Philadelphia Confession* of 1742 (*PC [1742]*) and the *New Hampshire Confession* of 1833 (*NHC [1833]*), shaped Baptist life. The second confession fed directly into the *BFM (1963)*.[2]

James Carter and Walter Shurden chronicle both the SBC's confessional history and responses to the concept of confessionalism as well as to particular documents.[3] Three facts are clear. (1) The SBC was organized in 1845 without a doctrinal statement. As the founders declared, "[w]e have constructed for our basis no new creed, acting in this matter upon a Baptist aversion for all creeds but the Bible."[4] (2) The SBC worked and expanded its work for eighty years without a confessional statement. (3) Nevertheless, during the decade preceding adoption of the *Baptist Faith and Message* in 1925 (*BFM [1925]*), Baptists of the SBC drafted, adopted, and circulated several documents that were confessional in nature.[5] These documents subsequently shaped the approach, content, and emphases of the *BFM (1925)*.

Eight documents comprise the soil that produced both the *BFM (1925)* and the *BFM (1963)*. Three documents served as forerunners for the *BFM (1925)*. In 1914, the SBC adopted its first confession of faith, the *Pronouncement on Christian Union and Denominational Efficiency*.[6] The fifth and final article of that document concerned the separation of church and state, declaring that "Soul freedom and civil liberty are twin blossoms on the stalk of Christian faith."[7] The article also expressed the willingness of Baptists in the SBC to cooperate in moral, civic, and social movements.

The *Fraternal Address of Southern Baptists* followed in 1920 as a second forerunner to the *BFM (1925)*.[8] The document included eight doctrinal statements, called "the fundamentals of our faith and the peculiar beliefs and observances that characterize us." The summary statement concerning the Bible declared that "the Scriptures are the sufficient, certain, and authoritative revelation of God in all matters of faith and practice, and that obedience to their teachings is binding upon all men." The article on the atonement stated that Christ "redeems [men] unto God and righteousness." Similar to the earlier document, this one defined religious freedom as one of "the inalienable rights of men" and claimed that "all religious denominations should stand on an equality before the civil power."[9]

In response to doctrinal agitation, the Foreign Mission Board of the SBC adopted a doctrinal statement in 1920 to guide its mission appointees.[10] Though brief, the confession was fairly complete. It did not, however, follow the *NHC (1833)*. The document contained thirteen affirmations, including one on civil government: "[I believe] That civil government being ordained of God, due obedience and subjection should be rendered to the government under which I may live and that prayers should be offered for rulers; but that God alone is Lord of the conscience and He has left the soul free to worship after its own dictates."[11]

In 1923, the SBC adopted another document, *Science and Religion*, as its response to intense sentiment against evolution. The statement was originally the concluding section from the presidential address of E. Y. Mullins. The SBC adopted the statement as the Convention's position on evolution.[12]

Moreover, some of the themes embodied in the *BFM (1963)* are evident in the writings of E. Y. Mullins.[13] The *NHC (1833)*, for example, did not include an article dealing with Christian responsibility in the social order; the *BFM (1925)*, however, did include such an article, as did Mullins's "Social Axiom."

Between the adoption of the *BFM (1925)* and the adoption of its revision in 1963, four additional documents entered the SBC's life: (1) the *Report on Interdenominational Relations* of 1938; (2) *A Pronouncement upon Religious Liberty* of 1939; (3) the *Reply to World Council of Churches* of 1940; and (4) the *Statement of Principles* of 1945 and 1946.[14] The fourth document resulted from the presidential address of W. W. Hamilton and the report of the Social Service Commission in 1942. Themes common to both the *BFM (1925)* and the *BFM (1963)* ran throughout the document.

One additional document, *Baptist Ideals* of 1964, articulated much of the understanding of Christian life in the *BFM (1963)*.[15] The statement from 1964 was prepared for the celebration of the 150th anniversary of the organization of the first national Baptist body in the United States. It was prepared by a committee chaired by Ralph A. Herring, pastor of the First Baptist Church of Winston-Salem, North Carolina, and eighteen leaders and scholars of the SBC. The document described the Baptist concepts of religious authority, the individual, the Christian life, and the church. The document concluded with a section entitled, "Our Continuing Task." As James E. Carter notes, however, "[t]hough a rather comprehensive statement the Baptist Ideals were never presented to the Southern Baptist Convention nor adopted by it."[16]

II. The Vision-Statements

The moral and ethical themes contained in the SBC's confessional heritage can be seen throughout the *BFM (1963)*.[17] James Carter classified the articles into two types: "theological" and "methodological."[18] One finds ethical content in both types. Three of the "methodological" articles deal specifically with moral and social issues: "The Christian and the Social Order," "Peace and War," and "Religious Liberty."[19] Five of the document's "theological" articles contain themes or emphases that are foundational for the moral vision of the confession. Three articles provide key insights: "Man," "Salvation" (specifically, its second section on sanctification), and "Kingdom of God."[20] Additionally, two of the document's articles, "The Scriptures" and "God" (specifically the third section, "God the Holy Spirit"), contain affirmations central to an understanding of the document's vision of the moral life.[21] Four other "methodological" articles also offer some insight into the moral vision of the *BFM (1963)*: "The Lord's Day," "Evangelism and Missions," "Stewardship," and "Cooperation."[22] These articles contain statements and emphases that one must examine in order to delineate the moral and ethical vision of this confession of faith. Thus, fifteen of the confession's articles, the lion's share of the document, contain grist for the ethicist's mill.

Two different ways of developing an ethic are included in the one document. In one approach, the basic ethic (either biblical or theological) is articulated first. Then, it is followed by the applied ethic. This pattern marked much of the work of T. B. Maston, C. W. Scudder, William M. Pinson, Jr., and Henlee Barnette during earlier years. In the second approach, the applied ethic is woven into the theology and is integral to it. In this approach, a writer begins with a doctrine such as "The Christian Understanding of Man" and articulates an ethic that grows from it. The work of Karl Barth and many continental treatments of ethics exemplify this methodology.

III. The Moral and Ethical Vision

How, then, does the *BFM (1963)* understand Christian moral life? How does it describe personal morality and social ethics? What is its moral, social, economic, political, and cultural vision?

One might formulate responses to those questions in varied ways. As one approach to the task, an ethicist might analyze, exegete, and interpret each of the fifteen pertinent articles of the confession. As another approach to the task, an ethicist might delineate and characterize and, thereby, articulate an overview of ethical perspectives contained in the document. Each of the approaches has its merits, but I have adopted the latter approach.

First, the moral and ethical vision of the *BFM (1963)* anchors moral life in a trinitarian God who is moral and calls and empowers people to live Godlike lives.

Second, the *BFM (1963)* articulates an ethic for the redeemed.

Third, the *BFM (1963)* identifies resources that faith gives to believers, to enable them to live the Christian life, especially the Bible and the Holy Spirit.

Fourth, the *BFM (1963)* contains an ethic that is both personal and social. The confession primarily emphasizes action in the social order, applications of the law of love, actions concerning peace and war, the defense and pursuit of religious liberty, and behaviors related to "the Lord's Day." The document also references Christian character, moral and spiritual perfection, love for others, and loyalty to Christ. These emphases, however, are far less prominent and receive far less attention than the social ethic. Thus, the *BFM (1963)* focuses attention on that which the believer *ought to do* or on actions, more than on character or the kind of person the believer *is to be*.

Fifth, the *BFM (1963)* casts a vision of the moral life, without articulating a large number of specific actions designed to implement that life. The *BFM (1963)* identifies some areas of life that call for attention and action, but generally does not set forth strategies or action-plans. When the confession deals with "the Lord's Day," nevertheless, it does specify actions, both negative and positive. In this article, believers are told to refrain from certain activities and are instructed to use the day for certain activities and purposes.

Sixth, the moral and ethical vision of the *BFM (1963)* embodies an approach to the moral life that is primarily deontological, although it does include some teleological themes. Behavior, in terms of ethics, may be described as either rule-formulated (deontology) or goal-formulated (teleology). Both rules and goals are found in the Bible, and both are found in the Old and New Testaments. Each approach calls for a particular kind of response. Deontological formulations call for obedience and are permeated with the language of "should" and "ought." Teleological formulations, on the other hand, call for reaching the goal that is set out or called for, and are permeated with images such as "the chief end of man" and "pressing toward the mark." In the *BFM (1963)*, the article on the social order contains six sentences, with the word "should" as central to four of them. No less than eight of the articles include words such as "duty," "ought," and "should," or point to command, spiritual necessity, obedience, and obligation. Teleological language is also included, but much less frequently, and with much less prominence. The article on "Man," for example, speaks of "fulfill[ing] the creative purpose of God." The paragraph on "Sanctification" talks about "progress toward moral and spiritual perfection."

Seventh, the *BFM (1963)* presents a vision of the ethical agent that includes the divine origin of humankind, a realistic assessment of human fallenness, and a hopeful understanding of human potential through the grace and power of God.

Eighth, the moral and ethical vision of the *BFM (1963)* presents a separationist view of the church and its relationship to the world, but includes some transformationist perspectives.[23] The first model emphasizes both the necessity that the Christian live by the Kingdom of God quite apart from an involvement in the world and the believer's ability to do so. The second model believes that the structures of life can be converted and changed. The *BFM (1963)* incorporates emphases from both models, perhaps because Anabaptist and Calvinist theologians alike have shaped Baptists.

Ninth, the moral and ethical vision of the *BFM (1963)* contains a realistic understanding of the Christian's moral task, as well as a sober analysis of the world in which that task is to be enacted. Here is the task: to "seek to make the will of Christ supreme in his [the Christian's] own life and in human society." Here is the realism: a world marked by greed, selfishness, and vice; a world populated with the orphaned, the needy, the aged, the helpless, and the sick; a world in which industry, government, and society as a whole are not yet under the sway of righteousness, truth, or brotherly love; a world in which the spirit of war prevails and the spirit of peace languishes; a world in which government seeks to play the role of God, and the church is tempted to use the power of the state to do the works of God.

Tenth, the moral and ethical vision of the *BFM (1963)* incorporates emphases that belong to "basic" ethics and topics that belong to "applied" ethics.

Eleventh, the moral and ethical vision of the *BFM (1963)* demonstrates that the faith and message that belong to Baptists are ethical as well as doctrinal.

IV. Influence of the Vision

The *BFM (1963)* has now been part of the SBC's life for more than three decades. "It is clear that [it] has been used more extensively than the older statement."[24] The document from 1963 has been widely distributed as "information for the churches" and has been printed frequently in pamphlets, annuals, and literature. The SBC's institutions, agencies, and publications as well as state conventions have used the confession as "guidelines" for their work.

Nevertheless, one cannot discover clear evidence for the influence or impact of the moral and ethical vision of the *BFM (1963)* among Baptists of the SBC. One can see evidence, however, that certain ethical content and concerns found in the confession of faith are expressed widely throughout the SBC's life. The common life of Baptists in the SBC, in some respects, parallels their common statement of faith.

No extended discussion of the ethical content of the confession exists. Herschel Hobbs wrote a small commentary on the *BFM (1963)* but allotted less than three pages to "The Christian and the Social Order," less than five pages to "Peace and War," and less than four pages to "Religious Liberty."[25] Hobbs's treatments of ethics in the document were cursory, at best, and hardly influential in the common life of Baptists.

The Sunday School Board of the SBC plans and promotes a "Doctrinal Study Week" each year, often with the topic derived directly from the *BFM (1963)*. The study has centered, however, on neither the moral and ethical vision of the confession nor the articles that deal with the social order, peace and war, and religious liberty.

The SBC has adopted numerous resolutions concerning moral issues during the national conventions. Yet, those resolutions do not anchor their "Wherefores" and "Be It Therefore Resolveds" in the *BFM (1963)*.

The SBC has an agency for moral and social concern, the Christian Life Commission. Nonetheless, that agency was birthed out of concerns and commitments that predated the *BFM (1963)*.[26] For more than a half century, the Convention funded and participated in the Baptist Joint Committee on Public Affairs, a multidenominational group committed to religious freedom and separation of church and state; that organization, however, was also born from forces other than the *BFM (1963)*.

The SBC's Home Mission Board (HMB) has a Department of Christian Social Ministries, itself the result of a concern expressed in the fifteenth article of the *BFM (1963)*.[27] The HMB, however, established the department in response to mission-initiatives, rather than in response to the presence or power of the confession of faith.

All six Convention-sponsored seminaries have departments of ethics and professors; in some instances, those seminaries offer advanced work in the discipline. The presence of these departments, however, is to be attributed to influences other than the *BFM (1963)*.

Baptists of the SBC, within the geographical boundaries of state conventions, often participate in cooperative efforts that address moral and social issues. For example, Baptists are often active in groups such as Texas Alcohol and Narcotics Education, Inc., the Louisiana Moral and Civic Foundation, or the Christian Civic Foundation of Missouri. These groups, however, came into existence beyond the influence of the *BFM (1963)*. Furthermore, Baptists tend to take part in them for pragmatic and immediate reasons.

Thus, the SBC's one major confession of faith is largely a document unknown, a call unheard, a resource unused, a guideline unfollowed, a vision unheeded. In terms of its view of the moral life, the *BFM (1963)* is a confession of faith that Baptists in the SBC may know by name, but not necessarily in terms of its message.

V. Assessing the Moral and Ethical Vision

Like all human documents, the *BFM (1963)* has its limitations, its strengths, and its weaknesses. Assessment of the document can help Baptists in the 1990s find strength and direction for the Christian moral life and the moral action of churches alike.

A. Strengths of the *BFM (1963)*

First, the *BFM (1963)* reminds believers that concern for behavior is integral to the faith of the church. In a world where "anything goes" is often the rule of life, this confession of faith reminds Baptists that behavior is the concern of the Lord of life and the Lord of the church. During a time when the Christian life is often understood in terms of "the deeper life," emotional religious experiences, religious self-actualization, or psychological well-being, this confession of faith calls believers to behave in ways that are consistent with the New Testament and its Lord. This confession of faith calls Christians, individually and corporately, to take the *doing* of life as seriously as they take the doctrine of the church.

Second, the *BFM (1963)* reminds believers that they may not legitimately limit the responsibility and work of the church only to evangelism and missions. It calls believers to engage in social action as well as in evangelism and missions. In a time when "church growth," largely understood as numerical, is touted as the chief, if not the only, purpose of the church, the *BFM (1963)* calls God's people to engagement with the evils of society, ministry to the hurts of humankind, and the pursuit of personal and social righteousness.

Third, the *BFM (1963)* anchors moral life and action in one's relationship to God and the truth of Christian scriptures. Clearly, one may anchor values in many authorities or philosophies, but the *BFM (1963)* calls Christians to anchor values and actions in a personal relationship with God and response to the truth of the Bible.

Fourth, the *BFM (1963)* puts believers in touch with the ethical heritage and history of the people called "Baptist," especially Baptists of the SBC. People living with eyes set only on "now" and/or "tomorrow" can lose touch easily with their history, can lose sight of those factors that create their uniqueness, and can become something other than the people God called them to be. The *BFM (1963)* engages its readers with a legacy rich, powerful, and unique in many respects, and it can renew and reinvigorate all who take it seriously.

B. Weaknesses of the *BFM (1963)*

Nevertheless, the *BFM (1963)* is a human formulation and has weaknesses as well as strengths. It reflects the time and social setting of its framers. The document expresses the less-than-perfect vision of the *men* who drafted it. It deals inadequately with some of the issues it addresses. It does not treat topics that press for attention in the 1990s. The moral and ethical vision of the Baptist Faith and Message is inadequate in several ways.

First, it does not embody a clearly systematic treatment of the Christian moral life.

Second, it does not speak of the role of the church in moral formation or in social action.

Third, the document focuses on what one ought to do more than what kind of person God wants one to be. Those concerned with character, character-formation, and character-education find little substantive help in the *BFM (1963)*.

Fourth, the document has the imprint of a much simpler time and a less complex social order than Christian experience at century's end.

Fifth, the confession of faith seems to assume that Christians "know" right and wrong in most instances. Thus, the *BFM (1963)* leaves them with limited help or with no assistance whatsoever.

Sixth, both the confession's heavy emphasis on duty and its inadequate development of teleological emphases are liabilities in *The Sibling Society*, in which all vertical authorities are either suspect or rejected.[28]

VI. Scoring Baptists' Practice of the Moral Vision

Because Baptists in the SBC have accorded the *BFM (1963)* a central place in their common life, one is entitled to assess, as much as is humanly possible, the degree to which Baptists practice what they profess to be important. Were one recording scores, the results would be mixed.

Baptists in the SBC have been uneven in their implementation of the agenda set forth in the confession's fifteenth article, "The Christian and the Social Order." For example, Baptists have worked in behalf of "the orphaned, the needy, the aged, the helpless, and the sick" with a significant measure of faithfulness. Baptists have not sought, with intensity or intentionality, however, to "bring industry, government, and society as a whole under the sway of the principles of righteousness, truth, and brotherly love."[29] Likewise, the document's tenth article, "The Kingdom," declares that "Christians ought to pray and to labor that the Kingdom may come and God's will be done on earth." A survey of Baptist life, however, suggests little focused labor in behalf of the Kingdom where justice, peace, and righteousness prevail; little intentional pursuit of the heavenly Kingdom come on earth. Furthermore, Baptists have been slow to work cooperatively with others in the pursuit of civic righteousness or social concerns.

Likewise, the SBC's record in racial relations is checkered.[30] The confession's statement on "Man" powerfully declares both "the sacredness of human personality" and that "every man possesses dignity and is worthy of respect and Christian love." The SBC has spoken more than once on the issue of race. The SBC was the first major denomination in the United States to affirm the Supreme Court's decision in 1954 on school desegregation. In 1968, the Convention adopted "A Statement Concerning the Crisis in Our Nation," perhaps its most powerful, courageous, and prophetic statement.[31] The Convention has implemented its concern for race relations through the work of the Christian Life Commission, the Home Mission Board, and the American Baptist Seminary. Throughout their tenure, Foy Valentine at the Christian Life Commission and Arthur Rutledge at the Home Mission Board provided consistent, visionary, and courageous leadership in racial relations. Yet, racism continues to thrive among Baptists of the SBC, as long as many individuals and churches resist racial reconciliation and efforts in behalf of racial equity in the United States.

Along the same lines, the *BFM (1963)* states that "[i]t is the *duty* of Christians to seek peace with all men on principles of righteousness."[32] Baptists of the SBC, however, have most often been "hawks" and have often opposed "doves." The denomination that twice formally declared its opposition to the war-spirit is far from being a peace-church.[33]

Furthermore, the doctrine of sanctification that finds a prominent place in the confession's fourth article, "Salvation," is virtually absent from the ethical message of Baptists of the SBC at century's end. Baptists apparently believe that the vision of perfection is both antiquated and outdated. Thus, Baptists in the SBC appear to drift with the moral tide and take things easy.

Baptists of the SBC in the 1990s have largely abandoned the vision of the Lord's Day, as expressed by the *BFM (1963)*. Something happened to Sunday about the middle of the twentieth century. Sunday became a holiday, not a holy day. Now it seems that anything goes on Sunday, even for church folks. For many people in the larger society and in Baptist churches, Sunday is only one of seven days in the week. For many people, Sunday is business as usual.

In matters related to religious liberty, many Baptists in the SBC appear to be deserting both the *BFM (1963)* and their birthright.[34] Until fairly recent times, one could count on the SBC to pass strongly-worded resolutions of opposition to such things as tax support for parochial schools and governmental involvement in prayer in public schools. A significant weakening of that united front, however, has occurred within the past decade.[35] Furthermore, the SBC ended its fifty-year partnership with the Baptist Joint Committee on Public Affairs, the most tenacious watchdog of religious liberty in the United States, in the late 1980s. At the same time, the Christian Life Commission, also an ardent advocate for the separation of church and state until 1988, aligned itself in opposition to the Baptist Joint Committee on Public Affairs and in concert with groups that want to link the power of the state with the purposes of the church.

At yet another point, Baptists of the SBC appear to be unfaithful to their heritage. The confession's seventeeth article, "Religious Liberty," declares that "[t]he gospel of Christ contemplates spiritual means alone for the pursuit of its ends."[36] During the 1990s, however, many leaders in the SBC have resorted to political methods and means to accomplish their religious and/or spiritual goals.[37] A host of highly visible leaders in the SBC and their fellow travelers have formed alliances with political parties, political action groups, politicians, and partisan-alliances, in order to achieve their goals. In this, they have departed the faith of Baptists. The greatest apostasy of the church in the 1990s may be the reliance of the church on secular means, political tricks, and manipulative tactics to try to accomplish its goals.

Conclusion

The *BFM (1963)* links God, self, and neighbor. Personal morality and social ethics, according to this confession of faith, should mirror one's doctrine. In this understanding, the document is true to biblical religion.

Each generation, however, must decide best how to relate its faith properly and wisely in the world. Each generation must determine how best to fulfill its calling and the mission of the church in its time. For these tasks, the *BFM (1963)* offers guidance, example, and encouragement.

The heart of the Christian's assignment and the ethical vision of the *BFM (1963)* are condensed in the lyrics of a hymn written by Thomas Jackson, a former Baptist pastor in Virginia. The first stanza affirms that

"We are called to be God's people, Showing by our lives His grace" and that God's people are the "sign of hope for all the race." The final stanza declares:

> We are called to be God's prophets,
> Speaking for the truth and right;
> Standing firm for godly justice,
> Bringing evil into light
> Let us seek the courage needed,
> Our high calling to fulfill,
> That we all may know the blessing
> of the doing of God's will.[38]

Notes

[1]"Committee on Baptist Faith and Message," in *Annual of the Southern Baptist Convention: One Hundred Sixth Session in Kansas City, Missouri, 7-10 May 1963*, by the Executive Committee, Southern Baptist Convention (Nashville: Southern Baptist Convention, 1963) 63, 269-81 ("Proceedings," Thursday Morning, May 9, Items 112-124) (hereafter, cited as *BFM [1963]*).

[2]See the following: "The New Hampshire Confession, 1833," in *Baptist Confessions of Faith*, rev. ed., William L. Lumpkin, ed. (Valley Forge PA: Judson Press, 1969) 360-67 (hereafter, cited as *NHC [1833]*); "The Philadelphia Confession, (1742)," in *Baptist Confessions, Covenants, and Catechisms*, vol. 11, Library of Baptist Classics, ed. Timothy George and Denise George (Nashville: Broadman and Holman, 1996) 56-93 (hereafter, cited as *PC [1742]*).

[3]James E. Carter, "A Review of Confessions of Faith Adopted by Major Baptist Bodies in the United States," *Baptist History and Heritage* 12 (April 1977): 83-91; Walter B. Shurden, "Southern Baptist Responses to Their Confessional Statements," *Review and Expositor* 76 (Winter 1979): 69-84.

[4]William B. Johnson, et al., "The Southern Baptist Convention, To the Brethren in the United States; to the congregations connected with the respective Churches; and to all candid men," in *Proceedings of the Southern Baptist Convention in Augusta, Georgia, 8-12 May 1845* (Richmond VA: H. K. Ellyson Printer, 1845) 19.

[5]See "Report of Committee on Baptist Faith and Message," in *Annual of the Southern Baptist Convention: Seventieth Session in Memphis, Tennessee, 13-17 May 1925*, by the Secretaries, Southern Baptist Convention (Nashville: Marshall and Bruce, 1925) 70-76 ("Proceedings," Second Day–Afternoon Session, May 14, Item 53) (hereafter, cited as *BFM [1925]*).

[6]"Pronouncement on Christian Union and Denominational Efficiency," from "Report of Commission on Efficiency to the Southern Baptist Convention," in *Annual of the Southern Baptist Convention: Fifty-Ninth Session in Nashville, Tennessee, 13-18 May 1914* ("Proceedings," Fourth Day, Morning Session, May 16, Item 97), by the Secretaries, Southern Baptist Convention (Nashville: Marshall and Bruce, 1914) 73-78 (hereafter, cited as *PCU [1914]*); also, see

James E. Carter, "Southern Baptists' First Confession of Faith," *Baptist History and Heritage* 5 (January 1970): 24-38.

[7]*PCU (1914)* 76.

[8]*Fraternal Address of Southern Baptists* (Southern Baptist Convention, 1920) (hereafter, cited as *FASB [1920]*); James E. Carter, "The Fraternal Address of Southern Baptists," *Baptist History and Heritage* 12 (October 1977): 211-18.

[9]*FASB (1920)* 5-6, 12.

[10]"A Statement of Belief," from "Appendix A: Seventy-Fifth Annual Report of the Foreign Mission Board," in *Annual of the Southern Baptist Convention: Sixty-Fifth Session in Washington, D. C., 12-17 May 1920*, by the Secretaries, Southern Baptist Convention (Nashville: Marshall and Bruce, 1920) 197-99 (hereafter, cited as *SB [1920]*); also as "Statement of Faith, Foreign Mission Board, S.B.C., 1920," in *A Sourcebook for Baptist Heritage*, ed. H. Leon McBeth (Nashville: Broadman Press, 1990) 485-87.

[11]*SB (1920)* 197; also in McBeth, *Sourcebook*, 485-86.

[12]"Science and Religion," in *Annual of the Southern Baptist Convention: Sixty-Eighth Session in Kansas City, Missouri, 16-20 May 1923* ("Proceedings," Wednesday–Morning Session, May 16, Item 11), by the Secretaries, Southern Baptist Convention (Nashville: Marshall and Bruce, 1923) 19-20 (hereafter, cited as *SR [1923]*).

[13]E. Y. Mullins, *The Axioms of Religion* (Philadelphia: Judson Press, 1908); idem, *Baptist Beliefs* (Louisville KY: Baptist World, 1912); idem, *The Christian Religion in Its Doctrinal Expression* (Philadelphia: Judson Press, 1917); and E. Y. Mullins and H. W. Tribble, *The Baptist Faith* (Nashville: Sunday School Board, Southern Baptist Convention, 1935) 99-109.

[14]"Report on Interdenominational Relations," in *Annual of the Southern Baptist Convention: Eighty-Third Session in Richmond, Virginia, 12-15 May 1938* ("Proceedings," Thursday, Afternoon Session, May 12, Item 15), by the Southern Baptist Convention (Nashville: Southern Baptist Convention, 1938) 24-25 (hereafter, cited as *RIR [1938]*); "A Pronouncement upon Religious Liberty," in *Annual of the Southern Baptist Convention: Eighty-Fourth Session in Oklahoma City, Oklahoma, 17-21 May 1939* ("Proceedings," Saturday–Morning Session, May 20, Item 82), by the Executive Committee, Southern Baptist Convention (Nashville: Southern Baptist Convention, 1939) 114-16 (hereafter, cited as *PRL [1939]*); "Reply to World Council of Churches," in *Annual of the Southern Baptist Convention: Eighty-Fifth Session in Baltimore, Maryland, 12-16 June 1940* ("Proceedings," Friday–Afternoon Session, June 14, Item 66), by the Executive Committee, Southern Baptist Convention (Nashville: Southern Baptist Convention, 1940) 99 (hereafter, cited as *RWCC [1940]*); "Statement of Principles," in *Annual of the Southern Baptist Convention, 1945*, by the Executive Committee, Southern Baptist Convention (Nashville: Southern Baptist Convention, 1945) 21, 59-60 (hereafter, cited as *SP [1945]*); "Statement of Principles," in *Annual of the Southern Baptist Convention: Eighty-Ninth Session in Miami, Florida, 15-19 May 1946* ("Proceedings," Thursday–Morning Session, May 16, Item 27), by the Executive Committee, Southern Baptist Convention (Nashville: Southern Baptist Convention, 1946) 38-39 (hereafter, cited as *SP*

Mirror of Doctrine 159

[1946]). Also see "A Declaration on Religious Liberty," in *Sixth Baptist World Congress, Atlanta, Georgia, 22-28 July 1939: Official Report*, ed. J. H. Rushbrooke (Atlanta: Foote and Davies, 1939) 14 (Thursday, Eleventh Session, 27 July 1939, Item 95); also included as "Appendix Two," in Henry Cook, *What Baptists Stand For* (London: Kingsgate Press, 1947) 182.

[15]*Baptist Ideals* (Nashville: Sunday School Board of the Southern Baptist Convention, 1963) (hereafter, cited as *BI [1963]*); also included as "Appendix VII," in *The Baptist Identity: Four Fragile Freedoms*, Walter B. Shurden (Macon GA: Smyth & Helwys, 1993) 103-115.

[16]James E. Carter, "Twentieth-Century Southern Baptist Confessions of Faith," An Address to the Historical Commission, Southern Baptist Convention, Nashville, 24 April 1984.

[17]*The Baptist Faith and Message* (Nashville: The Sunday School Board of the Southern Baptist Convention, 1963) 3-19; also, *BFM (1963)* 269-81.

[18]James E. Carter, "The Southern Baptist Convention and Confessions of Faith, 1845–1945" (Th.D. diss., Southwestern Baptist Theological Seminary, 1964) 138.

[19]*BFM (1963)* 280-81 (articles 15, 16, and 17).

[20]Ibid.., 272-73, 276-77 (articles 3, 4, and 9).

[21]Ibid.., 270, 272 (articles 1 and 2).

[22]Ibid.., 276, 278, 279-80 (articles 8, 11, 13, and 14).

[23]For helpful discussions of these two models and their theological roots, see Robert Webber, *The Secular Saint* (Grand Rapids: Zondervan, 1979) 75-103, 135-65.

[24]Carter, "A Review of Confessions of Faith," 91.

[25]Herschel H. Hobbs, *The Baptist Faith and Message* (Nashville: Convention Press, 1971) 129-31, 134-38, 141-44.

[26]See Leon McBeth, "The Origin of the Christian Life Commission," *Baptist History and Heritage* 1 (October 1966): 29-36.

[27]*Encyclopedia of Southern Baptists* (Nashville: Broadman Press, 1958) 2:1648, s.v. "Christian and Social Ministries, Home Mission Board Program of," by T. E. Carter.

[28]Robert Bly, *The Sibling Society* (Reading MA: Addison-Wesley, 1996).

[29]C. William Junker, "Christian Social Services," in *Contending for the Right to Know* (Franklin TN: Providence House, 1996) 95-96.

[30]Norman Alexander Yance, "Southern Baptists and Race Relations, 1947–1977: Changing Attitudes from Harry Truman to Jimmy Carter," *Journal of Religious Thought* 35 (Spring–Summer 1978): 45-54; Leon McBeth, "Southern Baptists and Race Since 1947," *Baptist History and Heritage* 7 (July 1972): 155-69; Junker, *Contending for the Right to Know*, 96, 104-107, 132-33, 151-54, 163, 235.

[31]"Recommendation No. 24: A Statement Concerning the Crisis in Our Nation," from "Report of the Executive Committee," in *Annual of the Southern Baptist Convention: One-Hundred Eleventh Session in Houston, Texas, 4-7 June 1968* ("Proceedings," Wednesday–Morning Session, June 5, Items 21, 39, 40; Wednesday-Afternoon Session, June 5, Items 91-109), by the Executive

Committee, Southern Baptist Convention (Nashville: Southern Baptist Convention, 1968) 55, 60, 66-69; also as "Southern Baptist Convention Statement on Racial Crisis in America, 1968," in *Sourcebook*, McBeth, 523-25.

[32]*BFM (1963)* 280 (article 16, "Peace and War") (emphasis mine).

[33]Claude Howe, "Baptists and Peacemaking," *Review and Expositor* 79 (Fall 1982): 607-21; Ken Sehested, "Conformity and Dissent: Southern Baptists on War and Peace Since 1940," *Baptist History and Heritage* 28 (April 1993): 3-18; and Kent B. Blevins, "Southern Baptist Attitudes Toward the Vietnam War in the Years 1965–1970," *Foundations* 23 (July–September 1980): 231-44.

[34]See H. Wheeler Robinson, "The Passion of the Baptists for Liberty," in *The Life and Faith of the Baptists* by H. Wheeler Robinson (London: Kingsgate Press, 1946) 123-38; and Junker, *Contending for the Right to Know*, 96, 100-103, 125-27, 137-41, 163, 179-80, 181-82.

[35]As an example, see "Religion Bill Praised and Denounced at Hearing," *Alabama Baptist* 161 (1 August 1996): 1; and "Religious Groups Divided over Amending Constitution," *The Report from the Capitol*, 51 (No. 16) (13 August 1996): 1.

[36]*BFM (1963)* 281.

[37]See Bob Allen, " 'From Carter to Clinton': Clergy More Open to Politics," *Word and Way* 133 (28 March 1996): 7; Junker, *Contending for the Right to Know*, 182-83.

[38]"We Are Called to Be God's People," lyrics by Thomas A. Jackson, tune ("Austrian Hymn") by Franz Joseph Haydn (1797), in *Baptist Hymnal* (Nashville: Convention Press, 1991) 390, verses 1 and 3; also in *Baptist Hymnal* (Nashville: Convention Press, 1975) 405.

Chapter 6

In Search of the One, True Church
Ecclesiology in
The Baptist Faith and Message (1963)

Bill J Leonard

Introduction

The nature of the church—ecclesiology—was an extremely important issue for the earliest Baptists. It shaped their identity, their schisms, and their responses to the world around them. What does ecclesiology mean to contemporary Baptists, particularly those related to that entity known as the Southern Baptist Convention (SBC)? How do Southern Baptist churches understand the nature of the church? Is the Convention's confession of faith, the *Baptist Faith and Message (BFM [1963])*, a document for use primarily by local churches, or does it define essential dogma for the denomination and its employees, or both?[1] How does the confession impact Southern Baptist ecclesiology? Such questions inform this particular article on the church and the confession.

In America, eighteenth-century and nineteenth-century Baptists often utilized confessions of faith in founding congregations throughout the South. While affirming the ultimate authority of Holy Scripture, many of these churches were organized around three "man-made" documents. These included a confession of faith (usually the *Philadelphia Confession* of 1742 or the *New Hampshire Confession* of 1833), a church covenant, and rules of decorum. The confession outlined basic beliefs, the covenant established ideals for personal and interpersonal relationships among members, and the rules of decorum defined the conduct of church business.[2] More recently, however, the confession of faith has become a crucial element in denominational self-definition, a tool for determining and monitoring the orthodoxy of those employed by the Convention.

To examine the *BFM (1963)* and its statements on the church is an intriguing exercise at this point in time, when Southern Baptists confront major transitions in their ideological and organizational life. These transitions are intricately related to questions regarding the nature of the church. The Convention itself was organized in 1845 without an official confession of faith. Eighty years later, when the *BFM (1925)* was originally approved, the denomination seemed determined to define itself as both a national organization and a connectional body, linking congregations throughout the South. When the confession was revised in 1963, the denominational system of the SBC was perhaps at the strongest and most unified point in its history. In 1925, many local churches continued to manifest mistrust of national and regional denominational "hierarchies," viewing them as potential threats to congregational autonomy. In 1963, a substantial majority of SBC-affiliated churches were convinced that they could retain their local autonomy while participating extensively in the denominational structure. During the last decade of the twentieth century, however, numerous churches in the SBC, across the theological and geographical spectrums, have redefined their relationships to denominational entities beyond the local church. Some minimize the name "Baptist," preferring more generic designations such as "Peoples' Church," or "Community Church" to identify their congregations. Others are re-examining the nature of the authority, ministry, and mission of the church, local and national. Still others are attempting to relate to numerous Baptist entities, old and new.

To deal with the nature of the *Baptist Faith and Message* itself is also an important exercise in the 1990s. Although the *BFM (1963)* is often promoted as a primary source of denominational unity, it now seems clear that the confession offers no panacea for curing the divisions created by the so-called denominational "Controversy," which began around 1979.[3] Many "conservative-" and "moderate-" oriented individuals, churches, associations and state conventions continue to affirm the *BFM (1963)*, while redefining their relationships with the denominational system in ways that often loosen rather than strengthen connectional ties. While doctrinal unity centered in the *BFM (1963)* is widely celebrated, significant spiritual and organizational fissures remain.

My own experience is a case in point. When I became a professor at the Southern Baptist Theological Seminary (SBTS) in Louisville, Kentucky, in 1975, I was asked to sign the *Abstract of Principles*, the school's own confession of faith.[4] Approved in 1859, the *Abstract* was the first confessional document ever used by a Southern Baptist institution. By the 1980s, as the denominational Controversy descended on Louisville, the faculty of SBTS was required to affirm the *BFM (1963)* alongside the *Abstract of Principles*. Still later, faculty members were asked to "reaffirm" both documents. None of the confessional reaffirmations kept the seminary from being enveloped in a continuing controversy, ultimately losing a significant number of its faculty and student body. In 1992, I became a professor of religion at Samford University in Birmingham, Alabama, and, with other religion faculty, affirmed the *BFM (1963)* "and its preamble." Yet, those affirmations did not keep the university from either redefining its relationship with the Alabama Baptist Convention or returning its governance to a self-perpetuating board of trustees. Similar circumstances have occurred at educational institutions throughout the SBC. In the 1990s, it seems that merely affirming confessions of faith cannot bring peace and unity to a troubled people. Perhaps

I. Early Baptist Ecclesiology

the attention given in this volume to the meaning of the confession will help us understand something of our continuing denominational dilemma.

Any discussion of the nature of ecclesiology in Southern Baptist life must first examine the way in which the earliest Baptists understood the doctrine of the church and articulated that doctrine in their confessions of faith. There is no doubt that questions regarding the nature of the church were at the heart of early Baptist identity. Those who formed the first Baptist communities were concerned about defining the church, its membership, and its mission in the world. For example, the General Baptists, led by John Smyth and Thomas Helwys, were influenced by the English Separatist assertion that the church was a gathered community of Christian believers united to God and one another through a covenant. For them, the church was a covenanting community of Christian believers. Smyth himself held that "the church of Christ is a company of the faithful; baptized after confession of sin and of faith, endowed with the power of Christ."[5] Likewise, these first General Baptists believed that each congregation so gathered was irrefutably part of the body of Christ. In what was probably the first Baptist confession of faith, Thomas Helwys wrote the following:

> That as one congregacion hath CHRIST, so hath all, 2. Cor. 10.7. And that the Word off GOD cometh not out from anie one, neither to anie one congregacion in particuler. I. Cor. 14.36. But unto everie particuler Church, as it doth unto al the world. Coll.1.5. 6. And therefore no church ought to challeng anie prerogative over anie other.[6]

Baptists, like other Protestants of the seventeenth and eighteenth centuries, debated the nature of the church in terms of its membership. Most Baptists rejected the idea set forth by the Anglican and Catholic establishments that the church on earth was composed of both wheat and tares, the saved and the unsaved. Thus the "gathered church" included only believers, those who had experienced a work of divine grace in their hearts and had testified to it in the community of faith. For many Baptists, therefore, the visible church on earth was identical with the invisible church in heaven. Particular Baptist Calvinists agreed with this idea in principle, yet they also acknowledged that the elect were known to God alone, and that members of the earthly community could be certain that they were in that number.

The *Orthodox Creed* of British Baptists (1678–1679) represented an early effort to synthesize these ideas. It suggested that the invisible church is an elect community known only to God. The visible "Catholick (universal) church" "is made up of several distinct Congregations," the "marks" of which include: "Where the Word of God is rightly Preached, and the Sacraments truly Administered," all carried out with proper discipline and ministry.7

The early Baptists also debated whether church membership was closed or open to those who had not received believer's baptism by immersion. They were divided over whether to admit members who were baptized but unimmersed "professors" of Christian faith. They also could not agree on whether to welcome such persons to the Lord's Table in Baptist churches. Many of these issues are evident in the *BFM (1963)* and its statements on ecclesiology.

Nineteenth-century Baptists in the United States confronted yet another ecclesial controversy related to the Landmark movement and its insistence on the absolute authority and autonomy of the local congregation. Landmark Baptists developed an ecclesiology based on what they believed to be a historic "trail of blood" and martyrs running from the New Testament into the present. Landmarkists insisted that Baptists were the only true church, alone maintaining the definitive "marks of the church" throughout Christian history. Perhaps no other single movement so impacted the *BFM's* statements on the church. The repercussions from these ideas shaped the SBC's ecclesiology in powerful ways as evidenced in the *BFM (1963)*.

II. The Confession and the Church: Specific Articles

The *Baptist Faith and Message* was not merely a statement of faith for use in the Southern Baptist Convention. Drawn from the *New Hampshire Confession* of 1833, it represented a *via media*, a middle way, between varying theological views held by diverse segments of the Southern Baptist Convention. In some respects, the *BFM (1963)* was not unlike the *Orthodox Creed* among seventeenth-century Baptists, an effort to delineate dogmas in a way that would unite diverse, often differing, ideological and geographical subgroups within the SBC. Theologically, the *BFM (1963)* reflects a modified Calvinist/modified Arminian outlook, retaining the Calvinistic language of election, justification, and sovereignty within the framework of general atonement, freedom of the will, and immediate human participation in the salvific process. Ecclesiologically, it represents something of a modified Landmarkist approach to issues of local autonomy, ordinances, and democratic idealism. In its formal statement on "The Church," the *BFM (1963)* declares the following:

> A New Testament church of the Lord Jesus Christ is a local body of baptized believers who are associated by covenant in the faith and

fellowship of the gospel, observing the two ordinances of Christ, committed to His teachings, exercising the gifts, rights, and privileges invested in them by His Word, and seeking to extend the gospel to the ends of the earth.[8]

This initial declaration reflects the influence of the Landmarkist insistence that the only church is a local congregation.[9] Landmark leaders such as J. R. Graves, J. M. Pendleton, and A. C. Dayton used Greek word studies to make their point. Largely ignoring the broader references to the church as "Body of Christ," "People of God," and "household of faith," they focused largely on the word *ecclesia*. As they saw it, that New Testament word, translated as church in English, referred only to a local congregation. The true church was a visible church only. Graves wrote:

> The only church that is revealed to us is a visible church, and the only church with which we have anything to do, or in connection with which we have any duties to perform, is a visible body.... Christ never set up but one kingdom; and if this is visible, he has no invisible kingdom or church, and such a thing has no real existence in heaven or earth. It is only an invention to bolster up erroneous theories of ecclesiology.[10]

The impact of Landmark ideas is clearly evident in the confessions of both 1925 and 1963. At the same time, the confession's reference to the church as "associated by covenant" reflects the idea of the church as a covenanting community of believers. Thus, it extends the early Baptist emphasis on the church as composed of believers—those who can testify to a work of grace in their hearts and lives. Interestingly, the document does not utilize the classic signs of the true church in Reformed theology—where the Word is preached and the sacraments rightly administered—but describes the true communion of faith as observing the "ordinances," committed to Christ's teaching, exercising gifts, rights, and privileges, and extending the gospel to the all the earth.

The second paragraph affirms the congregational nature of Baptist polity, but with a decidedly North American twist. In this statement, congregational autonomy is placed in the context of "democratic processes under the Lordship of Jesus Christ." Though implicit in much Baptist congregationalism, the use of the terms "democratic processes" owes much to the Americanization of Baptist polity. Likewise, the assertion that "[i]n such a congregation, members are equally responsible" suggests a congregational egalitarianism that may run contrary to certain contemporary emphases on ministerial authority or the role of pastor as "undershepherd."[11]

The final sentence in the article reflects the nature of the *BFM* as *via media*. It declares that "[t]he New Testament speaks also of the church as the body of Christ which includes all the redeemed of all the ages."[12] This declaration clearly contradicts the Landmark denial of any form of the church beyond its local setting. It also is an acknowledgment, however hesitant, that there are other members of the Body of Christ, beyond Baptist believers and churches. Unlike Landmark ecclesiology, this statement gives at least limited recognition to the broader categories for describing the church in the Christian scriptures.

A. The Ordinances: Baptism and the Lord's Supper

1. Baptism

The *BFM's* article on "Baptism and the Lord's Supper" begins with the avowal that "Christian baptism is the immersion of a believer in water in the name of the Father, the Son, and the Holy Spirit."[13] This is a classic declaration that reflects a significant element (no pun intended) of Baptist identity. Although immersion was not normative for the earliest Baptists, by the 1640s, British Baptists were insisting on that mode as a depiction of Christian/Baptist identity. Indeed, historian William Brackney says that, "[m]ore than any other characteristic of the Baptist tradition . . . believers' baptism by immersion was the functional essence of historic Baptist identity."[14]

Likewise, immersion was to follow "belief," an experience of grace in the life of the sinner. The article also requires baptism as "prerequisite" both to church membership and admission to the Lord's Supper. The way the sentence reads again reflects a middle way, offering the possibility of closed communion for members of the local congregation only, or permitting a more open communion, extending to all baptized believers (immersed only?) who might be present in any Baptist church when the Supper is celebrated.

Statements on the meaning of baptism—as "an act of obedience symbolizing . . ." or "a testimony . . ."—tend to reflect the human side of the event, what baptism means to the individual who receives it.[15] No attention is given to the meaning of baptism from God's side. As Martin Luther might have suggested, in baptism it is not that humans have chosen God, but that God has chosen them.

2. The Lord's Supper

Concerning the Lord's Supper, the *BFM (1963)* stresses the symbolic and memorial nature of the observance: "The Lord's Supper is a symbolic act of obedience whereby members of the church, through partaking of the bread and the fruit of the vine, memorialize the death of the Redeemer

In Search of the One, True Church

and anticipate His second coming."[16] This seems to reflect a more Zwinglian than Calvinist approach. Ulrich Zwingli, the sixteenth-century reformer of Zurich, suggested that the Lord's Supper is a memorial remembrance of Christ's death, His presence shared through the faith of the worshiping community. John Calvin, the reformer of Geneva, insisted that the Supper was an experience of Christ's "spiritual presence," known, as He promised, when the bread and the wine were shared by the church. This latter view was and continues to be affirmed by some Baptist groups.

Unfortunately, the idea of the Supper as symbolic memorial has led many churches to think of it as "only a symbol," thus minimizing the significance all together, rushing through the event, tacked on to the end of a church service. Many Baptists around the world continue to view the Supper as a "means of grace," a special experience of Christ's presence as promised in Holy Scripture and known through the Holy Spirit in the gathered community.

The reference to the elements as "bread and the fruit of the vine" reflects the impact of the temperance movement on nineteenth-century and twentieth-century Southern Baptists. The revision of the *BFM* in 1963 replaced the allusion to wine in the *BFM (1925)* with the phrase, "fruit of the vine," probably a more faithful, though less biblical, rendering of contemporary practice. Temperance sentiments have apparently created one instance of the Southern Baptist hesitancy to press the theory of biblical inerrancy to the limits in faith *and* practice! Likewise, the recent use of disposable communion kits for sanitary and logistical convenience may also distance the community of faith from the experience of the power of the Lord's Supper, whatever the community's theology of Christ's presence may be.

B. The Lord's Day

This often neglected segment of the *BFM (1963)* commits Baptists in the SBC to Sunday, as opposed to Sabbath, worship in religious observances both public and private. Its call both to refrain "from worldly amusements" and to rest "from secular employments," with "work of necessity and mercy only being excepted," no doubt has become one of the more "negotiated" elements of the *BFM (1963)*.[17] In the 1990s, even the most scrupulous Lord's-Day-Baptists often succumb to the allure of restaurant meals and shopping-center Sunday afternoons. Nonetheless, while the phrase "work of necessity and mercy only being excepted" has a more nineteenth- than twentieth- (let alone twenty-first-) century ring to it, its simplicity and piety betrays a wistful sanity.

C. The Kingdom

In the article on "The Kingdom" (of God), the *BFM (1963)* moves firmly away from the Landmarkist agenda. Landmarkist dogma rejected any concept of the Kingdom of God apart from its connection to the local Baptist congregation. Leon McBeth observes that, for Landmarkists, "the churches and the kingdom of God are coterminous."[18] Landmark leader, J. R. Graves, insisted that "the churches of Christ constitute the kingdom of Christ."[19]

The *BFM (1963)* makes no such reference, preferring instead to address the kingdom in terms of personal salvation and God's anticipated rule. Again, as a *via media*, it urges Christians "to pray and to labor" that the kingdom may come on earth, acknowledging that its "full consummation" awaits Christ's return. Does the phrase, "that the Kingdom may come and God's will be done on earth" (taken directly from the Lord's Prayer), demonstrate any influence drawn from the ideas and anticipations of Baptist social gospeler, Walter Rauschenbusch, and others like him? The reference to Christ's return "and the end of this age" affirms a general eschatology, while avoiding any attention to specific millennial theories.[20]

D. Evangelism and Missions

In its eleventh article, "Evangelism and Missions," the *BFM (1963)* sets forth the basic evangelical and missionary imperative that long characterized Southern Baptist unity, cooperation, and identity. It declares that both churches and individuals are called to "make disciples of all nations." Such a statement places Southern Baptists on the side of missionary endeavor in the historic debate over the role of human agents in the divine plan of redemption. Thus, many SBC-related churches in certain parts of Appalachia and the Southeast are often known as Missionary Baptist churches, in contrast to their non-missionizing Primitive or Old Regular Baptist neighbors. The article also reflects the impact of the revivalistic, conversionistic method of evangelism: "to win the lost to Christ by personal effort and by all other methods in harmony with the gospel of Christ." The emphasis here is on personal evangelism and the need for individual conversion.[21]

E. Education

Early in their history, Baptists of the SBC sought to create "an adequate system of Christian schools," founding colleges throughout the South, from Richmond, Virginia, to Waco, Texas. Almost from the beginning, these institutions encountered controversies over the content of that education and its impact on the churches. The articles on education in the *BFM* disclose such significant differences between the original text, the *BFM (1925)*, and its revision, the *BFM (1963)*. Perhaps no other article was revised so extensively, alterations largely overlooked by historians.

The *BFM (1925)*, approved by the SBC at the height of the Fundamentalist-Modernist controversy about evolution, reflects a highly progressive, optimistic view of Christian education.

> Christianity is the religion of enlightenment and intelligence. In Jesus Christ are hidden all the treasures of wisdom and knowledge. All sound learning is therefore a part of our Christian heritage. The new birth opens all human faculties and creates a thirst for knowledge.[22]

In the previous statement, it appears that Jesus Christ is exalted as the door of all learning. Christian faith encompasses all educational elements since all truth is God's truth.

In the *BFM (1963)*, the article on education was almost totally revised, no doubt impacted by the so-called "Elliott Controversy" and other developments in Baptist schools. In that article, Christ becomes the boundary and limitation of education. Indeed, the article states clearly that "[t]he freedom of a teacher in a Christian school, college, or seminary is *limited* by the preeminence of Jesus Christ, by the authoritative nature of the Scriptures, and by the distinct purpose for which the school exists."[23] Perhaps those differences in the two documents reflect Southern Baptists' own struggle with the nature and meaning of education and educational institutions, a debate about which there is no end in sight.

F. Cooperation

Given the current developments in the SBC, the *BFM's* segment on "Cooperation" may be one of the most poignant, even timely, elements of the document. It begins by acknowledging that "Christ's people" should unite in "associations and conventions" to achieve "the great objects of the Kingdom of God." It continues: "Such organizations have no authority over one another or over the churches. They are voluntary and advisory bodies designed to elicit, combine, and direct the energies of our people in the most effective manner."[24] These statements are especially poignant given the extensive organizational reconfiguration now evident throughout the traditional SBC system. As noted earlier, Baptist connectionalism in the SBC is in significant transition as churches, associations, state conventions, and educational institutions redefine their connectional relationships with other, often parent, bodies. Indeed, one of the most pressing issues for contemporary Southern Baptists involves the decision of many churches and groups to reevaluate their relationships with other "voluntary and advisory bodies." Conservatives were among the first to take such actions more than twenty years ago, when many of their churches began to "designate" some of their financial contributions away from agencies of the SBC that they considered too liberal. More recently, moderates have followed suit, limiting their gifts to the national SBC and funding local or newly organized entities such as the Cooperative Baptist Fellowship. The decision of the Baptist General Convention of Texas in 1995 to redefine a "cooperating church" in ways that permit financial support of the SBC, the Texas state convention, or other Baptist organizations is another indication of these realignments. Are these actions affirmed by the *BFM's* article on "Cooperation," even when they rankle various segments of denominational leadership?

Churches across the theological spectrum are currently establishing a variety of new networks and "associations" for education, publication, and evangelism. Many congregations permit their members to designate funds to an assortment of Baptist-related entities, inside and outside the traditional boundaries of the SBC. All these developments have theological, organizational, and financial implications for the SBC as it is now and as it will be in the future.

Conclusion

What does all this have to do with the *Baptist Faith and Message* and the nature of the church? First, it suggests that confessions of faith can only go so far in providing unity and security for religious communities. Churches are living organisms, ever changing, growing, and, especially in the case of the SBC, debating, the implications of written documents.

Second, given the burgeoning number of rebaptisms among Southern Baptist church members, the increasing use of disposable communion kits, and the influx of persons from other Christian traditions, should churches in the SBC renew study and dialogue regarding the nature of baptism and the Lord's Supper?

Third, in the past, the denominational system of programs and bureaucracies aided Southern Baptists in defining the nature of the church. As those resources become increasingly less uniform, Baptist bodies, particularly local congregations, will be compelled to reexamine their own ecclesiology, their reasons for cooperation, and their reasons for retaining Baptist identity, even the Baptist name. Such endeavors are essential for any people who would continue to struggle with what it means to be part of the Body of Christ, the one true church, apostolic, and universal.

Notes

[1] See "Committee on Baptist Faith and Message," in *Annual of the Southern Baptist Convention: One Hundred Sixth Session in Kansas City, Missouri, 7-10 May 1963*, by the Executive Committee, Southern Baptist Convention (Nashville: Southern Baptist Convention, 1963) 63, 269-81 ("Proceedings," Thursday Morning, May 9, Items 112-124) (hereafter, cited as *BFM [1963]*). Also see the precursor to the *BFM (1963)*: "Report of Committee on Baptist Faith and Message," in *Annual of the Southern Baptist Convention: Seventieth Session in Memphis, Tennessee, 13-17 May 1925*, by the Secretaries, Southern Baptist Convention (Nashville: Marshall and Bruce, 1925) 70-76 ("Proceedings," Second Day—Afternoon Session, May 14, Item 53) (hereafter, cited as *BFM [1925]*).

[2] Bill J. Leonard, "Types of Confessional Documents Among Baptists," *Review and Expositor* 76 (Winter 1979): 29-42.

[3] For a discussion of the historical and sociological roots of "The Controversy," see Bill J. Leonard *God's Last and Only Hope: The Fragmentation of the Southern Baptist Convention* (Grand Rapids: Eerdmans, 1990); and Nancy Tatom Ammerman, *Baptist Battles* (New Brunswick NJ: Rutgers University Press, 1990).

[4] "Abstract of Principles," from "Recommendation No. 3, Charter of the Southern Baptist Theological Seminary," in *Annual of the Southern Baptist Convention: Ninety-Seventh Session in St. Louis, Missouri, 2-5 June 1954*, ed. the Executive Committee, Southern Baptist Convention (Nashville: Southern Baptist Convention, 1954) 38-39 ("Proceedings," Wednesday Morning, June 2, Item 15).

[5] William H. Brackney, *Baptist Life and Thought: 1600–1980* (Valley Forge PA: Judson Press, 1983) 27. See "A Declaration of Faith of English People Remaining at Amsterdam in Holland, 1611," in *Baptist Confessions of Faith*, rev. ed., William L. Lumpkin, ed. (Valley Forge PA: Judson Press, 1969) 119 (article 10).

[6] "A Declaration of Faith of English People Remaining at Amsterdam in Holland, 1611," in *Baptist Confessions of Faith*, Lumpkin, 120 (article 12). Also cited in Brackney, *Baptist Life and Thought*, 48.

[7] "The 'Orthodox Creed,' 1678," in *Baptist Confessions of Faith*, Lumpkin, 318-19 (article 30); also, see Brackney, *Baptist Life and Thought*, 49, citing *An Orthodox Creed* (London: n.p., 1679) 40-41.

[8] *BFM (1963)* 275 (article 6, p 1).

[9] Leon McBeth, *The Baptist Heritage* (Nashville: Broadman Press, 1987) 450.

[10] McBeth, *Baptist Heritage*, 451, citing J. R. Graves, *Old Landmarkism: What Is It?* 32.

[11] *BFM (1963)*, 275 (article 6, ¶ 2). Larry E. High, "Bible Says Pastor Clearly the Church 'Ruler': Patterson," *Biblical Recorder* (26 November 1988) 6.

[12] *BFM (1963)* 275 (article 6, ¶ 3).

[13] *BFM (1963)* 276 (article 7, ¶ 1).

[14] William Brackney, " 'Commonly, (Though Falsely) called . . .': Reflections on the Search for Baptist Identity," in *Perspectives in Churchmanship*, ed. David M. Scholer (Macon GA: Mercer University Press, 1986) 80.

[15] *BFM (1963)* 276 (article 7, ¶ 1).

[16] Ibid, 276 (article 7, ¶ 2).

[17] Ibid, 276 (article 8).

[18] McBeth, *Baptist Heritage*, 451.

[19] McBeth, *Baptist Heritage*, 452, citing J. R. Graves, *Old Landmarkism: What Is it?* 33.

[20] *BFM (1963)* 276 (article 9).

[21] Ibid., 278 (article 11).

[22] *BFM (1925)* 74 (article 20); also in *BFM (1963)* 278; H. Leon McBeth, ed., *A Sourcebook for Baptist Heritage* (Nashville: Broadman Press, 1990) 514-15.

[23] *BFM (1963)* 278 (article 12, ¶ 2) (emphasis mine).

[24] *BFM (1963)* 279 (article 14).

Chapter 7

Principles Implicit in the Concept of Religious Liberty in *The Baptist Faith and Message (1963)*

William R. Estep

Introduction

Recently, the Southern Baptist Convention (SBC) has been accused of being a denomination devoid of both theological and historical roots. The casual observer of recent developments within the denomination might plausibly reach such a conclusion, but those who make any attempt to understand the Baptist heritage know how patently false such a statement is. While bias and ignorance are possible contributors to this misconception, it must be admitted that the majority of Baptists, or at least contemporary Baptists in the SBC, apparently are uninformed regarding the unique heritage of Baptists. Regardless of the reasons that possibly could explain this regrettable situation, the resulting identity crisis cannot be resolved until Southern Baptists undergo a reality check. This examination of the principles that underlie the seventeenth article of The Baptist Faith and Message of (1963) is designed to be a step in the process of such a reality-check.[1]

I. A Question of Baptist Identity

What constitutes the essentials of Baptist identity? This question can only be answered by a brief excursion into Baptist history and heritage. Such an excursion is necessary since the seventeenth article of the BFM (1963) was not the brainchild of Herschel Hobbs and his committee in 1963. Rather, that article embraces concepts rooted in a Baptist self-understanding at the origins of the movement four centuries ago.

Although an unknown number of English people were "excommunicated" by the "Ancient Church" of Francis Johnson at Campen and Naarden, Holland, for falling into the "heresies of the Anabaptist," it remained for John Smyth and his congregation in Amsterdam to articulate for the first time, in English, the principle of religious freedom.[2] In the year of his death, 1612, Smyth wrote the following in the eighty-fourth article of a hundred-article confession of faith:

> That the magistrate [government official] is not by virtue of his office to meddle with religion, or matters of conscience, to force or compel men to this or that form of religion, or doctrine: but to leave Christian religion free, to every man's conscience, and to handle only civil transgressions (Rom. xiii), injuries and wrongs of man against man, in murder, adultery, theft, etc., for Christ only is the king, and lawgiver of the church and conscience (James iv. 12).[3]

For Smyth and other English Baptists, the concept of religious liberty implied the separation of church and state. Following his return to England from Amsterdam, Thomas Helwys published a curious little book entitled *The Mistery of Iniquity*, which constituted the first petition addressed to King James I for religious liberty, not only for Helwys's congregation, but also for "Papists [Roman Catholics], Jewes, Turks, and pagans."[4] After Helwys's death in Newgate Prison, John Murton, who succeeded him as pastor of this first Baptist church (of record) on English soil, continued to champion the cause of religious freedom in at least five books until his own death in the same prison. Even before Murton's remarkable series of works, in which he took issue precisely on this point with John Robinson, pastor of the congregation of English Separatists in Leyden, Mark Leonard Busher, a citizen of London living in exile at Delf, Holland, wrote the most cogently argued book on the subject, *Religion's Peace*. He also entered a vigorous plea for Jews to be allowed to return to England, from which they had been banished in the thirteenth century. Smyth, Helwys, Murton, and Busher were later categorized as "General Baptists," since they believed that Christ died for all who would believe in him for salvation. By the time the General Baptists were baptizing by immersion, there arose in London a second group, which became known as Particular Baptists, because they held that Christ died only for the "elect." The Particular Baptists, too, joined the struggle for religious freedom.

The Particular Baptists published three notable confessions of faith in 1644, 1646, and 1677. The confession of 1644, known as the *First London Confession*, devotes five of its fifty-three articles to church-state relations. While these articles assure the reader that those publishing the confession are loyal citizens who obey the civil laws of the land, they cannot obey the religious laws that attempt to regulate the church-life of England and stifle the conscience. Even though they may suffer for their disobedience, they declare their willingness to defend the government even at the risk of life, material goods, and families for they "ought to obey God rather then [*sic*] men . . . ." The authors of this confession conclude it with a ringing affirmation of their commitment to this principle:

> And thus wee desire to give unto God that which is | Gods, and unto Cesar that which is Cesars, and unto all | men that which belongeth unto them, endevouring our | selves to have always a cleare conscience void of offense | towards God, and towards man. And if any take this that | we have said, to be heresie, then doe wee with the Apostle | freely confesse, that after the way which they call heresie, | worship we the God of our Fathers, beleeving all things | which are written in the Law and in the Prophets and A- | postles . . . .[5]

The framers of this *First London Confession* cited thirty-one biblical references to support their position on church-state relationships–twenty-nine from the New Testament and two from the Old Testament. A number of significant changes were made in the 1646 edition of the confession. Among these, the twenty-fifth article emphasizes that Christ is the "Savior of such sinners as through the gospel shall be brought to believe on Him." In the thirty-sixth article, a further departure from the modified Calvinism of the previous confession takes place. The Calvinistic fourfold ministry of pastors, teachers, elders, and deacons is replaced with a twofold ministry of "elders and deacons," as was the practice of the General Baptists.

The forty-eighth through the fifty-third articles were completely rewritten, thus reducing the total number to fifty-two articles with a conclusion added, incorporating the basic concepts of religious liberty presented in a more logical sequence. A phrase also was added, reminiscent of Smyth's confession from 1612: "And concerning the worship of God; there is but one lawgiver, which is able to save and destroy; *James 4:12*, which is Jesus Christ, who hath given laws and rules sufficient in His word for His worship"[6]

Twenty-one years later, the Particular Baptists felt compelled to send forth the *Second London Confession* of 1677, modeled after the *Westminster Confession* of 1646. After the restoration of the English monarchy in 1660, a fresh wave of persecution arose against all dissenters, including the Presbyterians, who had become so numerous that they could hardly be intimidated, even though they no longer had the political power of an established church in England. By the same token, they no longer presented a threat to other dissenters. In order to present a united front with the Presbyterians against the monarchy and the prelates of the Church of England, both the Congregationalists and the Particular Baptists published their own versions of the *Westminster Confession*, with certain alterations.

Although the *Second London Confession* (1677) represents a departure from the *First London Confession*, both in order of articles and content, it remained true to historic Baptist ecclesiology and commitment to religious liberty. The framers of the Baptist version of the *Westminster Confession* began the second of three sections in the twenty-first chapter as follows: "God alone is Lord of the Conscience, and hath left it free from the Doctrines and Commandments of men which are in any thing contrary to his Word, or not contained in it."[7]

Baptists in the North American English colonies reflected the same commitment to the separation of church and state and religious liberty that was true of their English brethren. In the *Bloudy Tenent of Persecution*, Roger Williams, founder of Providence Plantations and the first

Baptist church in the colonies, presented numerous arguments for religious freedom.[8] Williams's position was derived not from his political theories, but from a theology grounded in the New Testament. He was convinced that the coercive powers of the state should never be used in an attempt to compel citizens to become Christians, for conversion was the work of the Word and the Spirit. By "strong arm" tactics the state could compel conformity, but in the process only succeed in making hypocrites—not true Christians. He also contended that Massachusetts Bay Colony was not the New Israel that the Puritan, Dr. John Cotton, claimed, for the New Israel is not to be identified with any race or nation. Rather, Williams argued, it is made up of those of every race and nation who are born again by the Spirit of God through faith in Jesus Christ. One must not underestimate the importance of Williams for subsequent Baptist and American history, as Perry Miller writes:

> Just as some great experience in the youth of a person is ever afterward a determinant of his personality, so the American character has inevitably been molded by the fact that in the first years of colonization there arose this prophet of religious liberty.[9]

Williams was not the only Baptist spokesman to champion separation of church from state and religious freedom in New England. Dr. John Clarke, in his *Ill Newes from New-England* of 1652, tells of his imprisonment in Boston, along with Obadiah Holmes and John Crandall, for conducting a private worship service in the home of a blind Baptist by the name of William Witter. In his prison manuscript, Clarke penned the essence of his faith as a Baptist, which he includes in *Ill Newes*. Clarke was not only pastor of the Newport Baptist church, but joined with Williams both in founding the colony of Rhode Island and in securing its second charter.

The first Baptist confession of faith in the American colonies was presented in 1665 to the Court of Assistants in Charlestown, Massachusetts, by members of a Baptist church who were arrested along with their pastor, Thomas Goold, for conducting unlawful worship in his home. This confession was a brief digest of the *First London Confession*, including its ringing affirmation "if any take this to be heresie. . . ."[10]

On the eve of the Revolutionary War, there arose a number of champions of religious liberty in colonial America. By this time, the First Great Awakening had brought into the ranks of the Baptists thousands of new converts. Virtually all of these new Baptists had been members of the Congregational Church, the established church in the New England colonies, or the Church of England, which enjoyed the status of a state-church in the southern colonies. In spite of fierce opposition in New

England by colonial authorities and ministers of the "Standing Order" and in spite of severe persecution in the South, particularly in Virginia, Baptist converts multiplied, and new churches began in both sections of the country. With numbers on their side and the ground-swell of support of the patriots, who had political freedom uppermost in their minds, the Baptist message of religious freedom began to impact the revolutionary cause.

Among the Baptists, two major spokesmen emerged: Isaac Backus in New England and John Leland in Virginia. Thomas Jefferson, James Madison, and George Mason were capable and well-placed political leaders who were also allies of the Baptists in the struggle to free religion from the shackles of "a priest-ridden state" and to add an amendment to the Federal Constitution in order that religious freedom would not be stillborn in the birth of the new nation. Even with a delegation of his own, including James Manning, president of Rhode Island College, John Gano, pastor of the First Baptist Church in New York City, and leading Baptists and Quakers of Philadelphia, the Backus-led forces ran into a stubborn wall of resistance from the Massachusetts delegation to the Continental Congress in 1774.[11] The contrary situation prevailed in Virginia. The General Committee formed by representatives of both the Regular and Separate Baptists became a most effective force in bringing the cause to the forefront in the legislative process. Although Leland recognized, as doubtless did George Eve, Reuben Bledsoe, and John Waller, that the basis of Jefferson's commitment to religious freedom and that of other deists was fundamentally different from that of the Baptists, they still welcomed their support, apart from which there possibly would have been no First Amendment.[12]

There is little doubt that Baptists in America were not prepared to accept complacently halfway measures, as their united opposition to the General Assessment Bill in Virginia indicates. Their own experience of intolerance at the hands of state churches had been too bitter for those who had so recently won their freedom from England to give up the most basic of all freedoms for another yoke of bondage.

The first widely accepted confession of faith in the United States by the end of the nineteenth century was *The New Hampshire Confession* of 1833. Although its article, "Of Civil Government," constituted a very brief statement on religious freedom, it was almost identical to the eighty-fourth article of Smyth's confession in 1612.

> We believe that civil government is of divine appointment, for the interests and good order of human society; and that magistrates are to be prayed for, conscientiously honored and obeyed; except only in things opposed to the will of our Lord Jesus Christ, who is the only Lord of the conscience, and the Prince of the kings of the earth.[13]

At the height of the fundamentalist movement in the United States before it began to disintegrate after the Scopes trial in Dayton, Tennessee, the SBC was pressured into issuing a new confession of faith. The Convention had never adopted a confession of its own, although many of the churches then affiliated with the SBC had adopted the *New Hampshire Confession*. E. Y. Mullins, highly respected theologian and president of the Southern Baptist Theological Seminary, served as chairperson of the committee that reported to the Convention meeting in Memphis, Tennessee, 13-17 May 1925. The confession, which the committee presented for the approval of the Convention, used the *New Hampshire Confession* as its guide, which it revised and to which it added ten new articles.[14] The SBC, meeting in Kansas City, Missouri, in 1963, revised the confession once again, but left unchanged "Article XVII. Religious Liberty."

> God alone is Lord of the conscience, and He has left it free from the doctrines and commandments of men which are contrary to His word or not contained in it. Church and State should be separate. The state owes to every church protection and full freedom in the pursuit of its spiritual ends. In providing for such freedom no ecclesiastical group or denomination should be favored by the state more than others. Civil government being ordained of God, it is the duty of Christians to render loyal obedience thereto in all things not contrary to the revealed will of God. The church should not resort to the civil power to carry on its work. The gospel of Christ contemplates spiritual means alone for the pursuit of its ends. The state has no right to impose penalties for religious opinions of any kind. The state has no right to impose taxes for the support of any form of religion. A free church in a free state is the Christian ideal, and this implies the right of free and unhindered access to God on the part of all men, and the right to form and propagate opinions in the sphere of religion without interference by the civil power.[15]

Since 1963, the revision of the *BFM (1925)* has been published and distributed in tract form by the Sunday School Board of the SBC under the title, *The Baptist Faith and Message*. The foregoing brief historical sketch cannot begin to do justice to the Baptist commitment to the concepts of religious liberty and the separation of church and state. *One fact, however, seems abundantly clear: the separation of church and state as the only sure guarantee of complete religious freedom has been a Baptist conviction from the very beginning of the movement.*

II. Theological Roots

If the principle of the separation of church and state is essential to an authentic Baptist identity, what is the theological basis for this position?

As numerous confessions and Baptist writers have stated, it is based upon the revelation of God in Jesus Christ, to whom the apostles bear witness in the pages of the New Testament. Roger Williams wrote in the *Bloudy Tenent of Persecution* that "an enforced uniformity of religion in a given state" is a denial of the incarnation. Doubtless, his detractors were somewhat amused by this statement, for, of all people, they considered themselves the soul of orthodoxy and Williams, the heretic. They were also bewildered, because they did not understand the profound depth of his theology. Was he not saying that the God revealed in Jesus Christ is the God of the invitation, for Christ invites all men and women to salvation? Therefore, God forces no one to accept that which He freely offers in Christ.

Admittedly, not many Baptists have thought through the implications of a Christ-centered theology. Most of the early confessions quote Christ's words on rendering unto Caesar that which is Caesar's and unto God that which is God's and the parable of the wheat and the tares. Few Baptists, however, have linked these words to an incarnational theology. Yet, this is inescapable when the whole force of the New Testament witness is that *all authority* has been given to Christ the Lord. Smyth, Helwys, and the early English Baptists (General and Particular), as well as Roger Williams and the colonial Baptists in America, are one in affirming that Christ is the only Lord of the church and conscience. Whether recognized or not, the Baptist concept of religious liberty begins with a biblical christology.

The nature of saving faith and that of the gospel are very closely linked in the Baptist insistence upon complete religious freedom. The proclamation of the gospel is predicated upon an uncoerced response: faith that results from duress of any kind is a spurious faith. Salvation, Baptists have always taught, must be the result of a voluntary response to the gospel at the prompting of the Holy Spirit. This means that the individual is not only free to believe something, but must be free to believe nothing at all. If religious liberty means anything, it must mean freedom from religion as well as freedom for religion. This is one reason that, until the twentieth century, Baptists were exceedingly careful that a child reach the "age of accountability" and make his or her own personal faith-commitment to Christ before receiving baptism. To insure that this was the case, so far as the church was concerned, adults and children were asked to "give an account of their experience" in their own words in front of the members of the church gathered for the purpose. When this gradually ceased to be the custom, Baptists opened the doors to an unconverted membership, much as the Congregationalists had done with the "Halfway Covenant." In the confessions and preaching, however, the Baptist insistence upon a regenerate church membership still receives lip service.

III. A Unique Ecclesiology

The brief article on the church in the *BFM (1963)* is deceptively simple. There is no hint that the concept of the church set forth in this article was the most distinctive doctrine in the rise of the Baptist movement. Ecclesiology set Baptists apart from the state churches of the Reformation and even from the English Separatists (Congregationalists), with whom they had so much in common. Taking the New Testament as their guide, Baptists rejected infant baptism while insisting upon the baptism of believers only. This conviction, according to the Baptists, was not only found in the clear teachings of the New Testament, but was the only way to preserve the concept of a regenerate membership. A personal confession of faith followed by baptism assured that the nature of the church would be a fellowship of disciples sharing as equals in the ministry of the church under the "Lordship of Jesus Christ." Such a church could acknowledge no other Lord but its head, Jesus Christ. Not even the pastor could usurp the prerogative that God reserved for Christ alone. Pastors and deacons differed only in function from other members, not in authority, for all were disciples, brethren, priests, and servants. Baptists, who from their beginnings have rejected the authority of princes and kings in the life and worship of the church, could not be expected to accept another yoke of bondage, neither that of the denomination nor that of any other extra-ecclesial organization. The Landmark movement with all its faults and excesses simply reflected a longstanding Baptist aversion for any organization that attempted to exercise its authority over the local church. Associations were forced to disclaim any such intentions in order to elicit the cooperation of the churches.

Among Baptists in the SBC, the SBC can exercise no authority over the local church: the SBC can only recommend and withdraw fellowship from a disorderly church. When the Executive Committee was first proposed, many leaders expressed fear that the committee would take unauthorized actions in an attempt to control the denomination. Only after assuring its critics that the Executive Committee could never take any action not delegated to it by the Convention, was it approved. By such safe-guards, the churches have steadfastly refused to permit the SBC to assume the functions of a superchurch, that is, until 1995.[16] Until the present, it has never been accurate to refer to the SBC as the Southern Baptist Church, but only as a convention of autonomous churches, for the authority still resides within local churches under the Lordship of Christ.

IV. The Political Equation

The Baptist understanding of the nature of the church demands the separation of the church from the state. Although ordained of God, the state's functions are limited to the secular order. The state is not a church. As Thomas Helwys reminded James I, "The king is a mortal man & not God, therefore hath no power over ye immortal souls of his subjects, to make laws and ordinances for them, and to set Spiritual Lords over them."[17] Helwys, who had studied law at Gray's Inn (now the University of London's law school), went on to assure the king that "Baptists" were no anarchists. Not only would they pray for the king, but they would obey him as his loyal subjects. While Baptists have from their earliest confessions acknowledged their obligations to the state of their citizenship and their responsibility to participate in the political process where possible, they have also insisted upon the state's responsibility toward all its citizens, including those of differing religious persuasions.

The seventeenth article of the *BFM (1963)* delineates in a number of terse statements that which every church has a right to expect from the state: "protection and full freedom in the pursuit of its spiritual ends"; no favoritism toward any "ecclesiastical group or denomination"; "[t]he state has no right to impose penalties for religious opinions of any kind"; "[a] free church in a free state is the Christian ideal, and this implies the right of free and unhindered access to God on the part of all men and the right to form and propagate opinions in the sphere of religion without interference by the civil power."[18]

The references to the state in this article on freedom of religion imply a number of convictions historically held by Baptists concerning governments. The state is ordained by God to promote peace, justice, and freedom: although divinely sanctioned, the state is in no sense a church. The state is a secular institution for secular ends, but in no way does this free any state, regardless of its nature, from the obligation to function morally in guaranteeing the civil and religious rights of all persons. Although the state, in some form, is necessary for law and order in a given society, it is temporal. Only the Kingdom of God is eternal. Therefore, while the Christian is obligated to obey the laws of a given state, his or her ultimate loyalty belongs to God alone. As Baptist confessions have consistently and repeatedly stated, Baptists will serve God rather than humans, regardless of the consequences, for God only is the Lord of the conscience. This freedom that Baptists claim for themselves, they ask for all others as well.[19]

One of the reasons the Baptist World Alliance (BWA) was organized was to promote the cause of religious freedom in a global arena. In 1939, at its World Congress in Atlanta, Georgia, the BWA, in "The Atlanta Declaration," stated to the world the following:

> No man, nor government, nor institution, religious or civil, social or economic, has the right to dictate how a person may worship God, or whether he shall worship at all.
> Therefore no civil authority may of right make a law, decree, or regulation respecting an establishment of religion or affecting its free exercise.[20]

It is highly questionable whether one who rejects the principle of the institutional separation of church and state can consistently hold to religious freedom. If this is the case, can such a person legitimately claim to be a Baptist?

Notes

[1] See "Committee on Baptist Faith and Message," in *Annual of the Southern Baptist Convention: One Hundred Sixth Session in Kansas City, Missouri, 7-10 May 1963*, by the Executive Committee, Southern Baptist Convention (Nashville: Southern Baptist Convention, 1963) 281 (article 17) (hereafter, cited as *BFM [1963]*). Also see "Report of Committee on Baptist Faith and Message," in *Annual of the Southern Baptist Convention: Seventieth Session in Memphis, Tennessee, 13-17 May 1925*, by the Secretaries, Southern Baptist Convention (Nashville: Marshall and Bruce, 1925) 73-74 (article 18) (hereafter, cited as *BFM [1925]*).

[2] Champlin Burrage, *The Early English Dissenters in the Light of Recent Research (1550–1641)* vol. 1 (New York: Russell and Russell, 1912) 156.

[3] "Propositions and Conclusions concerning True Christian Religion, 1612–1614," in *Baptist Confessions of Faith*, ed. William L. Lumpkin (Philadelphia: Judson Press, 1959) 140 (article 84).

[4] Thomas Helwys, *The Mistery of Iniquity*, ed. H. Wheeler Robinson, for the Baptist Historical Society (Holland: n.p., 1612; reprint, London: Kingsgate Press, 1935) unnumbered page (reproduced from the copy presented to King James, now in the Bodleian Library).

[5] *The Confession of Faith, Of those Churches which are commonly (though falsly) called Anabaptists* (London: Matthew Simmons in Aldersgate-Street, 1644); also in *Baptist Confessions of Faith*, Lumpkin, 170-71.

[6] *A Confession of Faith of Seven Congregations or Churches of Christ in London, which are commonly (But Unjustly) Called Anabaptists (The Second Impression Corrected and Enlarged)* (London: Matth. Simmons, 1646; reprint, Rochester, New York: Backus Book Publishers, 1981).

[7] "The Assembly or Second London Confession, 1677 and 1688," in *Baptist Confessions of Faith*, Lumpkin, 279-80.

[8] Roger Williams, *The Bloudy Tenent of Persecution for Cause of Conscience Discussed, in A Conference betweene Truth and Peace*, ed. Edward Bean Underhill (London: n.p., 1644; reprint, London: J. Haddon, 1848).

⁹Perry Miller, *Roger Williams: His Contribution to the American Tradition* (New York: Atheneum, 1962) 254.

¹⁰Quoted in Nathan E. Wood, *The History of the First Baptist Church of Boston (1665–1899)* (Philadelphia: n.p., 1899), 65-66. Also, a more recent reprint is in Shelton Smith, Robert T. Handy, and Lefferts A. Loetscher, *American Christianity*, vol. 1 (New York: Charles Scribner's Sons, 1960) 171-72. There were twenty-three members when the church was constituted in 1665.

¹¹William R. Estep, *Revolution within the Revolution: The First Amendment in Historical Context, 1612–1789* (Grand Rapids: Eerdmans, 1990) 110.

¹²See Estep, *Revolution within the Revolution*, 120-79.

¹³"The New Hampshire Baptist Confession. A.D. 1833," in Philip Schaff and David S. Schaff, eds., *The Creeds of Christendom*, vol. 3, *The Evangelical Protestant Creeds*, 6th ed. (New York: Harper & Row, 1931; reprint, Grand Rapids: Baker Book House, 1990) 747-48; also in *Baptist Confessions of Faith*, Lumpkin, 366.

¹⁴*BFM (1925)* 71-76.

¹⁵*BFM (1963)* 281.

¹⁶See "Covenant for a New Century, The Spirit and Structure of the Southern Baptist Convention: The Report of the Program and Structure Study Committee," from "Sixty-Eighth Annual Report of the Executive Committee," in *Annual of the Southern Baptist Convention: One Hundred Thirty-Eighth Session in Atlanta, Georgia, 20-22 June 1995*, ed. Executive Committee, Southern Baptist Convention (Nashville: Southern Baptist Convention, 1995) 45-46, 151-76 ("Proceedings," Tuesday Morning, June 20, Item 30).

¹⁷Helwys, *Mistery of Iniquity*, xxiv.

¹⁸*The Baptist Faith and Message* (Nashville: The Sunday School Board of the Southern Baptist Convention, 1963) 19; also *BFM (1963)* 281.

¹⁹See George W. Truett, "The Baptist Message and Mission for the World Today," in *Sixth Baptist World Congress, Atlanta, Georgia, 22-28 July 1939: Official Report*, ed. J. H. Rushbrooke (Atlanta: Foote and Davies Company, 1939) 5, 22-36 (Sunday, Third Session, 23 July 1939, Item 21); quoted in full in Walter B. Shurden, *The Life of Baptists in the Life of the World*, (Nashville: Broadman Press, 1985) 115-16.

²⁰"A Declaration on Religious Liberty," in *Sixth Baptist World Congress*, 14 (Thursday, Eleventh Session, 27 July 1939, Item 95); also included as "Appendix Two," in Henry Cook, *What Baptists Stand For* (London: Kingsgate Press, 1947) 182.

Contributors

N. Larry Baker—Pastor, First Baptist Church, Pineville, Louisiana. Formerly, he served as Vice President for Academic Affairs and Dean of the Faculty (1986–1987), Academic Dean (1982–1986), Professor of Christian Ethics (1985–1987), and Associate Professor of Christian Ethics (1978–1985) at Midwestern Baptist Theological Seminary. He also taught Christian ethics at Southwestern Baptist Theological Seminary (1969–1975). In addition, prior to his present service as a pastor, he held the position of Executive Director-Treasurer of the SBC's Christian Life Commission (1987–1988). His publications include the book, *Mission Action Guide: Combating Moral Problems*. He received his education from East Texas Baptist University (B.S.) and Southwestern Baptist Theological Seminary (B.D., Th.M., Th.D.).

William R. Estep—Distinguished Professor of Church History, Emeritus, Southwestern Baptist Theological Seminary (1954–present). Previously, he taught at Los Angeles Baptist Seminary (1946–1947) and Union Baptist Seminary in Houston, Texas. He has taught history internationally as well: Seminario Bautista Internacional Teologico in Colombia, Ruschlikon Baptist Seminary in Switzerland, Seminario Bautista Teologico in Spain, Seminario Bautista Teologico in Peru, and Northwest Baptist Theological Seminary in British Columbia. His publications include numerous books, only some of which follow: *La Fe de Los Apostoles*; *The Anabaptist Story*; *Baptists and Christian Unity*; *Colombia: Land of Conflict and Promise*; *And God Gave the Increase*; *Anabaptist Beginnings, 1523–1533*; *The Lord's Free People in a Free Land*; *Renaissance and Reformation*; *Revolution within the Revolution: The First Amendment in Historical Context, 1612–1789*; *Whole Gospel—Whole World: The Foreign Mission Board of the Southern Baptist Convention, 1845–1995*. He received his education from Berea College (B.A.), The Southern Baptist Theological Seminary (Th.M.), and Southwestern Baptist Theological Seminary (Th.D.).

William L. Hendricks—Director of Baptist Studies and Lecturer in Theology, Brite Divinity School, Texas Christian University. He has taught systematic and biblical theology at Southwestern Baptist Theological Seminary (1957–1977), Golden Gate Baptist Theological Seminary (1978–1984), and The Southern Baptist Theological Seminary (1984–1994). He has also taught theology internationally at Taiwan Baptist Seminary, Malaysia Baptist Seminary, Yugoslavian Baptist Seminary, Hungarian Baptist Seminary, and Ruschlikon Baptist Seminary in Switzerland. His publications include several books: *The Letters of John: Tapestries of Truth*, *The Doctrine of Man*, *A Theology for Children*, *Deepening Discipleship*, *A Theology for Aging*, and *Who Is Jesus Christ?* He received his education from Oklahoma Baptist University (B.A.), Southwestern Baptist Theological Seminary (M.Div., Th.D.), and the University of Chicago (M.A., Ph.D.).

Bill J. Leonard—Dean of Wake Forest University Divinity School. Formerly he served as Chairperson of the Department of Religion and Philosophy at Samford

University (1992–1996). Previously, he taught church history at The Southern Baptist Theological Seminary (1975–1992). His publications include several books: *The Nature of the Church*; *Becoming Christian: Dimensions of Spiritual Formation*; *God's Last and Only Hope: The Fragmentation of the Southern Baptist Convention*; editor with George Shriver, *Encyclopedia of Religious Controversy in the United States*; editor, *Dictionary of Baptists in America*. He is currently writing a history of Baptists in America for Judson Press and editing a collection of essays on religion in Appalachia. He received his education from Texas Wesleyan University (B.A.), Southwestern Baptist Theological Seminary (M.Div.), and Boston University (Ph.D.). He also has done post–doctoral studies at Yale University.

Molly T. Marshall—Professor of Theology, Worship, and Spiritual Formation, Central Baptist Theological Seminary. She formerly taught Christian Theology at The Southern Baptist Theological Seminary (1984–1994). Her publications include the following books: *What It Means to Be Human* and *No Salvation Outside the Church? A Critical Inquiry*. She has done advanced studies at Cambridge University, Tantur Ecumenical Institute in Jerusalem, and Princeton Theological Seminary. She received her education from Oklahoma Baptist University (B.A.) and The Southern Baptist Theological Seminary (M.Div., Ph.D.).

Warren McWilliams—Professor, Auguie Henry Chair of Bible, Joe L. Ingram School of Christian Service, Oklahoma Baptist University. He has taught theology at Oklahoma Baptist University since 1976. Previously, he taught religious studies at Stetson University (1974–1976). His publications include several books: *Free in Christ: The New Testament Understanding of Freedom*; *The Passion of God: Divine Suffering in Contemporary Protestant Theology*; *When You Walk Through the Fire*; co-author with Jerry Lemon, *Teaching Guide for Acts: The Gospel for All People*; and *Christ and Narcissus: Prayer in a Self-Centered World*. He received his education from Oklahoma Baptist University (B.A.), The Southern Baptist Theological Seminary (M.Div.), and Vanderbilt University (M.A., Ph.D.).

Jeff B. Pool—Assistant Professor of Systematic Theology, Southwestern Baptist Theological Seminary (1992–present). Previously, he taught systematic theology at Phillips Theological Seminary (1989–1992). His publications include the following books: editor, *Through the Tempest: Theological Voyages in a Pluralistic Culture*, by Langdon Gilkey; *Against Returning to Egypt: Exposing and Resisting Credalism in the Southern Baptist Convention* (forthcoming); and co-editor with Kyle Pasewark, *The Theology of Langdon Gilkey* (forthcoming). He received his education from Wayland Baptist University (B.A.), Southwestern Baptist Theological Seminary (M.Div.), Texas Christian University (M.A.), and the University of Chicago (Ph.D.).